Indian Society through
Personal Writings

Indian Society through
Personal Writings

M. N. SRINIVAS

DELHI
OXFORD UNIVERSITY PRESS
CALCUTTA CHENNAI MUMBAI
1998

Oxford University Press, Great Clarendon Street, Oxford OX2 6DP

Oxford New York
Athens Auckland Bangkok Calcutta
Cape Town Chennai Dar es Salaam Delhi
Florence Hong Kong Istanbul Karachi
Kuala Lumpur Madrid Melbourne Mexico City
Mumbai Nairobi Paris Singapore
Taipei Tokyo Toronto

and associates in

Berlin Ibadan

ISBN 0 19 564560 X

Typeset by Guru typograph Technology, New Delhi 110045
Printed at Pauls Press, New Delhi 110020
and published by Manzar Khan, Oxford University Press
YMCA Library Building, Jai Singh Road, New Delhi 110 001

Dedicated with affection to
R. K. NARAYAN
in memory of our Mysore days

Acknowledgements

I thank the Director, other faculty members, and the administrative staff of the National Institute of Advanced Studies, Bangalore, for the facilities and help in the preparation of the typescript. Mr V. S. Parthasarathy has corrected the proofs and prepared the index of this book, for which I thank him. I must also thank my friend Mr C. N. C. Unni and his staff for their help in various ways.

I dedicate this book to my friend, R. K. Narayan. I am privileged to have been the first to read the typescript of his first novel *Swami and Friends*. I was lucky to have read it when I was young enough to look at the world through Swami's eyes. I have also had the pleasure of walking the streets of Mysore with Narayan, listening to the stories he was planning to write. The last occasion when it happened was in the closing months of 1956 when Narayan was our neighbour in Berkeley, California, and he, my wife Rukmini and I met frequently to exchange gossip, and also discuss the progress of his well-known novel, *The Guide*.

Bangalore   M. N. SRINIVAS

Introduction

Some of my more personal writings which shed light on Indian culture and society have been put together in this volume. Leaving aside the autobiographical essays (Chapters 1 and 2) and Chapter 3 which is a very idiosyncratic account of Bangalore, all the others are concerned with Rampura, a village in south Karnataka, where I did fieldwork in 1948 and the summer of 1952.

Chapter 4 provides a background to the study of disputes, while Chapters 5, 6 and 7 are the straightforward accounts of the disputes themselves. The disputes have a dramatic quality about them, and in their own way, inform the reader about the kind of life which Rampurians—and I guess, millions of other villagers—led, during the years 1948–52.

Chapters 8 to 11 have been culled from my book, *The Remembered Village*, which was written during the period following 24 April 1970, when my processed field-notes were destroyed by arsonists at Stanford, who attempted to set fire to the Centre for Advanced Studies in the Behavioural Sciences, where I was a fellow. I wrote a book based on the memory of my fieldwork in Rampura, and it may be referred to as a collection of facts recollected when the mind was far from tranquil. They represent ethnography of a different kind. Some purists may ask whether it is ethnography at all.

Chapter 3, 'Bangalore as I See It', is as I have already mentioned, an idiosyncratic if not capricious account of the city, written for the benefit of those who were total strangers to it. I was not at all keen on writing on Bangalore, especially as I was then in the midst of editing a book, but I was persuaded to agree almost against my will. I was told that I could just write what I liked about the city. But even writing a long essay for laymen cannot be accomplished without some reading about the city and its history, but since the essay had to be produced by a certain date, there were severe limits to my reasoning. But in spite of these constraints, I did enjoy writing about Bangalore, the association of my relatives with it, and my own early impressions of it. It was a journey into my origins. Further, parts of my essay referred to individuals who had contributed to Bangalore's intellectual life, and I enjoyed this too. I also refer very briefly to the recent and radical changes that are occurring in India's 'future city', and the swift deterioration in the quality of life of its inhabitants.

Chapters 1 and 2 are the really autobiographical pieces in the book. Chapter 1 was written in response to a request from Dr Peter Lengyel, editor of the *International Social Science Journal*, who wanted to mark the completion of twenty-five years of the Journal by publishing autobiographical accounts of some social scientists. I quote his words, 'For the present number (vol. xxv, no. 1/2, 1973), we have chosen a highly personal approach by asking a group of internationally prominent social scientists to contribute autobiographical "intellectual profiles". The resulting collection has its idiosyncrasies . . . but it also has the merit of spanning at least two generations and of drawing upon a great variety of origins and subsequent "intellectual trajectories". '

'My Baroda Days' was similarly written for the silver jubilee number of the *Journal of the M.S. University of Baroda*, to whose first issue also I had contributed a piece.

Biographies and autobiographies focus on the lives of particular individuals, but they also shed light on the cultural and social milieu of the subjects. Some novels also achieve this in a remarkable way. The knowledge and insights they provide are not quantifiable but not any the less valuable. In fact, the insights they provide are usually beyond the reach of a sociological study. Given this fact, I wonder why biographies, autobiographies and novels are not made use of in sensitizing sociologists to cultures other than their own. One reason may be that since their discipline claims to be a science, sociologists think that it ought to go in for more and more quantification, and mathematization, and not lean towards literature and history. This results in training in fieldwork being restricted to training in statistics, scaling techniques, constructing questionnaires to carry out surveys, conduct opinion polls, make content analysis etc. No attempt is made to train the student to be a sensitive observer, to watch out for changes in moods, and in the body language of the observed.

Sociology is a science in the sense that it studies human societies in space and time in a systematic and comparative manner, but it is also an art in the sense that it is much more than information and knowledge about societies. It strives to achieve *understanding*, and this is impossible without imagination and empathy. In some areas social knowledge involves not only the intellect but the emotions, not only the head but the heart.

Sociologists in India have been, by and large, preoccupied with the study of one or other part of their own culture and society but they have not yet tried to use their own lives as ethnographic data for analysis. The hazards in the use of such material are only too well-known: there is a desire to present oneself as a much nicer person than one is, and exaggerate one's achievements and deprecate or ignore the achievements of others, and so on. The temptation to exhibitionism, tear one's hair and beat one's breasts in public, cannot also be ignored, even though it is much less likely than the possibility mentioned earlier.

The focus in an autobiography is the narrative, or to use a cinematic cliché, the story line, but an anthropologist might be tempted to digress frequently into descriptions of rituals, festivals etc., which would be unwise, for the description would fall far short of what is required in ethnography, and at the same time weaken the reader's attention. The central theme in an anthropological autobiography should be the subject's progress through shifting cultural milieus which means that the light the narrative sheds on cultural and social changes, has to be incidental.

It is my plea that the movement from studying one's own culture or a niche in it, to studying oneself as an ethnographic field, is a natural one. In the west, anthropology started as a study of 'the other', generally a weaker, inferior and exploited 'other', but in India it has largely been a study of the self or the self in-the-other. And this should extend to include one's own life. 'Sociology of the Self' should be a rich field given the diversities and unities which the members of Indian civilization, are heirs to.

Contents

Itineraries of an Indian Social Anthropologist

I am concerned in this brief essay with narrating how I became a sociologist and how I grew in the discipline. I have brought in my personal and domestic life only to the extent that it is relevant to understanding my career. I have also not discussed my 'contribution' to sociology and social anthropology, but I have confined myself to describing my activities as an organizer of sociological studies in two Indian universities and elsewhere, and the work I did for strengthening the profession in India. I find even this difficult as I have to steer clear of the Scylla of egotism and the Charybdis of undue modesty. If the former is vulgar, the latter is dishonest.

I owe my career in sociology to my delicate health during my boyhood and adolescence. My high school and pre-university career was marred by chronic malaria which occasionally erupted into bouts of illness marked by high temperature and it was brought down only after swallowing quantities of quinine. I was scrawny and grossly underweight, and my relatives and family friends were of the view that I was too delicate for a serious course of study such as medicine or engineering. I did moderately well at the Secondary School Leaving Certificate Examination (1931) conducted by Mysore University and I could have opted for the two-year Intermediate course in science like many other students. In fact, there was a suggestion by a friend or relative that I should take chemistry, botany and zoology for my optionals as that would enable me to take up medicine. But this was vetoed by my eldest brother (hereafter referred to as EB), and he asked me to take up modern history, logic and mathematics instead. Incidentally, this ensured my staying in my home town of Mysore in my natal family till I completed the BA whereas I would have had to go to Bangalore if I selected science subjects. Left to myself, I would have dropped mathematics but my EB thought it essential for my future career.

I must mention here that I dreaded mathematics. I was no good at it even though I knew that much of my trouble arose from my not being able to see what was written on the blackboard. I was acutely myopic and it went untreated till I reached the first BA (Honours) class in social philosophy in Maharaja's College (1933–4). I was participating in a debate, and EB, who was among the audience, noticed that I was holding my notes within inches of my eyes. I was sent to an opthalmologist the next morning and he found that I had a reading of minus four in each eye.

Since I could not see what was on the blackboard, I would not follow a mathematics course, and I could not make up at home what I had missed in the class. But EB had two lecturers in mathematics among his wide circle of friends and as a result of his speaking to them, I occasionally got free tuition. But even with that help I managed only to scrape up enough marks for a bare pass at the Intermediate examination in 1933. This was my last tussle with mathematics and I had a sense of profound relief that my future was going to be unclouded by it.

From what I have said above it is obvious that EB made all the major decisions with regard to my educational career till I was practically in my late twenties. My father passed away in November 1934 but even when he was alive, decisions regarding education and career and other important matters were left to EB as he was the educated member of the family. He had an MA in English literature and taught at the Maharajah's High School in Mysore. (He later taught English in Mysore University.) He was regarded as a rebel and a heretic, and under the influence of his modern guru, had rejected many of the values and ideas of the orthodox Brahmins of those days. He even refused to get married on the ground that it would come in the way of his devoting himself to the welfare of his family. This was indeed an extraordinary decision to take, and while it was disapproved of it had earned him the respect of not only relatives but many others. Indeed, my mother occasionally used to compare him to the epic figure Bhishma who had sworn celibacy in order to assure the sons of his stepmother the right to succeed to the lineage throne.

EB's degree, his job and his refusal to marry made him the virtual head of our large family. His moral authority was such that it did not occur to us to question his decisions. My father was quiet and retiring by temperament, and as a man with limited education, he perhaps felt it beyond him to take decisions about his younger sons and daughters when there was an educated older son. One of his major ambitions was, however, to see all his sons and daughters become graduates.

I passed the Intermediate examination obtaining a third division, and a decision had to be taken about the course I should pursue for the bachelor's degree. Fate intervened in the person of Acharya, a friend of EB's, a Marxist and a rebel. EB asked Acharya what course I should take. He flipped the pages of the university handbook and gave his verdict—the honours course in social philosophy was a 'broad' humanizing one and good for me. I sent in my application for it and was admitted without difficulty. It was not a very popular course, and indeed, I came to know later that one or two lecturers in the Philosophy Department were busy trying to recruit bright students. They were able to bag only one first class, a cheerful youth with a happy-go-lucky temperament who found the course dreary beyond words.

There were two kinds of BA courses in 1930 in Mysore University— a two-year 'pass' course designed for large numbers who wanted to get a degree in the shortest possible time, and another, a three-year 'honours' course meant for a selected few who were expected to specialize in a particular subject. There were five students in my batch of honours students in social philosophy while in the pass course there were nearly a hundred and twenty.

The course I had chosen, was an ambitious one including papers in sociology, ethics and political thought, history of ethics, comparative religion, Indian social institutions, Indian ethics and Indian political theory. The 'minor' subjects, which were shed at the end of the second year, included social anthropology, social psychology, comparative politics and Indian economics.

Professor A. R. Wadia, who was the Head of the Department of Philosophy from 1917 to 1942, had devised the course, and he was more interested in ethics, sociology, political thought and social work than in pure metaphysics. Wadia had shown imagination and courage in introducing sociology, social anthropology, social psychology and politics in a philosophy course, and I expect that in this he had received encouragement from Dr Brajendranath Seal, one of the distinguished vice-chancellors of Mysore University. Seal was an erudite scholar, a polymath, and had taught 'Comparative Sociology' at Calcutta University in the years preceding the First World War.

Under Wadia's leadership Mysore proved to be one of the pioneers in introducing sociology in the undergraduate classes. This was no mean achievement for the contemporary academic climate in India was suspicious of sociology as a discipline. Indian academics, generally trained in English universities, shared the prejudices which their mentors displayed towards continental and especially American disciplines and ideas. The prejudice against sociology diminished only gradually during the post-Independence years and it would not be incorrect to state that it has not disappeared totally yet. The greatly increased exposure of Indian academics to American universities during the last forty years is an important contributory factor to the recent popularity of sociology. A belated realization of the insufficiency of a purely economic approach to development is another.

There were five students including me in my class and we could not help coming into close contact with our teachers. I was the youngest of the five, and much of ethics, political thought and comparative religion went above my head, but I found sociology, Indian social institutions and social anthropology interesting.

I must comment here briefly on Wadia. He was a very impressive man to look at, always well-dressed in a silk jacket, white duck trousers, black shoes and striped shirt and tie. Like most Parsis he was light-skinned. His curly hair was parted in the middle framing his round face. He wore a tooth-brush moustache and sported gold-rimmed glasses. He looked more like a powerful executive than a scholar. In fact, he had an air of authority about him, and his colleagues and students, whose respect and regard he enjoyed did not feel totally at ease with him. He was a stickler for discipline and he did not easily forgive lapses from rules. But everyone knew that he did not impose on others the standards and rules which he did not himself observe. He always lectured in his gown, and he never came to the class without preparation. He made an effort to get to know his students including the numerous students in the BA class. They were all invited to tea, in batches of eight or ten, on the eve of their final examination. He also made each one write an autobiographical essay for his archives. He was a real talent-spotter, and he did his utmost to encourage talented students, He was most generous in his appreciation of the abilities of his students, a quality which I am increasingly discovering to be rarer than I thought it was.

My relations with him were pleasant most of the time except on one occasion when he thought I was indulging in unnecessary verbal display instead of stating my arguments as simply as I could. I have not forgotten his pulling me up over this and giving me a 'B' instead of an 'A'. Again, it was typical of him that while he was genuinely sorry at my missing a first class in my final homours examination by a narrow margin, he refused to give the necessary 'grace' marks like other heads of departments. He wanted me to get the marks on my own and not as a result of his friendly feeling towards me. I felt sore at that time but I now think that he acted rightly.

It is indeed curious the way in which my career has been influenced first by Wadia's and later by Dr V. K. R. V. Rao's intervention. While Wadia was instrumental in bringing me to Baroda (and India), my leaving Baroda for Delhi in March 1959 was at the instance of Dr Rao, then Vice-Chancellor of Delhi University. My migration to Bangalore from Delhi in May 1972 to take up the joint directorship of the new Institute for Social and Economic Change was again the result of Dr Rao's intervention.

To return to Wadia, in September 1943, he was a member of the selection committee to choose two lecturers in the Department of Sociology in Bombay. I appeared before the committee and I was included in the panel, but eventually two others, both several years senior to me, were chosen. Wadia and Radhakrishnan both encouraged me in my efforts to go to Oxford after I had finished at Bombay. Again, Wadia was responsible for my returning to India as Professor of Sociology in the new University of Baroda, where he was Pro-Vice-Chancellor. At Wadia's suggestion, Radhakrishnan wrote to the Vice-Chancellor Mrs Hansa Mehta, on my behalf.

Wadia left Baroda in June 1952, barely a year after I had joined the university. He settled down in his native city of Bombay and was actively involved in academic and public affairs till a year or so before his death in 1971. We kept in touch with each other till 1970 when I left Delhi for a fellowship at the Centre for Advanced Study in the Behavioural Sciences, Stanford.

Wadia wanted me to succeed him as Director of the Tata Institute of Social Sciences but I did not think that I had the qualifications to preside over an institute specializing in social work. He saw my point of view and did not press me.

I passed the BA (Honours) examination in the summer of 1936, and as I have mentioned, my results were a bitter disappointment to me. But looking back, I feel that the stars were kind to me in denying me the first-class degree I had worked for but which I am now certain I did not deserve. I was an extremely unintelligent examinee and did not know the first thing about preparing for an examination. I thought I had to read conscientiously every text book that was prescribed to us. All first-class students in arts subjects concentrated on certain topics, if not questions, but such gambling was not in my nature. But I became aware of my short-comings as an examinee only long after I had ceased to take examina-tions. With a first-class degree I might have landed a teaching job in Mysore University and this I am certain would have meant an end to my development as a sociologist. Several of my peers with far brighter aca-demic records and who were appointed to teaching posts in Mysore in the 1930s, became bitter and frustrated men as they found that promo-tions within the university and elsewhere in the state were based on such criteria as caste and kinship and not on merit. Brahmins in particular were discriminated against on the ground that they had been a privileged group historically, and had enjoyed a near monopoly of government jobs till the 1920s. The principle of caste quotas and reservations for government jobs was introduced in the 1920s, and in 1936, when I graduated, Brahmins were eligible to apply for only one of every five advertised jobs.[1]

My second-class degree also saved me from sitting for the Mysore Civil Service examination, which was being held after a long interval. Two probationary assistant commissioners were to be selected on the basis of performance at the examination, and every graduate who regarded himself as bright, or whose parents regarded him as bright, took it. I knew that I stood little or no chance of getting into the service, as some very able and mature students whom I knew were competing. Besides, I was so tired after three years of continuous work for the

[1] Those interested in obtaining more information about the Backward Class Movement in South India may see my *Caste in Modern India* (Bombay: Asia Publishing House, 1962) and *Social Change in Modern India* (Chapter IV, Berkeley and Los Angeles: University of California Press, 1966). See also A. Beteille, *Castes: Old and New* (Bombay: Asia Publishing House, 1969) and M. S. A. Rao, *Tradition, Rationality and Change* (Bombay: Popular Prakashan, 1972).

honours examination that the prospect of facing another highly competitive examination was distasteful. Another important consideration was EB's disapproval of my entering government service (except as a teacher). I welcomed his suggestion to go to Bombay to take the MA course in sociology and work in addition for a law degree during the evenings.

G. S. Ghurye was the professor and head of the Department of Sociology at Bombay and he had been one of my examiners at BA. And as it happened I had secured 66 per cent marks in the sociology paper set and evaluated by him. Wadia gave me letters for Ghurye, and Dr N. A. Thoothi, reader in the department. Professor M. H. Krishna, who had taught me social anthropology, was enthusiastic about my working under Ghurye. According to him, Ghurye was the best man in sociology in India.

The University School of Economics and Sociology in Bombay as it was then known was something unique in the academic life of India in the 1930s. It comprised two departments, economics and sociology, and the first professor and head of the Department of Sociology was the brilliant biologist and town-planner, Sir Partick Geddes. Both the departments did only postgraduate and research work. In 1936, there was a combined course in economics and sociology for the MA, and the head of the Economics Department, Professor C. N. Vakil, was also the director of the school. There were more than twenty students who were working for the Ph.D., most of whom had full or part-time jobs. Those were days when doctoral fellowships were unknown.

In view of my honours degree in sociology, Ghurye suggested that I submit a dissertation for the master's degree instead of writing papers at the end of two years' attendance at lectures. I chose as my theme 'Marriage and Family among the Kannada Castes in Mysore State'. I completed it before the end of 1938 and it was published in 1942 under the title *Marriage and Family in Mysore*. It was favourably reviewed in professional journals including *Nature*. In retrospect, however, the book appears immature and its style brash, and I was glad when it went out of print in the 1950s.

Ghurye exercised an important influence on my career and I therefore present here a brief idea of the scholar and man. He was a student of Sanskrit right up to MA degree and won the coveted chancellor's Gold Medal in 1918 for his performance at the MA examination. His exposure to sociology occurred only subsequently when he attended

Geddes' lectures in the university. It speaks much for Geddes' abilities as a teacher that he was able to discover Ghurye's potentialities as a sociologist, especially as Sanskrit students in Indian universities inhabit a world of their own, far removed from the world of others. After a year with Geddes, Ghurye was given a scholarship by the University to proceed for higher studies in London under Hobhouse, then the Martin White Professor of Sociology. Ghurye left London for Cambridge after six months as he found the erudite Hobhouse dull and uninspiring. In Cambridge he came under the twin influences of Haddon and Rivers. Ghurye developed an enormous admiration for Rivers, and his premature death in 1922 from strangulated hernia, Ghurye regarded, not only as a tragedy for anthropology but as a personal misfortune. Ghurye also liked to recall Haddon's devotion to anthropology, and his kindness to students.

Ghurye's approach to anthropological problems as well as his interests were decisively influenced by Rivers. The foundations of one of Ghurye's most important books, *Caste and Race in India*, were laid in one of the several papers he submitted in fulfillment of the Ph.D. degree titled, 'The Ethnic Theory of Caste'. Ghurye's interest in kinship, and in purely ethnological problems (e.g., 'The Disposal of the Human Placenta in India') were derived from his apprenticeship at Cambridge. I may add here that Ghurye combined fruitfully the ethnological and Indological approaches, a combination for which his earlier Sanskritic training had eminently qualified him. He did not stop with this, however. He undertook, for instance, a study of the sex habits of clerks in Bombay, and he published a critique of Kinsey much later.

Ghurye seemed to be completely under Rivers' intellectual influence even during the period I knew him, 1936–44. He even defended Rivers' espousal, along with Elliot-Smith and Perry, of the theory of the Egyptian origin of important cultural phenomena such as mummification in widely-separated parts of the world. His attachment to his master made him harsh towards Malinowski who had criticized Rivers' 'kinship algebra'. While Ghurye was unappreciative of the significance of the functionalist revolution in social anthropology, he regarded Radcliffe-Brown as a 'seeded functionalist' in contrast to Malinowski. I have a suspicion that this was at least partly due to Radcliffe-Brown's having been a student of Rivers.

One of the abiding lessons which Ghurye had learnt at Cambridge was the indissoluble link between social anthropology and the fieldwork tradition. While he himself never undertook any serious fieldwork he, more than any other teacher, contributed to basing sociology and social anthropology in India on sound fieldwork. From his chair in Bombay, he directed a one-man ethnographic survey of India, an operation which was conducted with little or no financial resources. The way he went about it was interesting. Bombay being the most cosmopolitan of Indian cities, Ghurye's MA and Ph.D. students came from diverse regions and economic backgrounds. He encouraged them, wherever possible, to take up the study of problems in their regions for their master's and doctoral dissertations. This meant that they combed the existing literature in English and in the local language for data, and supplemented it with fieldwork. In this way he managed to get dissertations written on such themes as 'Hindu Culture in Sind', 'Muslims of UP', 'Harijans in Bombay', and 'Prabhus and Kolis in Maharashtra'.

Ghurye's students also undertook village studies but these were more similar to the studies carried out by the agricultural economists than to the intensive studies undertaken by anthropologists since the 1950s.

Ghurye encouraged those students who had a Sanskrit background to describe and analyze social life and culture in ancient India. Thus, K. M. Kapadia wrote on 'Hindu Kinship' and S. V. Karandikar on 'Hindu Exogamy' and Mrs Karve used her knowledge of Sanskrit as well as fieldwork in her *magnum opus, Kinship Organization in India*.

I was only nineteen when I first met Ghurye and I must have sounded naive and woolly, with my mind full of half-digested ideas from the books that I had read. But on the other hand I was enthusiastic and one of his few full-time students. Ghurye's first assignment to me was a critical review of Hobhouse's *Morals in Evolution*, a book which I found monumentally dull. I don't know if I produced the review, and if I did, what Ghurye thought of it. I am certain, however, that I did not displease him over it as I was allowed to proceed to the master's degree by submitting a thesis instead of answering eight question-papers at the end of two years. I knew that a dissertation gave me a better chance to show my abilities than an examination. There was no sharp deadline for a dissertation, and I did not have to compete with thirty other students as I would have had to if I had to 'take papers'.

During the academic year 1936–7, I spent more of my time in preparing for the first law examination than on sociology and I made up for this by devoting 1937–8 wholly to my MA. I read the usual gazettes and census reports, and volumes on the tribes and castes of Mysore, Kannada folklore and even fiction. I printed a questionnaire at my own expense and did fieldwork for a very brief period in a village. I met priests and others who were in a position to give me information on customs and rituals.

A few months before I was due to submit my dissertation Ghurye told me that some changes were in the offing in the university, and that I should alter my registration from MA to Ph.D. But a few days later he told me to go ahead with MA. The reason became clear after a while. The university instituted two research fellowships and one research assistantship in each of the two departments. I was awarded a fellowship in June 1940 to carry out a field study of the Coorgs of South India. Ghurye had read about the Coorgs in Richter's *Manual of Coorg* and he had been intrigued by their distinctive appearance, dress, warlike culture and ancestor-shrines. He wanted me to study them for my Ph.D. which I did.

While the field study of Coorgs in their forested mountains had its appeal for me, I was troubled by the fact that I was becoming a chronicler of customs and not the theoretician of society which I wanted to be. I must explain here that at that time I had a few friends who were Gandhian ideologues who did not have any sympathy with my anthropological interests. My excitements did not make any sense to them nor did they visualize my studies leading me to a fat salaried job. All this bothered me not a little and I thought I should take up a 'theoretical' subject for my Ph.D. I went to the late Professor M. Hiriyanna in Mysore, whose understanding of Indian philosophy was profound, and asked him whether a person who did not have a knowledge of Sanskrit could make a study of how the relation between the individual and society was formulated in Indian thought. Hiriyanna said I could undertake such a study. But the project was nipped in the bud by Ghurye who told me that no fellowship would be forthcoming if I chose a theme which did not involve fieldwork. Ghurye took a dim view of my hankering after 'theory'.

I was bitter with Ghurye at that time but in retrospect I cannot help being thankful to him for being firm about fellowships being available for fieldwork only. For the development of sociology in India fieldwork was fundamental, and quite apart from that, I remember Ghurye telling me that one could not understand the 'nexus of social relationships' without fieldwork experience. The comment was all the more remarkable coming from an armchair scholar.

From our beginnings as a custom bootmaker, Merrell has been setting the standard in technical hiking boots that stand up to the harshest conditions.Our hiking heritage and passion for the outdoors are the inspiration for every boot we make. With hiking boots, rugged walking shoes, sport sandals and backcountry/telemark ski boots, **Merrell takes you where you want to go**™.

Depuis nos débuts en tant que manufacturier de bottes sur mesure, Merrell a établi un niveau de qualité supérieure qui résiste aux conditions les plus sévères pour ses bottes de randonnée techniques. Notre héritage pour la randonnée et notre passion pour le plein-air nous servent d'inspiration pour chaque botte que nous fabriquons. Avec ses bottes de randonnée, ses souliers de marche robuste, ses sandales sports et ses bottes de ski de fond et de télémark, **Merrell vous porte "de plain-pied vers de nouvelles aventures"**™.

MERRELL' Footwear is warranted against defects in workmanship and materials for one year from date of purchase. Merrell Sport Sandals are warranted against defects in workmanship and materials for 90 days from date of purchase. If you feel your Merrell Footwear may have a quality defect, bring them and your receipt to your Merrell Dealer. She/he will process your return immediately. Working with your dealer, Merrell has set up an effective, no-hassle system to process your claim as quickly as possible. Products not covered under warranty will be returned to the dealer. Please allow 3 to 5 weeks for turnaround.

For more information or other inquiries contact:

USA / ÉTATS-UNIS
Merrell/Division of Karhu USA, Inc.
Ship: 34 River Road
Essex Junction VT
05452-3808

Mail: P.O. Box 4249
Burlington VT 05406

Pour plus d'information ou autres renseignements, communiquer avec:

CANADA
Merrell/Division of Tropsport Acquisitions, Inc.
1200 55th Avenue
Lachine (Montreal)
Quebec H8T 3J8

Envois: 1200 55ième
Avenue
Lachine (Quebec)
H8T 3J8

Courrier: 59 Lindsay
Dorval (Quebec)
H9P 2S6

Les chaussures sont garanties contre les défauts de pièces et de main-d'oeuvre pour une période d'un an à partir de la date d'achat. Les sandales sports Merrell sont garanties contre les défauts de pièces et de main-d'oeuvre pour une période de 90 jours à partir de la date d'achat. Si vous sentez que vos chaussures Merrell ont un problème de qualité, rapportez-les avec votre reçu chez votre marchand Merrell. Il procédera à votre retour de marchandise immédiatement. Merrell a mis sur pied un système facile et efficace avec votre marchand afin qu'il puisse traiter votre réclamation le plus rapidement possible. Les produits qui ne sont pas couverts par la garantie seront retournés au marchand. S.V.P. allouer 3 à 5 semaines de délai de livraison.

Ghurye took trouble over the preparation of his lectures but I found them dull and repetitious. In contrast to his lectures, however, he was stimulating in informal talk. He talked about all kinds of things including sex and he was frank and uninhibited. I got into the habit of dropping into his room whenever I had a doubt or difficulty and Ghurye was generous with his time. (I sometimes felt that he welcomed an intrusion.) The discussion frequently strayed far afield and this gave me an idea of the man behind the scholar. There was no doubt about his dedication to his teaching and research. But he made up his mind on many matters and he would not change it.

My field study of the Coorgs could not be as deep or thorough as I wanted it to be as, within a few weeks of my first trip to Mercara, the capital of Coorg, I came down with a serious stomach upset which went undiagnosed for several weeks and for which, I discovered, there was no cure. I had to live with it. I was, therefore, forced to collect my data in short hit-and-run trips. But eventually I did manage to collect a certain amount and this was submitted in a two-volume study, nearly 900 pages long, in December 1944, when I bade good-bye to Bombay which I had come to love and went to Mysore.

My fellowship had come to an end in June 1942 and I was immediately appointed to a research assistantship in the department which lasted till June 1944. The duties of my new post required me to assist Ghurye in his research including undertaking tours to collect data. One part of the data or folklore collected during the tours, I was, however, allowed to publish under my own name. I went on two field trips as assistant, one to Tamil Nadu in 1942 and the other to Andhra in 1943, and thanks to my nodding acquaintance with both Tamil and Telugu, I was able to do reasonably well in both areas. My ethnographic range increased as a result.

My relations with Ghurye started souring in 1943 and this continued for several years. I shall not go into this here. I would only like to acknowledge my indebtedness to him for driving home to me the cruciality of fieldwork in sociology and for making me get off the high horse of theory and speculation and always keep the 'ethnographic reality' before me. I had also obtained some intellectual discipline by working with him, of which I stood badly in need. On the negative side, however, more than eight years of apprenticeship under Ghurye had left me with a feeling of deep dissatisfaction. I had started out wanting to be a theorist of society but had ended up by becoming a conjectural historian and a collector of discrete ethnographical facts without being able to integrate them into a meaningful framework. My interest in ideas had been starved.

On the material side also my position was unenviable. I had an MA and L.L.B., and I had submitted my thesis for the Ph.D. but there was no job in sight. Worse still, there was no prospect of a job in sociology. A well-meaning family friend suggested that I should join the war-time Civil Supplies Department of the Government of India but the suggestion did not appeal to either EB or me. I then thought of pursuing my studies abroad. But funds for higher studies abroad were very scarce in those days, and my efforts to secure financial aid failed. But EB was nothing if not generous and so was another brother, G. He gave me about Rs 6,000 which was enough to cover my passage to England and my expenses during the first three or four months.

I had applied for admission to the Ph.D. course at Oxford as well as Columbia but I heard only from Oxford, which admitted me to the B.Litt. course in the first instance with provision for its later conversion to the D.Phil. with retrospective effect. I had been asked to submit a theme for my dissertation and I had chosen something like 'Culture Patterns among Three South Indian Ethnic Groups, Coorgs, Todas and Chenchus'. Professor Daryll Forde was then deputizing for Radcliffe-Brown who was away in Sao Paulo in Brazil doing fieldwork.

I reached Oxford on 11 May 1945, exactly a month after leaving Bombay, to find that Radcliffe-Brown had returned from Brazil. My initial encounters with him were far from happy and in no way predictive of the future cordial relations between us.

A day or two before disembarking, my spectacles had been badly damaged during a game of deck quoits. A fast return had knocked them off my face, shattering to smithereens one eye-piece while the other was badly cracked. It had not occurred to me to carry a spare pair and I was too myopic to do without the use of even one cracked eye-piece. I did not realize what an odd sight I presented to everyone as I went about the ship in that state. I must have looked even odder after disembarking at Tilbury, a black man in a white country walking about with a cracked eye-piece. I met the severe-looking and immaculately dressed Rector of Exeter, Dr Barber, immediately after arriving at the college, and he at once asked me to go to the nearest optician who said he needed at least a fortnight to fit me with new glasses.

I stood before Radcliffe-Brown soon after I had seen the optician and he scrutinized me slowly through his monocle. I felt awkward and foolish and wished to God I had kept off deck quoits.

I did not know that sometime previously an Indian anthropology student had disturbed the even tenor of Oxford's academic life by his political activities. He was not a bright student, he was aggressive, and had made trouble for the dons and others in charge of him. In those days Indian students, most of them coming from well-heeled families had a reputation for political extremism, and this did not endear them to the British with whom they came into contact.

Radcliffe-Brown probably thought that I was another potential packet of trouble, and my appearance could not have decreased his unease.

Beneath these superficial considerations there was a more important reason for R-B's initial prejudice against me. R-B (as he was generally called) thought poorly of Ruth Benedict's idea that each culture had a pattern, that these patterns could be classified (e.g., Apollonian and Dionysian), and that such patterning had a profound influence on the behaviour of the members of the culture. According to R-B, Benedict had selected facts which suited her theory and ignored inconvenient ones, and apart from this, her theory was the antithesis of the 'scientific' approach. He was a positivist who was convinced that sociology was a science like biology or other natural sciences, and that human social behaviour was governed by universal laws which it was the business of the sociologist to discover by systematically comparing institutions from diverse societies. Also, R-B's structural approach had led to the downgrading if not elimination of culture. The source of Ruth Benedict's heresy was traceable to Wilhelm Dilthey, the German philosopher, and R-B had little use for Dilthey and his kind.

R-B's temperamental affinity with the French sociologists was as marked as his antipathy to the German. While he could not lecture without referring to Durkheim, Mauss, Hubert, Loisy, Levy-Bruhl and Granet he rarely mentioned Marx or Weber. The only German sociologist whom he mentioned and with respect was Simmel.

His antipathy to German intellectuals was probably linked to certain events in his personal life but I shall not go into them. I shall remain content to say that while I learnt of R-B's disapproval of my research topic soon after becoming his student, the source and depth of that disapproval were revealed to me only gradually.

I attended his lectures during the remaining part of the summer term and remember interrupting a lecture occasionally to offer a pseudo-historical explanation to a phenomenon for which Radcliffe-Brown had already suggested a functional one. I must have grated on the nerves of one who had all his life waged a crusade against 'conjectural history'.

While R-B disapproved of my research topic he did not try to persuade me to change it. He asked me to read a few books including Bateson's *Naven*, Margaret Mead's *Sex and Temperament in Three Primitive Societies* and to attend his lectures and seminars. And before leaving for his mountain home in Wales for the long vacation he asked me to write a paper on the concept of 'pattern of culture' for him to look at after his return. I worked hard that summer reading whatever I could find on 'patterns of culture' and I had a longish paper ready for R-B when he returned to Oxford at the beginning of the Michaelmas term. He took a few days to read it, and I was naturally worried and anxious about his reaction. But to my great relief, R-B told me that he was satisfied with my paper and that I could go ahead with my topic. This was indeed my moment of triumph but suddenly I heard myself telling R-B that since I had won my point I wanted to know what he really thought I should be doing for my Ph.D.? He replied that it was a waste of my time and talents to be working on 'patterns of culture' and that instead I should try to examine the relation between religion and society among the Coorgs of South India. In fact, he had been reading my voluminous manuscript, and he found that it contained considerable material on religion. He told me that it was written in very good English and he wondered how Indians who had never left their native shores were able to master such an alien and difficult tongue. Had I been taught by English teachers? I replied that I had been taught English in a neighbourhood school by ill-qualified teachers. I had never really studied the language but had picked it up as I went along.

I think that R-B's object in suggesting that I analyze the material on religion in my Coorg thesis from the functionalist point of view was to teach me in a way that I would never forget the fruitfulness of his approach in contrast to the futility of my pseudo-historical approach. The idea was attractive, even challenging, but I was scared that he might want me to visit Coorg again. The last thing that I could think of then was the luxury of another field trip. Besides, I had protracted my student life too long and I wanted to get a job and start contributing to the family income instead of being a drain on their hard-won resources. R-B assured me that the material in my thesis was enough for a D.Phil. thesis, and armed with that assurance, I went ahead.

Sometime in September 1945, I learnt that G, the brother who had been financing my studies at Oxford, had died suddenly of pneumonia. Apart from my personal grief at the loss of one who was very close to me, I was overwhelmed by the financial implications of the event. My immediate reaction was to take the first boat home but in those days getting a berth on a boat was extremely difficult. I was utterly miserable for a few weeks at the end of which I was lucky enough to obtain a Carnegie research grant (for overseas students) of £300 for 1945–6 with a possibility of renewal for another year. It happened this way, a few days after I had heard the news of my brother's death, an Indian friend drew my attention to an announcement in the *Oxford Gazette* calling for applications for Carnegie research grants from overseas students. I promptly sent in an application and was interviewed by Sir Humphry Milford a few days later. I do not think my performance at the interview was scintillating and I was really surprised to get the grant. But I also knew that R-B had written a note on my behalf. I may add here that my grant was raised to £400 for 1946–7.

Freed from immediate financial worries, I was able to devote all my time to my thesis, and I found the writings of Durkheim, Radcliffe-Brown, Evans-Pritchard, Gregory Bateson exciting. In the course of time I became an enthusiastic convert to functionalism *a'la* Radcliffe-Brown. I had the feeling that I had at last found a theoretical framework which was satisfactory but like all new converts I was a fanatic. I suppressed my natural scepticism, one of my few real assets, to accept such dogmas as the irrelevance of history for sociological explanation, the unimportance of culture and the existence of universal laws.

As I looked at my material from the functionalist viewpoint, I found it falling into a pattern. The data was no longer unrelated and disorderly. The different levels of reality were clearly discernible as were the links between them. In retrospect, one of the troubles with my analysis was that everything was too neatly tied up leaving no loose ends. I must also add that my data, collected from a different point of view, was too thin for the kind of analysis I was attempting.

The year 1945–6 was R-B's last at Oxford. A few new students had joined the institute in October 1945 but the class was still small enough to make personal contact possible between teacher and student. Dr Meyer Fortes joined the institute as Reader some time after the beginning of the term. He had specialized in kinship and I found his lectures and seminars stimulating.

Before R-B left Oxford at the end of the Trinity term in 1946, I had completed two long and difficult chapters on 'The Ritual Idiom of the

Coorgs', and had started working on the cult of the patrilineage (or *okka* as it was called). R-B approved of these chapters and indeed he thought so well of them that he had put in a kind word about me to his successor, Professor (now Sir) Evans-Pritchard. He had made my transition to Evans-Pritchard (to be referred to as E-P) smooth.

E-P's style offered a profound contrast to R-B's. He did not seem to enjoy lecturing or presiding over seminars but he came into his own in a small group of students, colleagues and friends where he was free from the constraints of the set lecture and seminar. It was usual for a small circle of his students, and occasionally one or two others, to meet in one or other of the pubs near the Institute of Social Anthropology or at his house in Headington Hill, and discuss anthropology and everything else under the sun over tankards of beer. I came to know E-P the man as well as the scholar in these pub sessions, and looking back, I am amazed how he was able to give so much of his time to his students, and during a period when he was so extraordinarily creative.

He had the gift of establishing contact with human beings of diverse cultures and this was due in part at least to his deep and almost instinctive acceptance of all mankind as one in spite of racial and religious barriers. He was a conservative Englishman at heart but an odd conservative who could place himself in the position of the black man, the transhuman Nuer and the feuding Sànusi chief. I found it easier to communicate with E-P than with other white scholars, some of whom were known for their sympathy for India and for leftist causes generally.

Perhaps the ease which I felt in communicating with him was due in part at least to the latter's conversion to Catholicism sometime during the war. My Ph.D. theme was a religious one and our discussion could not ignore matters of faith and belief. We talked about Hinduism, Catholicism and Islam, and our talks were not only intellectually rewarding but increased our understanding of each other.

E-P was no doubt a staunch Catholic but there was also a deep streak of scepticism in him. This may sound paradoxical but it was true. He distinguished between the analytical potentialities of an idea and its truth-values. Functionalism had proved to be very useful in social anthropology but that did not necessarily mean that societies were actually integrated wholes. His scepticism was creative.

E-P's assertion that social anthropology was a moral and not natural science, and that its methods approximated to those of history, represented a rejection of R-B's basic position. He gave expression to these ideas in his well-known Marrett Lecture (1950) which gave rise to an excited debate. I think E-P did a service to anthropology by his 'revolt', for sociologists have not to date discovered any general 'laws', and R-B's dismissal of history as more or less irrelevant to sociological explanation is untenable. Further, sociological understanding and interpretation are similar to the historical except for the fact that the sociologist collects his data from direct observation whereas the historian relies on other people's observations and interpretations. As the 'primitive' or pre-literate world shrinks under the impact of modern technology, and as social anthropologists turn more and more to studying ancient civilizations and modern Western societies, E-P's ideas are likely to prove increasingly relevant.

But I was unhappy with certain side-effects of E-P's ideas. There was an unstated downgrading of the achievements of modern social anthropology and of the fieldwork tradition which had been built up by generations of anthropologists. Thanks to their methods and the ideas they pursued, social anthropologists have been able to build up a body of knowledge and theory about such basic institutions as the family, lineage, kinship system, caste and class and religion which cannot be ignored.

A few of E-P's more enthusiastic admirers even advanced the view that since the anthropologist selected his facts and interpreted them, the fieldworker was far more important than the field. I am stating the view too baldly and crudely without the sophistication which usually went into its exposition but I have no doubt that ultimately this was what was meant. This view is too absurd to merit rebuttal and it is also unfair to E-P who is one of the greatest of modern fieldworkers, as anyone who has read his *Witchcraft, Oracles and Sorcery among the Azande* or the Nuer trilogy can testify.

The continued denigration of R-B as thinker and man was another by-product of his stance. The advocates of the relevance of the historical dimension forgot only too easily that they were intellectually standing on the shoulders of the man whom they were downgrading. There was a failure to place themselves in R-B's position and view social anthropology as it appeared to him at the time he reached a position of influence. (Isn't this what Collingwood recommended in his *Autobiography?*) R-B rejected the diffusionism of the wilder variety which his mentor Rivers had come to espouse in his last days, and he tried to steer British anthropology in a new direction, that is, towards the French. This was also what Malinowski, another great British anthropologist, tried to do.

I was awarded the D.Phil. degree in July 1947, and before I sailed home E-P told me that he was trying to create a lectureship for me in Indian Sociology in Oxford and would I be interested? I was naturally delighted though in my confusion I was not able to tell him how I felt. Later in November I heard from him that I had been appointed and that I could spend the first year of my job doing a study of a multi-caste village in Mysore, a project which he knew I wanted very much to undertake.

I spent the best part of 1948 in making a field study of Rampura, a village 22 miles from Mysore.[2]

I shall skip my field experience and refer briefly to my second spell at that academic Arcadia, Oxford. My teaching load was light, being only forty-eight lectures a year, half of which were seminars on Indian Sociology. The 'light' load enabled the teacher to try to live up to the high scholarly standards which Oxford expects from its dons. The long vacations were ideal for intensive study and writing, and I was able to get my Coorg thesis ready for publication before I said good-bye to Oxford in June 1951. I had a few good friends in whose company I felt at home and in the sunshine of whose friendship I basked. But underneath my seeming contentment I was homesick for the sun and warmth of India. And I also realized that if I did not make an effort and pull myself out of Oxford before it was too late, I would probably not return home.

Throughout the year 1950 I was bothered by the nagging desire to return home. It was at this time that new universities were coming into existence and new chairs in sociology were being founded. Baroda was one of these new universities, and my old teacher Wadia was Pro-Vice-Chancellor there. To cut a long story short, I was appointed to the professorship in Baroda and I was asked to 'report myself to duty' as the phrase goes, on 15 June 1951.

I had kept E-P informed about my desire and plans, and he agreed with my view that I should return to my native country. But after I had burnt my boats in Oxford I was seized with all kinds of doubts and fears. I walked about with the feeling that I was really committing academic *hara-kiri* in giving up Oxford to go to a university which had just been

---

[2] The story of my research in Rampura is told in *The Remembered Village* (Oxford, New Delhi, 1976). Some of the chapters in this volume sketch my time at Rampura.

started. I even thought of going back on my decision but I lacked the courage to mention this to anyone. Indeed, all through my first year at Baroda I was occasionally plunged into moments of depression about the kind of academic life I had opted for, and even nourished fantasies about being transported back to Oxford by some unexpected turn of events. But looking back over the years I have no doubt whatever that I did the right thing in leaving Oxford and returning to a university in my own country. I am only too keenly aware that had I continued at Oxford I could have been a much more rigorous scholar and written more books and papers, but I am also certain that I would have experienced an emotional and spiritual desiccation which would have affected my work as well as my relations with those with whom I came into contact. Human social relations are the stuff of an anthropologist's analysis, and alienation from one's society and culture cannot but have consequences on his perceptions and interpretations. This is not to ignore the great contributions to the social sciences made by exiles and expatriates, and 'marginal' members of societies. Sociology is in a sense the offspring of collective as well as personal misery.

Leaving aside the problematic question of the kind of contribution I would have been able to make had I continued at Oxford, I have no doubt that by returning home I have been able to have certain satisfactions which I would not have had if I had remained abroad. One of the most important of these has been helping in the creation of a small body of scholars all of whom have been trained in India, are active in research and teaching and who are trying to apply the methods and techniques of social anthropology and sociology in the analysis of problems of a vast, diverse and complex society such as India which is also undergoing rapid change. This has had effects on the Indian sociological scene.

I have also been able to help in the setting up of two Departments of Sociology, first at Baroda and then at Delhi. I spent nearly eight years in Baroda and at the end of the period I had a small but good team of scholars, and some funds for fellowships and a building. But before the building could be started I left Baroda to take up the new chair of sociology established at Delhi University. The department grew rapidly and in a short period of ten years it was recognized as a centre of advanced study in sociology by the University Grants Commission. This meant funds for a new building, additional staff, strengthening the library, more fellowships and research, and visiting fellowships. The department is now better able to function as a national centre for teaching and research.

Even after twenty years of academic life in India, I have not been able to overcome my dislike of administration and committees. In fact, as I grow older my dislike of both has increased rather than diminished but I have not been able to shake them off. But it is also true that but for my involvement in committees both in Delhi University and outside I would not have been able to do my bit for promoting sociology in the universities and outside them.

I must add here that once in a while I participated in the work of a committee that was satisfying. The Indian Council of Social Science Research was one such committee, and I feel happy that facilities and opportunities are now available to Indian social scientists which were unknown even a decade ago. Again, in my role as president of the Indian Sociological Society between 1966–9, I was able to assist in the coming together of those two organizations, the Indian Sociological Society (ISS) and the All-India Sociological Conference, to form a single professional body. The society's finances needed strengthening and this was also achieved to some extent. The secretariat side of the society and its journal, the *Sociological Bulletin*, were reorganized and the constitution of the ISS altered to enable it to meet the new and increased demands made on it by a larger body of members.

One of the things to which I paid continuous attention both at Baroda and Delhi was devising a suitable syllabus in sociology. Any syllabus has to take note of local conditions including the kind of students who come and the specializations and interests of teachers. But I did want the syllabus to be rooted in Indian conditions in order to enable the student to relate what he read to his experience and at the same time I wanted some material on Asia and Africa included for purposes of comparison and contrast. I got a few classics prescribed for intensive study. After a few years, I was able to introduce books dealing with change, and entire courses on specialism such as 'sociology of kinship', 'political sociology' and 'sociology of religion'.

Several Indian sociologists and anthropologists who had jobs abroad and who wanted to return home wrote to me seeking help and I think I was of some help in enabling a few to settle down in India. This gave me satisfaction as their return helped to strengthen the profession in India.

As head of the department at Delhi, I was further to assist students from various countries: from the United States, the United Kingdom, France and Germany, Japan, Philippines and Australia to come to India to do field studies in various parts of the country in fulfillment of their

Ph.D. requirements. In a few cases l was even able to direct their attention successfully to the study of important problems or groups. The department's growing reputation attracted foreign students for the MA and M.Litt. degrees. It is no exaggeration to say that Delhi became a regular port of call for social anthropologists and sociologists from all over the world.

I have always believed that while natives enjoy certain undeniable advantages in studying their own society they also labour under serious disadvantages, the existence of which is not usually acknowledged. This can be reduced to some extent in a vast and diverse country such as India where scholars from one region can work in a different region—which is not sufficiently common. It is therefore essential, in the interests of sociological adequacy, to have a given society studied by members of diverse cultures. Only in this way can the element of subjectivity be reduced.

This fact together with the other that sociologists and social anthropologists all over the world have a commitment to certain common interests and values had made me believe that they form an invisible college. Their status as citizens of particular countries is not in any way invalidated by their membership of the 'invisible college'. I consider it necessary to state this as I hear the view expressed increasingly that developing countries should erect barriers against free contact with social scientists from developed countries in order to safeguard their academic interests and their national integrity.

As I have stated at the beginning, I shall not discuss here what I think is my contribution to the analysis of Indian society and culture as distinct from my contribution to the organization and development of the discipline. I would like, however, to emphasize that I have refused to make a distinction between social anthropology and sociology in teaching and research. This distinction has its origin in Western political and academic history, and it does not make sense to apply it in a country such as India where tribes have on the whole enjoyed some form of contact with the more advanced groups. A considerable proportion of India's population is backward, and many of the beliefs and practices of the backward sections are to be found even among the so-called advanced sections. In other words, there is a continuity in traditional India between tribes and castes and any imported distinction between social anthropology and sociology does violence to social reality.

As could be expected, I have emphasized also the crucial character of fieldwork experience in the training of sociologists. The method of participant observation, evolved by Malinowski, has been used to great advantage in the understanding of local communities, ethnic and other groups, and social situations in complex societies. Indeed, participant observation and the quantitative techniques associated with macro-studies can be used in a mutually complementary way. Thus, macro-studies describe the behaviour of large categories and aggregates in specific matters while micro-studies provide insights into relationships and motivations in small units. Properly used, micro-studies can provide hypotheses to be tested by macro-methods while the latter yield perspectives as well as problems to be tackled by new micro-studies. In short, the two can be brought together in a mutually creative relationship.

As a scholar progresses in his academic life, he finds to his dismay an increasing amount of his time being spent on matters other than his studies and research. Ever since my return home in 1951, I have been torn between two conflicting desires, one, to make such contribution as I could to the building up of a national sociological tradition, and the other, to my own study and research. I am aware that the latter has suffered and I have also been accused of having become a 'committee man'. I have no regrets whatever for the time I have spent on committees but during the last six or seven years I have been feeling acutely the need to catch up to some extent with the flood of new literature and to write up my Rampura material and to pursue some ideas and hunches. I thought, perhaps prematurely, that after building up the department in Delhi I would be able to concentrate on my work. But that proved to be illusory. I hope that my movement away from Delhi to Bangalore in the South will give me more time for my work.

My occasional escapes abroad have been helpful in reducing the feeling of academic illiteracy from which I suffered (and still do). I must not fail to mention here my two long visits to the Centre for Advanced Study in the Behavioural Sciences (1964–5 and 1970–1) where I was able to get away from my routine cares to concentrate on study and research. The Centre is really a dream place for scholars, and I found its staff always kind, considerate and helpful. I must express my indebtedness to them.

Before I end this autobiographical essay, I must give expression to my feeling that I am really lucky in that my work has had some influence on other scholars engaged in the analysis of Indian society and culture.

I have also had more than my fair share of honours. If anything I feel that now I should be more active in research in order to justify the honours conferred on me. I am also aware that while honours give a scholar great pleasure, total involvement in creative research with all its heartbreaks and anxieties brings with it a satisfaction which is altogether different and is more gratifying.

My Baroda Days

I joined the Maharaja Sayajirao University of Baroda as its first professor of sociology on 15 June 1951, the day the university reopened after the summer vacation. Only a week previously I had been teaching at Oxford. I must confess that my sudden elevation to a professorship at Baroda from a lectureship at Oxford had not greatly elated me. Oxford was a great centre of learning, and my job was a permanent and comfortable one, my teaching duties being such as to allow me adequate time to pursue my research. I had friendly colleagues, and the professor and head of the department, Evans-Pritchard, was particularly kind to me. In fact, he had got the post of university lecturer in Indian Sociology created with a view to my being appointed to it, and he had promoted my interests in other ways as well. I was full of doubts and uncertainties at the switch from Oxford to Baroda. Baroda was *terra incognita* to me, the only person I knew there being my former teacher at Mysore, Professor A. R. Wadia. He had joined the M.S. University at the time of its establishment in 1949 as its Pro-Vice-Chancellor.

I flew from London on 12 June to arrive in Bombay the next day, some time after noon. London was cool, and I wore my woollen, three-piece suit for the flight from London to Bombay. (My books and luggage were coming later by boat.) When I landed at Santa Cruz, it was extremely sultry, the outbreak of the monsoon being imminent. My hosts who had come to meet me were very amused by my three-piece: I was living up to my reputation for impracticality, for living in a world of my own and ignoring the world around me. In the evening my hostess took me at my request to a *khadi* shop near Sandhurst Road, and I was measured for three cotton suits, which would not be ready till at least a week later. In the meanwhile I had to stew in my woollen clothes!

I caught the Dehra Dun express to Baroda on the 14th night—the train was to become very familiar to me during the next eight years—and arrived in Baroda on the 15th, a little before dawn. Some time in the morning I called on the Dean of the Faculty of Arts, Mr G. B. Pandya, and the Registrar, Mr B. K. Zutshi. I must also have called on Professor A. R. Wadia, the Pro-Vice-Chancellor, and Mrs Hansa Mehta, the Vice-Chancellor but I have no recollection of it. All that I remember is the sticky heat of pre-monsoon Baroda and going from one office to another.

My first problem was to find a place to stay. Professor Wadia, whom I had met at Oxford a few months earlier, had assured me that I would be allotted a university flat but that it would take some time. The housing situation in Baroda was difficult. Sindhi refugees had come in large numbers following the Partition of the sub-continent and Baroda was one of the cities they had moved into in a big way. New buildings had not come up fast enough to meet the needs of an increased population. (All over India war-time scarcities continued into the early fifties.)

The only place for me to stay at was the Circuit House, formerly the guest house of the Maharaja of Baroda, and in 1951, the property of the Government of Bombay with which Baroda state had been merged after independence. During its heyday, the princely guests of the Maharajah had stayed at the Circuit House, and the furniture, crockery, cutlery, and service had been originally intended to meet their needs. But in 1951 only a few officials of the Government of Bombay 'camped' in the Circuit House when they had work in Baroda and they were charged an absurdly small sum for rent and food. The income from the guests was nowhere near enough to keep the place in the style it had been used to: the curtains were torn in places, the sofas sank when one sat on them, and rats scurried on the floor. Valjee, the cook, bemoaned the fate which had overtaken the Circuit House, and had nothing but ill-disguised contempt for the new type of guests. Some of the princely life-style had rubbed off on him. He used to import cheroots by the thousands from Trichinopoly and I used to see him smoking them at night sitting on the steps of the dining room, after the guests had eaten. It is probable that he was used to a drink during the princely days. After the merger, prohibition was extended to the former territories of Baroda state.

Professor Wadia had played a crucial role in my appointment to the professorship at Baroda. A chair in Sociology had been created as both he and the Vice-Chancellor, Mrs Hansa Mehta, were enthusiasts of the subject. I sent in my application for the chair, and was selected even though two very senior scholars, Professors Radhakamal Mukherjee and Kewal Motwani, had also applied. In retrospect, it appears to me that it was only natural that Professor Wadia should want me as I had been his student and I had kept in touch with him afterwards. But Mrs Mehta had taken a risk in selecting an unknown young man in preference to Professor Radhakamal Mukherjee. Mrs Mehta was an unusual person: she wanted Baroda University to be a centre of excellence and to be different from other Indian universities. She had created new faculties such as Home Science, Social Work, and Fine Arts, and there was widespread criticism of this decision. She had selected young men and women from all over the country to staff the departments. She took a keen interest in the university's functioning and activities, and she had to intervene frequently to see that scholars were able to get on with their work and that the administrative staff did not block their way. Several of the latter were men with small minds and could block any attempt at change but they all had a wholesome fear of Mrs Mehta. The fact that her husband, Dr Jivaraj Mehta, was minister for finance in the Government of Bombay, and a member of the syndicate of the M.S. University, made Mrs Mehta's task somewhat easier.

In due course, I received a letter from the university appointing me professor of sociology on a salary of Rs 700 per month and asking me to report to duty on 15 June and adding that the university would not pay my travel costs. At the Oxford end, even though I had taught during the entire academic year, I was not entitled to vacation salary since I was not returning to my post in October (1951) when the new term would begin. The move from Oxford to Baroda had considerably impoverished me.

Professor Wadia visited England in May 1951, and I invited him to have dinner with me in my college, Exeter. His visit gave us a chance to talk about Baroda and the work I was expected to do. During my undergraduate days at Mysore University, Professor Wadia had a reputation as a strict disciplinarian, and neither his students nor his colleagues felt totally at ease with him. The martinet in him surfaced during our brief encounter. He said to me that he hoped I had not picked up bad habits like smoking or drinking at Oxford. But he was surprised that I continued to be a vegetarian! As a Parsi, Professor Wadia was fond of meat, and considered smoking a terrible vice. But he was very un-

Parsi in condemning the consumption of alcohol. Forgetting all this, I had ordered a bottle of claret for dinner and we shared it. Perhaps drinking at the high table in Oxford was excusable. Professor Wadia had happy memories of a post-graduate year he had spent in Oxford and had great respect for Oxford and its institutions.

My first few days in Baroda were spent in a daze. I felt self-conscious in my heavy woollen suit, and carrying the jacket on my arm only increased my predicament. I perspired freely. Since I was not a government official, I was charged a high rate at the Circuit House and I wondered how long I would be able to afford staying there. The food was not to my taste, and the fact that Valjee was contemptuous towards his guests made his food even less appetizing.

I had been given a room next to the Dean's office in the Faculty of Arts (formerly Baroda College). I had to ask the Dean for everything: extra chairs, stationery, library grant, and an assistant to help me secure the things needed for the department, etc. Mr Pandya was on the whole helpful but there were severe limits to his ability to help. Besides, it was not easy to talk business with the Dean. One had to spend a lot of time making petty talk, and generally make oneself agreeable, before mentioning what one wanted done. Visiting him in his flat was regarded as evidence of friendship and not as an intrusion.

I think that on the whole I played the game on the right lines for the Dean let me have the assistance of a tutor in History or Political Science to prepare a list of books and journals for ordering. I was also allowed to ransack other collections in the Faculty of Arts for my departmental library. For instance, in one of the domes of the Baroda College building I found a huge pile of dust-covered books. Rummaging through the pile, I found several useful volumes, including the *Encyclopaedia of Islam* (4 volumes). When the head of the department of Urdu came to know that I had found a set of the *Encyclopaedia of Islam* he went to the Dean and said that the volumes ought to be in his department and not in that of Sociology. The Dean requested me to hand over the volumes to the head of the department of Urdu even though he thought that they would be better used in my department.

When I came to know Mr Pandya better, he talked about his problems and colleagues. It was not enough to listen to him, he expected one to agree with him. Once he confessed to me that he had accommodated the two new professors next to him in order 'to keep an eye' on them. He was pleased to learn that I did not want to be Dean at any price.

I had to teach an introductory course in Sociology to second year students in the Home Science Faculty. They were all girls in their teens, and their knowledge of English was very poor. I found it difficult to teach them. I had to stop frequently to explain the meanings of words I used. But the students' problem was not only linguistic—they were far too young, and ill-equipped. Besides, it was my first experience of teaching at such an elementary level. It needs a highly experienced and skilled teacher to teach absolute beginners.

My main task was, however, in the Faculty of Arts where I was teaching the BA course. Since Sociology was a new subject and not well-known locally, only two students, A. M. Shah and I. P. Shelat, registered themselves. Shah went on later to become Professor of Sociology at Delhi while Shelat went into Social Work after graduation. Narayan Sheth joined the BA in 1952 and later became Professor at the Indian Institute of Management at Ahmedabad. Another student to pursue a career in Sociology was Ramesh Shroff. He joined the Gujarat Vidyapeeth in Ahmedabad and became Reader in Anthropology. He died prematurely.

Soon after I had joined, two students who had graduated with Sociology from the University of Bombay wanted me to start an MA course in Sociology for them. I refused. I thought I could not undertake to teach, single-handed, the MA course comprising eight papers. Also, I did not want to teach the MA course as prescribed by the University of Bombay which I would have had to do, if I had admitted the students immediately, before I had worked out my own syllabus, and got it passed through appropriate committees. One of the two students was quite aggressive and even hinted that he could bring pressure on me to start the course. That settled it. I was not going to budge.

Three teachers in the Faculty of Social Work registered themselves for the Ph.D. with me while a fourth came from the Department of Archaeology. I found that none of these students had the kind of training which I would have liked them to have had before going on to do a Ph.D. The only thing I could do to help them was to start a course of seminars where there could be wide-ranging discussion. The seminars were held at various places, in my office, in my apartment in Adhyapak Nivas (university apartment house) or sometimes, when the weather was nice, on the lawn in front of my apartment. The seminars proved to be popular with the students and also helped me to get to know them better. They were perhaps the first seminars to be held in the university, long before an expensive 'seminar culture' took hold of the country.

If I may anticipate events, within a few years Sociology became a popular subject, especially at the BA and Ph.D. levels. Sociology was also taught in the Faculties of Home Science, Engineering and Technology. Before I left Baroda for Delhi in February 1959, the department's staff had increased, the nucleus of a library had come into existence, and it had become customary for students to take up a theme involving fieldwork for the Ph.D. A few months before my departure, the UGC granted money for a new building, for expansion of the library, for carrying out fieldwork, and finally, for creating a few additional posts and scholarships.

Soon, Baroda came to be recognized as a new centre of teaching and research in Sociology, the sociology that was taught there being distinct from that in other departments in the country. Sociologists and anthropologists from the USA and UK also visited the department, and interacted with the staff and students. Several students of the department obtained post-graduate degrees and pursued careers in Sociology. A few names, besides those mentioned earlier, come to my mind: Y. V. S. Nath, H. R. Trivedi, P. T. Thomas, B. V. Shah, K. R. Unni, R. S. Gandhi, V. H. Joshi, Tarun Sheth, E. M. Masihi and A. R. Shah.

I was able to pay some attention to the task of working out a suitable syllabus for students of Sociology in Indian universities, a task which continued to occupy my attention throughout my teaching career. When I joined Baroda it was usual for universities in Western India to copy blindly the Sociology syllabus of Bombay University. I did not want to do that: for one thing, that syllabus had not been revised for some years, and secondly, I had my own conception of Sociology which I wanted reflected in my syllabus. I wanted students to have a firm knowledge of Indian social institutions and in a comparative context. Secondly, I found American textbooks of Sociology really ethnocentric, un-comparative, and failing to distinguish between Sociology and Social Work. Also, I found the separation of Social Anthropology and Sociology untenable, particularly in the Indian context. Finally, I wanted students to study intensively, at least at the Master's level, a few classics on the subject. And all this had to be done while paying attention to the background of the students.

The train that carried me to Baroda from Bombay also carried the newly-appointed Professor of Economics, S. Chandrasekhar. I had a glimpse of him—though at that time I did not know who he was—as I got off the train. He had arrived with masses of luggage, an American wife in a sari, and his three-year-old daughter. He had resigned his job in Annamalai to join Baroda. We were thrown upon each other during the first few months of our stay, and more important, we became linked in the minds of the citizens of Baroda. That was because we were both South Indians with foreign degrees appointed to newly-created chairs, and we had travelled by the same train. And when I moved to the Circuit House I found that Chandrasekhar was my neighbour. After a fortnight at the Circuit House Chandrasekhar rented a house in Goya Gate and persuaded me to move in with him as we would be able to share costs. We both cycled daily from Goya Gate to the Faculty of Arts. This continued till I moved into Adhyapak Nivas. I was, needless to say, relieved to be finally on my own. Chandrasekhar seemed annoyed that the university authorities had allotted me a flat before he was allotted one.

Before the university came into existence, there was in Baroda, a cluster of colleges and other institutions providing the infrastructure for the creation of a university: a college teaching arts and science, a college of commerce, a teachers' training college, and an Oriental Institute. There was also an institution for technology and another for music. The teachers in these institutions were all employees of the Government of Baroda earning small sums and working long hours. Understandably, they looked on the new and well-paid employees of the university with a little less than love. The fact that many of the newcomers were 'outsiders' only added to their sense of grievance. The term 'outsider' had an elastic meaning. Not only South Indians, Bengalis and Punjabis qualified for the status but everyone from outside the boundaries of old Baroda state. The Professor of Gujarati who was from Ahmedabad, told me that he was also regarded as an outsider.

The university had come into existence in 1949 and had collected staff from all over India. Some of these men and women had been educated abroad. The new faculties of Home Science, Social Work, and Fine Arts in particular had attracted men and women trained in the USA. The behaviour and life-style of the university staff, in particular, of the women who wore sleeveless blouses, used lipstick and smoked cigarettes, were criticized by the townsfolk who were, by and large, very conservative. Two local Gujarati newspapers reported, not always accurately, the happenings on the campus to satisfy and titillate the curiosity of the townsfolk. The Maharashtrian youth who brought me my newspaper every morning stopped by occasionally to report on any interesting item concerning the activities of my lively colleagues on the campus.

Professor Chandrasekhar was Professor of Economics but his area of specialization was Demography. He had founded, when in Annamalai, an Institute of Population Studies. When he came to Baroda, the Institute came with him. Chandrasekhar liked to lecture on population problems, and within a few weeks of his arrival, he had lectured on India's population problems in Baroda, and a few nearby towns.

Since there was already in existence a Department of Economics in the Faculty of Arts, some teachers of Economics, called on their new boss in the Circuit House. Chandrasekhar sat in an easy chair on the veranda and received his callers. He was an outgoing man who liked meeting people, and during his stay in the US he had met several well-known academics and distinguished Indians, about whom he liked to talk. He had a sense of the absurd and this came into play very occasionally. When in such a mood he was amusing. On other occasions, however, it was just a litany of names.

People could not help noticing the contrast between the two new professors. Chandrasekhar's public lectures, his outgoing attitude, and his American wife, all attracted the attention of the university staff and even those outside. The fact that he was the head of an established and fairly big department, brought him into contact with many teachers, students and parents. The presence of several American-educated teachers in the university was also a factor in his quick acceptance by them. My innate shyness and my overdeveloped sense of privacy, were regarded as typical of a British-trained, especially Oxford-trained, Indian. I was, aware, however, of what was happening around me.

A few months after my arrival, Professor T. K. N. Menon, the Dean of the Faculty of Education, told me that the Vice-Chancellor had confided in him about her fears for the development of Sociology. She had found me so shy and retreating that she wondered how I would be able to build up an active department. She contrasted me with the Professor of Economics who had so much 'go'. It is probable that Mrs Mehta regarded Chandrasekhar as a typical product of the dynamic educational system of the USA and me of the stodgy and conservative educational system of England. She was widely reputed to be prejudiced against the British system of education. Her own children had been educated in the USA, and her son had married an American girl.

But relations between Chandrasekhar and the M.S. University went sour fairly soon. He left the university years before I did. But his fortunes continued to rise. He became an MP, and then minister of state for Health and Family Planning in Delhi, and finally, Vice-Chancellor of his former University, Annamalai. He also visited the US, frequently.

I needed to have more teachers in my department if I wanted to start teaching a Master's course in Sociology. But this was a matter beyond the Dean's jurisdiction. Once I broached the subject with Professor Wadia while out on a walk with him. He told me firmly that nothing would be forthcoming for at least another year. I had to manage as best I could. Professor Wadia was used to university teachers teaching between ten to fifteen periods a week, and research did not occupy a central place in his scheme of things. Further, the moment I asked the question he became a tough Pro-Vice-Chancellor who was used to saying no to importunate heads of departments.

It was at that walk or a little later that Professor Wadia told me that he was quitting Baroda at the end of that academic year. Apparently something had gone wrong in his understanding of his agreement with the university. I also gathered that Professor Wadia did not admire Dr Jivaraj Mehta's style of functioning. He advised me to apply for Professor Ghurye's chair in Bombay when it fell vacant. He did not know that Ghurye's dislike for me was intense, and that the last thing he wanted was for me to succeed him.

Professor K. T. Shah, the well-known economist, was a member of the syndicate of the M.S. University, and he had precise ideas about what I should be doing. He told Mrs Mehta that he wanted to talk to me, and I went and met him in a room in the administration building. He told me, in a rather long and rambling monologue, that he wanted me to do a sociological study of Manu's *dharmashastra*. It was the most important task before Indian sociologists, and if I am not misinterpreting him, he wanted the entire department to be engaged in the study of the *dharmashastra*. I listened to him patiently but kept my thoughts to myself. He became annoyed. He said that he was almost totally blind and he could not see my face to judge my reactions. I felt sorry for him but the more dominant feeling, I must confess, was resentment at the interference in my teaching of Sociology. Further, at that moment, I was engaged in a public controversy on the urgent need to carry out intensive field studies of communities in different parts of the country, and stressing the distinction between Indology and Sociology. There was a tendency in Indian sociological circles to mistake Indology for Sociology.

I think I had another encounter with Professor Shah. He must have written me off as a hopeless case.

The university appointed a Visiting Committee consisting of Professor Kellock of Wilson College, Bombay, Mr Ramanlal Vasantlal Desai, and the Vice-Chancellor to report on teaching in the Faculty of Arts. (I do not know what the precise terms of reference of the Committee

were.) The Committee met the teachers in the common room one afternoon and the two outside members asked the heads of departments
about teaching and other conditions in their respective departments. Mr
Desai asked me how many periods I was teaching per week; and I told
him six (or five). He replied that I ought to be teaching twenty-six
periods a week. I took him up on that and told him that since I was expected to do research as a part of my duties, any such teaching load was anta-
gonistic to research. I added that I was determined to go on with my research. I am afraid I had lost my cool and the assembled teachers did
not fail to notice it. Luckily for me, Mr Keilock expressed himself in
favour of my views.

I was annoyed that Mr Desai had tried to tick me off before my
colleagues, and I later mentioned it to Mrs Mehta. She asked me to
ignore what he had said. She added that he might have had an axe to
grind. Sometime later a friend of mine met him and Mr Desai assured
him that he had a high opinion of me but he had only expressed his
convictions regarding how many periods a teacher should be teaching.
Mr Desai had a reputation as a radical and novelist, and he was also a
member of the syndicate. However, he had never taught in a university.

There were two ways of meeting the Vice-Chancellor, one formal, and
the other, informal. In the former, one rang up her secretary and took an
appointment and saw her in her office in the university. The second was
to drop in on her in the evening when she sat in a chair in her beautiful
garden turning over the pages of a book or journal that had recently
arrived. I came to know about the latter method some weeks after my
arrival, but I thought that only those who were close to her were entitled
to take the liberty of dropping in on her. I knew that she worked hard and
I thought that she should not be disturbed in her privacy.

But once, in response to a request for an appointment, she asked me
to see her in her house in the evening. When I met her, I found her more
relaxed than when she was in her office. Also, there were no interrup-
tions. She was relatively informal and free, and talked about many
things besides the matter that had provoked me to request her for the
interview.

After this meeting, I started dropping in on her occasionally, drank
her *masala cha*, and talked about the needs and problems of the
department. She came to know me better. She sanctioned the appointment of a clerk-typist, a research assistant, and a reader. The 'kitchen

block' of the old Baroda College Hostel was made over to the department. Some money was sanctioned by the Vice-Chancellor for making minor changes in the building and for providing it with fans, curtains etc. My colleagues gradually woke up to the fact that the department had expanded substantially commanding facilities which others with ten times the number of students and older, did not have. A low profile which was natural to me, had paid off.

My choice for the readership in Sociology, was Dr I. P. Desai, who was then a lecturer in Sociology at Deccan College, Poona. Dr Desai was my senior by several years but we had known each other from our days as students under Professor Ghurye in the department of Sociology in Bombay University. We had a joking relation with each other and, underlying the joking relationship, respect. I knew that I. P.'s ideas of Sociology were different from mine in some ways but I regarded it as a factor in his favour. I wanted someone who would supplement my skills.

There was another reason why I thought I. P.'s appointment was essential. I did not see myself as staying for a long time in Baroda, and I did not want to leave a vacuum behind me after my departure. I. P. was from the region, and sufficiently senior to take over the department from me, which he did when I moved to Delhi in February 1959.

I knew that my request for the creation of a reader's post would not be easily granted. There were several departments in the university which antedated mine and which had not expanded at all. From the point of the university, a request for a lectureship made sense but not a request for a readership. I sounded out Mrs Mehta and she was not at all enthusiastic. I told Professor Ghurye that I was trying to get I. P. to Baroda but he did not like the idea either. He told me his reason for it and if he had any ideas of convincing me, he achieved only the opposite.

I informed Mrs Mehta that I could not start a Master's course in Sociology without a reader, and that I would like Dr I. P. Desai to occupy the post. She took a little while to agree to the proposal but, characteristically, matters moved quickly after her approval. I. P. joined me early in the academic year of 1952. Since I knew that I. P. was a sensitive person, I never told him about the problems I had in getting him to Baroda.

Mr Y. V. S. Nath, who had obtained an M.Sc. in Anthropology from Delhi, joined the department as research assistant even before I. P.'s joining. Nath was able to help me in preparing lists of books and journals, in the planning of courses of study, and finally, in teaching. If

I remember correctly, it was he who took Sociology classes for students in the engineering faculty. Nath went to do a study of the Bhils of Ratanmals. It may be described as one of the first modern studies of an Indian tribal group by an Indian. H. R. Trivedi did a similar study of the Mers of Saurashtra.

As I came to know Mrs Mehta better, my regard and respect for her increased. She wanted higher education to be more relevant to the needs of a developing country such as India. The starting of the Faculties of Social Work, Home Science and Fine Arts were expressions of her desire for a more relevant system of higher education. These faculties were staffed with several American-trained men and women whose life-styles did not meet with the approval of local townspeople and the conservative members of the teaching staff. (One story that did the rounds in the early fifties was that a few women teachers in the Faculty of Social Work went to Ranoli village on the outskirts of Baroda. They were dressed in jeans and shirts, had short hair, wore lipstick, and were smoking cigarettes. They were sitting on a culvert, and after watching them for a while, a few villagers walked up and asked them, 'Tell us, are you men or women?')

When these faculties were criticized, Mrs Mehta understandably defended them. But to be fair, Mrs Mehta also encouraged all those who had talent and commitment. For instance, my archaeologist colleague, Dr Subba Rao, was a fine and energetic digger though somewhat inarticulate, and he never lacked funds for his projects. He was promoted from senior lecturer to reader and then to professor in a relatively short period of time. She also gave considerable encouragement to the department of Gujarati. She was proud of Gujarat and its culture, but she was no small-minded chauvinist. She had an all-India vision.

Under her leadership, the M.S. University began to be recognized by the cognoscenti as an innovative centre of higher learning. And all this was achieved in a relatively short period of time. Of course, some of this was due to the fact that Mrs Mehta had real power, and that she could take quick decisions and implement them. Behind her stood her powerful husband, Dr Jivaraj Mehta. Also, the development took place at a time when student and teacher strikes had not become endemic. It was a period of relative calm, and on the whole, national optimism.

My relations with Mrs Mehta were uniformly good except on two occasions. Once I yielded to the pressure of my colleagues and signed a letter which they had written to the Vice-Chancellor. I forget what the exact issue was, but I had come to the conclusion that it was on the whole reasonable. When the letter reached the Vice-Chancellor she sent for me and asked me how I could have signed such a letter. Her argument was that I as 'a scholar' should have kept out of it. I told her that the letter was a reasonable one and as a teacher in the university, I felt that I should sign it. She was not convinced. It was all 'political'. She was so angry that the matter became undebatable.

My decision to leave Baroda for Delhi in 1959 was not liked by Mrs Mehta. The department had a good and growing reputation, and I understood Mrs Mehta's disapproving my leaving. I had to pay the university Rs 2,000 to obtain its consent to my leaving since I had not completed two years after my return in November 1957 from a year's leave in the US. What surprised me, however, was Dr Jivaraj Mehta's writing a letter to the Vice-Chancellor of Delhi advising him against encouraging me to move to Delhi. His letter only annoyed the Vice-Chancellor.

A few years after leaving Baroda I ran into Mrs Mehta at a meeting in Delhi and I was delighted at being able to have a pleasant chat with her. She showed no trace of annoyance at my having left Baroda. Her natural graciousness had surfaced when we met. She looked well, and her mind was as alert as ever.

Looking back, I think of my Baroda days with satisfaction and nostalgia. I learnt the lessons of department-building there, lessons which were to prove useful to me in Delhi. It was in Baroda that I had made the transition from Oxford to a university—a new one at that—in my own country. I also made some lifelong friendships in Baroda, friendships that have been a source of joy, solace and happiness.

Bangalore as I See It

I moved to Bangalore from Delhi early in May 1972 to help start an institute for research in the social sciences. I have stayed in the city since then. My contacts with Bangalore, however, go back to my childhood, and Bangalore has been a part of my consciousness ever since I can remember. I, therefore, begin my account of the city with my earliest encounters with it.

My mother's mother lived in Bangalore with her older daughter, Srirangamma (later known to Bangalore as Akkayya, literally; elder sister), who lived in a bungalow on Fifth Road, Chamarajpet. (Chamarajpet was one of the earliest extensions of the city, even before Basavangudi and Malleshwaram.) As long as grandmother was alive, my mother used to visit Bangalore during the summer holidays but the visits became much less frequent after grandmother's death. I did accompany my mother on more than one visit but what is tantalizing is that I only remember unconnected bits and pieces of events occurring at different points of time. It is like having only a few unrelated snapshots, to make the best of. At the same time to try and make them more coherent than they are, is to falsify them.

My aunt's bungalow was set in a large compound, the land sloping to the south. In fact, the road occupied the crest of the valley, the house being a few feet lower than the road. I remember a few croton plants with multi-coloured leaves between the gate and the steps leading to the front veranda. Two rooms flanked the veranda at either end, while the front door led to a large hall which was again flanked by rooms. Between the front part of the house and the kitchen and dining room there was a large yard, running the entire width of the house, and open to the skies. The kitchen was again a few feet lower than the front part, and steps descended from the back of the hall into the yard and the kitchen. At the far end of the compound were the coachman's quarters, and there was also a covered shed for the horse and Victoria—a horse-drawn carriage. My aunt was in the government and as befitted a high official she was driven around in such a carriage. (Cars had not yet become common: I recently learnt that in the 1920s only one gentleman in Chamarajpet owned a car, and he was an engineer who had retired from service in Bombay Presidency. My aunt eventually graduated to owning a second-hand Ford in which she toured the state on work.) Apart from the coachman's quarters, I remember a guava tree with plenty of tiny fruits which I used to eat, making myself sick in the process. There was a large, hairy white dog called Julie on whose back I used to sit and ride. The dog was the favourite of my cousin Raju, who was a contemporary of my older brother, Gopu. I remember Gopu telling me that Raju used to go in search of the sloughed-off skin of cobras to feed Julie with. Such a diet was supposed to make a dog ferocious and Raju wanted Julie to be the local champion dog which meant that every other dog had to be scared of him. However that might have been Julie was most patient with me! I think Raju did really roam the area around Kempambudhi tank in search of sloughed-off cobra skins.

Srirangamma ought to have a place in the cultural history of princely Mysore. She, along with her aunt, her father's younger brother's wife, Rukminiamma, were the first two women in South India to become graduates and that was before World War I, when all colleges in princely Mysore were affiliated to the University of Madras. When aunt and niece received their BA degree at the same convocation ceremony in Madras, they were taken in a procession by the local gentry, with musicians at the head, and the good women of Triplicane waving *arati* to honour the two women who had brought credit to their sex and community. (Iyengars were concentrated in Triplicane.) I heard this from my mother who was proud of the achievement of her older sister, and her aunt.

Both Srirangamma and Rukminiamma rose to high positions in the

Government of Mysore. Srirangamma was a high official in the Department of Public Instruction, while Rukminiamma had a long innings as the principal of Maharani College in Mysore. Both married men who supported their wives' careers, and who were content to stay in the wings, while their more important spouses occupied the centre of the stage. Both outlived their husbands, and lived to a ripe old age enjoying the respect of the people around them. What is astonishing is that people seemed to have accepted without much fuss a revolutionary change of role for women, and their spouses.

As I said earlier, I have recollections of my grandmother: she was a widow with shaven head, always dressed in a light brown jute sari with an inch-wide red border. Her head was covered by a part of the sari, and someone must have taught me to tease her which I did, and which used to annoy the old lady. I have faint recollections of my aunt's husband who used to shout periodically asking me not to run around the terrace in the hot afternoons while he slept in a room below. I have also recollections of Raju's sisters, Jaya and Padma, more of Padma than of Jaya. But it is all so fragmentary.

I remember a visit to Cubbon Park, walking around clumps of bamboos, and watching the water flow in the canals and also a visit to the museum, looking at things kept in glass cases. There was also a visit to the house of S.D.S. Iyengar, my mother's maternal uncle's son—a big bungalow set in a big garden with very many potted plants, and sculptures of deities on granite slabs, presumably from a temple, standing at strategic points in the garden. Only after May 1972, when I settled down in Bangalore, did I learn that that bungalow was 'Clovelly', now part of the Woodlands Hotel complex. S. D. S. Iyengar, after a distinguished career in the Mysore Electricity Department, moved to Ooty as the head of the Pykhara Power Project.

Raju lived in Akkayya's (Srirangamma's) house along with his sisters Jaya and Padma. Their father, M. G. Varadachar, was a lawyer, whose brilliant career was cut short, when he was only in his thirties. He fell a victim to influenza which came in an epidemic form in 1918–19. Varadachar was my maternal uncle, younger than Akkayya and older than my mother. My mother was full of stories of his brilliance, wealth, and popularity—they were part of our family's folklore. However, quite recently, I came across a brief account about him in a collection of twenty biographical sketches in Kannada, *Jnapaka Chitrashale*, by his friend and admirer, D. V. Gundappa (Kavyalaya, Mysore, 1969), and it is evident from the account that Varadachar was a gifted and unusual person. His fortune had risen rapidly at the Bar, and there had been every chance of his becoming a judge of the Mysore High Court. (In fact, his partner in law practice, C. S. Doreswamy Iyer, rose to become the Chief Justice of the Mysore High Court.)

Varadachar was a keen student of English literature, particularly poetry. He was a poet himself, but only a few of his poems in English were published. The notebook containing his other poems, was lost as also his thesis on Browning which he intended to submit for the MA degree (of Madras University). I remember reading a few of his poems in praise of Ramakrishna and Vivekananda in the last volume of the *Collected Works of Swami Vivekananda.* Varadachar was a devotee of Ramakrishna and Vivekananda, and a daily visit to the Ramakrishna Mutt, near his home in Appajappa Agrahar, was part of his routine. He was also a brilliant and witty speaker and he attracted big audiences. He was a patriot, deeply concerned about political and economic events of the day. He used to visit his maternal uncle, B. Ramaswamy Iyengar, the ophthalmologist regularly, where a few friends of the latter gathered during evenings to discuss political, economic, religious, literary and aesthetic matters. Incidentally, Ramaswamy Iyengar, was the first Superintendent of the Minto Eye Hospital. He and his brother's son, S. D. S. Iyengar, both went abroad for higher studies, the uncle to London to become an opthalmologist, the nephew to the United States where he became an electrical engineer, and both were thrown out of their caste on return. No Iyengar would give them his daughter, and both married Bengalis, emancipated Baidyas who had embraced the Brahma Samaj. The uncle married the older sister while the nephew married a younger sister. The life-styles of the uncle and nephew were highly westernized, totally different from that of their kinfolk who had not crossed the seas. Ramaswamy Iyengar was not allowed to perform the funeral rites of his mother to whom he was greatly attached. My eldest brother recalled the elderly gentleman writhing on the floor unable to control his grief at his mother's death. He was not allowed to go near her let alone touch her!

To return to Varadachar: his interests were many, perhaps too many. He was interested in amateur theatricals. T. Raghavachar, a lawyer from Bellary, with a keen interest in acting which included Shakespearean plays, was a friend and so was Tarabai, the 'lady sandow' of Maharashtra, who used to haul up huge blocks of granite with her long tresses. One of my earliest recollections of childhood is witnessing her lifting granite blocks secured to her hair, at one of her performances in Bangalore. And as already said, D. V. Gundappa, journalist, scholar, critic and poet, who has made important contributions to Kannada literature, was a great friend of Varadachar. There were numerous others, many of whom became friends of my aunt. Some of the influence wielded by Srirangamma was, I now realize, due to the admiration evoked by her gifted brother, and also the respect which Ramaswamy Iyengar commanded in society.

After Varadachar's death, his children Jaya, Padma and Raju, lived with our aunt, Srirangamma, in Chamarajpet. This was rendered inevitable by the fact that their mother, Seshamma, had predeceased Varadachar. Raju died of typhoid when he was only nine, and my mother grieved that her distinguished father's lineage had come to an end.

One of my childhood recollections of Bangalore relates to my efforts at learning how to swim in the Kempambudhi tank. My cousin Padma, several years older than me, used to go to the tank to swim and I went with her on a few occasions. At about fifteen feet from the bank, an iron pole rose from the bottom of the tank, and a few swimmers used to clutch the pole while talking and joking among themselves. One morning it occurred to me that it would be nice to join them. Yielding to the impulse of the moment, I left the shallow waters close to the bank and plunged into the tank with a view to reaching the pole. I did not know that the bank sloped steeply to the bottom, and I did not know how to swim. I did swallow a few mouthfuls of water and would certainly have gone down had not an elderly instructor swum over to me, hauled me up and deposited me near the bank to the accompaniment of much shouting and abuse. I have no recollection of what happened subsequently. One would have thought that after the incident I would have been ordered never to go near the tank, but that did not happen. On another occasion I started exploring the hillock adjacent to the tank with a view to finding a short cut to the road on the other side. I went up a snaking, uneven path to see a man in ochre robes sitting in the shelter of an overhanging rock, got frightened, and then followed a circuitous path which seemed to lead nowhere. I was lost, and this time I was even more frightened. Once again, I have no recollection of how I got back home and what happened to me after I got back. My mother was a disciplinarian and she could not have been an idle spectator of my doings for long.

A few months ago I visited the tank area—it is now a filthy, stinking swamp, and the hillside is covered with houses. Some days after my visit, I read a report in the papers about plans to get the swamp properly drained. But what will happen to the tank-bed? Will it become a housing estate, commercial complex, park or playground?

Akkayya was a dominant personality even during her husband's life, and it never occurred to anybody to think of her husband as the head of the household. She presided over a large household consisting of her husband, mother, two sons and an unmarried daughter, and her nieces and nephew—that was when she stayed in Chamarajpet. When she moved to her own bungalow in Malleshwaram, the household addition- ally included one or more women whom she had taken under her wing. Her official position conferred on her the power to appoint women teachers at the lower levels in government schools, and there were lots of women wanting such jobs. They were invariably either widows or women deserted by their husbands for one reason or another. In the course of her professional career, Akkayya did rehabilitate many un- fortunate women, and the women and their relatives were grateful to her. She travelled all over the state on official work, and I am certain that she helped poor and unfortunate women everywhere.

Akkayya was indeed a privileged person. As one of the two first women graduates of South India she was widely respected and sought after, and her official position only enhanced her public importance. Intellectuals such as D V. Gundappa and A.N. Krishna Rao, the lawyer- actor T. Raghavachar, and journalists and officials all knew her. Akkayya was a household name in the Bangalore of 1920s and 1930s. She also introduced Pandit Taranath to Bangalore. Taranath was a nationalist, ayurvedic doctor, musician, orator in Urdu, Kannada and English, lover of Ghalib, founder of an *ashram* in the 1920s on the banks of the Tungabhadra near Raichur; and Guru Taranath influenced many important people including T. Raghavachar; K. S. K. Iyengar, Profes- sor of Mathematics in Central College; A. N. Krishna Rao; and his cousin, Raja Rao, author of *Kanthapura*.

My last childhood memory of summers in Bangalore is a restless and uncomfortable rail journey to Mysore. I had high fever, and felt hot and miserable with an unquenchable thirst. I was prostrate on the bench in a third class compartment, and both my parents were with me. My father frequently got down at intermediate stations to get me bottles of Spencer's soda. However, I remember the unslakeable thirst and the nightmarish agitation of my parents. I do not remember the ending of the journey. My father was an employee in the Mysore Power and Light (as the Department of Electricity was then called), and he rarely took leave from his job. I must have caught the fever in Bangalore—it must have been malaria—and a letter or telegram must have summoned him. My illness worried my parents greatly: I was regarded as a delicate child, and anxiety about my health surfaced at the slightest provocation.

CRICKET AND BANGALORE

Cricket became a serious interest in my life during the years 1930–5. I was introduced to the game when I was in the first year (IV Form) in the Maharajah's High School, Mysore. Maharajah's was a government high school, and to be a student there meant prestige among peers. Games were compulsory and I had to stay back at school to play. Thus one evening I was introduced to the game of cricket—my previous school, Sadvidya Patashala, had not catered to sports. After the game, as I was returning home, I heard two or three boys from IVA, discussing the progress of a cricket match being played somewhere. They were on the other side of the road, and the one nearest me said, 'They were 2 wickets down 30' or something like that. The boys were from Lakshmipuram, an affluent part of Mysore, and the boy who made the remark appeared particularly sophisticated to me. But I found his statement mystifying. How does one calculate the fall of wickets? Does 2 down 30 mean 10 down 150? My puzzlement marked the beginning of an interest in the game, and during the next five years, I spent a great deal of my time and energy on cricket. It led me to other things, but the fever (or passion) died as suddenly as it had arisen in 1935. Perhaps my preoccupation with my Final Year BA Honours studies (1935–6) was responsible for it. Or, may be, I suddenly grew up.

Within a year or so of the incident mentioned earlier, I became familiar with the game. I changed my school at the end of the IVth Form, and joined Marimallappa's High School, which was derisively referred to as 'Marimallappana Doddi' (cattle-shed), as it had the reputation of being a home for mediocre students with very little ambition, though contrary to this popular perception, I found several students who were bright and wanted to do well in life. Since the school was close to my house, I could spend the evenings playing cricket. Marimallappa's had a good cricket team whose star was Y. S. Ramaswamy, a leg spinner of real talent, who once took all the 20 wickets in a Dasara Tournament final match played against the Bangalore Wesleyan High School. I was a spectator at that match. Ramaswamy later on went to play for the

Hindus, in the Pentangular in Bombay. It was during my Marimallappa days (1929–31), or very soon after, that I started my own team, Bradman's XI. My team won a small shield in a junior tournament, with a fellow-student at Marimallappa's, A. C. Somanna, scoring 103 not out, in the final. Somanna was an all-round sportsman, hailing from Coorg, and he represented the state in football. He later played regularly for a prominent Calcutta football team.

In June 1929, my eldest brother Parthasarathy, known to his innumerable students and friends as 'Pachu', a teacher of English, was transferred from Malleswaram High School in Bangalore to Maharajah's in Mysore. (He later became a lecturer in English in Mysore University.) He had a great love for sports but his passion was cricket. Indeed, it was he who popularized among younger cricketers what was then the 'new technique' in batting. Previously, batsmen used to stand at the crease with their feet planted wide apart, with the bat placed mid-point between the legs, and the stumps open to the bowler. A batsman was expected to hit, and no distinction was made between using a straight bat and a cross bat. Pachu popularized a stand in which the batsman's feet were close together and close to the bat, and while batting, the wickets were covered by the legs, whenever necessary. A batsman had to play a straight bat, a stroke made with a cross bat being regarded not only as unaesthetic but wrong. Pachu brought an ethical fervour to his cricket teaching, and did not hesitate to shout at 'wrong-doers'. He was also a determined patron of those he considered talented and went all out to help them.

With Pachu's arrival at Mysore, I became more knowledgeable about the game of cricket. He encouraged my interest in the game though he never tried to get me included in any team. I have referred earlier to my being regarded as delicate in health, and if I had a good Kannada novel to read, I did not feel like stirring out of the house. Pachu thought this was unhealthy, and he wanted me to spend the evenings playing a game, or exercising in the gymnasium.

It was during my first year at Marimallappa's (1929–30), that the Maharajkumar of Vizianagaram, known to cricket-lovers as 'Vizzy', toured India with his team which included the famous English opening pair, Jack Hobbs and Herbert Sutcliffe. The team was visiting Bangalore to play a local side, which included P. E. Palia, the Parsi cricketer from Bombay who had recently made Mysore his home. Pachu was keen to witness the match, and so was I.

We caught the night train from Mysore and reached Bangalore early on the following morning. It had rained during the night and everything was wet. The chief means of public transport in Bangalore in those days was the *jutka*—a torture chamber for both man and beast, a technological anachronism which survives to this day—and no *jutkawala* was willing to take us to 17th Cross, Malleswaram: '*Bahut door hai, sab; rasta to bahut ujhaad hai, godha ko mushkil hota hai; wapas ane' ko badha nai milta hai, sab* ('It is too far, the road is too steep, it will be difficult for the horse to pull, and I will not get a fare for the return journey') and so on. After these objections, he quoted an absurdly high fare, and fifteen minutes or more were spent in bringing it down to what one could afford. After edging into the coop-like interior, one was asked continuously to shift one's bottom to see that the balance (*mooki*) of the *jutka* was not upset. Both of us sat on a wet gunnysack cloth spread over a mattress of wet, green grass–fodder for the horse, and we progressed slowly towards 17th Cross, the smell of green grass in our nostrils, our bottoms damp from the improvised seat and a cold wind blowing through the vehicle. We were greeted at the entrance to Akkayya's house, which she had named Kusuma Bhavan, by our cousin Kittanna, he said 'I expected you fellows would turn up.' He knew of Pachu's passion for cricket just as we knew that he would not miss a single horse race in Mysore or Bangalore. After a hot bath, a sizzling cup of strong coffee, and breakfast, we were both on the road again, this time our destination was the Parade Ground where the match was being played. Surprisingly, I remember very little of the game. The sky was overcast, the sun showing up for brief periods. The wicket was wet, and so was the outfield. There was, however, some play. I remember Hobbs and Sutcliffe in their cream-coloured flannels, contrasting with the white (cotton) uniform of most others. Neither of them got a big score. They treated Palia's bowling with circumspection—he did take 3 or 4 wickets. Hobbs thought so well of Palia's bowling that he was invited to be a member of Vizzy's team, and later, a member of the first Indian official team to tour England in the summer of 1932, a team which included C. K. Nayadu, Amar Singh, Ramji, Lal Singh, and several others. But Palia did not have a particularly good tour. As I mentioned earlier, Palia was a friend of my brother Pachu, and he knew that I had a collection of cricket photographs from papers all over the world. He brought me a souvenir of the tour: a tiny, dealwood bat on which all the members of the team had signed. (Amar Singh's signature began with a small 'a'.) When I became uninterested in cricket, I neglected the souvenir, and all the signatures became smudged and indistinct. After that I threw the bat away.

I was also a spectator of the match between the visiting MCC team and the Mysore State Cricket Association team in 1934. The MCC team was led by C. F. Walters and the State team by one Captain T. Murari, an unknown personality. The visitors' attack was led by the paceman, 'Nobody' Clarke of Northants. He was assisted by another paceman, equally lethal, from the other end. The local batsmen had never faced the kind of pace bowled by Clarke and company. P. A. Kanickam, who had a great reputation locally as a batsman and hitter ran to the square leg umpire when he saw how fast the ball was. So did a few others, including the Captain, Murari. The crowd, initially dismayed, soon saw the absurdity of the encounter. A few people started shouting, *Murari avanu parari* (Murari, oh, he fled). Walters scored 160 runs which included 2 sixes. The match was a disaster as far as the local team was concerned.

Until independence, keen rivalry marked the relations between Bangalore and Mysore, and one of the areas in which it was expressed was sports and athletics. The conflict was particularly acute in the annual inter-collegiate tournament named after a well-known professor of Chemistry and cricketer, M. G. Srinivasa Rao, father of M. G. Vijayasarathy, a prominent sportsman and athlete of Bangalore. (Much later both Vijayasarathy and his son, M. V. Nagendra, became test match umpires.) In the 1930s Mysore University was a small and manageable entity, with only four colleges, two each in Bangalore and Mysore. Mysore had Maharajah's and the Medical colleges, and Bangalore had the Central and Engineering colleges. Maharajah's and Central College each had an attached intermediate college, and for purposes of the tournament, the intermediate college was merged with the older entity. The two professional colleges did not count for much in sports and athletics with the result that the conflict between Mysore and Bangalore really meant a conflict between Maharajah's and Central College. The M. G. S. Rao tournament was an integral part of the academic life of the university in those days, while a few even thought that the university existed for the tournament.

I was drawn into this vortex of rivalry from the day I joined the Junior Intermediate class in June 1931. My interest in cricket had added an edge to my partisanship. Interestingly, the first article I published in my life was a description of the cricket match between Maharajah's and

Central College played on the Central College grounds. I had gone to Bangalore as a Maharajah's fan. I had been smuggled in as a part of the Bangalore contingent, and enjoyed the hospitality of the Central College hostel without being entitled to it. I saw our team go down, and many years later, I came to the conclusion that the side which I supported was fated to lose.

My interest in cricket, if I am right, led me to take an interest in the sports page of *The Hindu*, which was then the most widely-read English newspaper in South India. After I joined the University, I started visiting the University Union's reading room where I could read a host of papers and journals including *Tit-Bits*, John O' London's *Weekly*, and *Punch*. I discovered Neville Cardus, and long after my interest in cricket had waned, I enjoyed reading his writings. But eventually even he palled—his style was too rich, too allusive and too erudite for my liking. Cricket would have died of boredom but for Kerry Packer's recent invention of one-day cricket in which cricketers, dressed in loud and ugly uniforms played limited-overs matches. But even with such matches, cricket throughout the year can be boring except to cricket fanatics. But then cricket, like everything else today, has become the handmaiden of consumerism.

It was when I was studying in the Intermediate College that I was bitten by the urge to write. I did get a couple of things published in popular weeklies which were then coming out in Madras, and soon after, I began writing about cricket, and very occasionally, also about other sports. I am not exactly proud of this phase of my career but the point that is pertinent here is that writing about cricket brought me into contact with Bangalore. I do not know how it happened but for a few months during the early 1930s, the *Tainadu*, the leading Kannada newspaper in Mysore State, published a half-column by me on cricket in English. The editor of the paper was P. Ramaiah, a widely-respected nationalist. My half-column was printed in the centre of the front page. I wrote the column under the pen name, Chamu, which was what I was called at home. It was indeed a most unusual thing to have happened: a patriotic, Kannada newspaper to publish my views on cricket and cricketers in English on the front page: I was an unknown student and I did not hail from an influential family. I was immature, partisan, fond of displaying my knowledge of cricket, and I threw my weight around. The fact that I had not asked for payment was perhaps a factor in my comments being published. But cricket fans did read what I wrote, and it did not make me popular with them. For instance, Safi Darashah, a prominent Bangalore all-rounder, who could not read Kannada, read my column in the *Tainadu*. Once, while on a visit to Mysore, he was beside himself with fury at one of my writings. I had compared M. B. Krishna Rao's century a few days previously to Victor Trumper's! (It must have been the result of reading too much Cardus.) He shouted, 'comparing M. B. Krishna Rao to Victor Trumper!' He was so angry that he could not say anything more. When bowling, Darashah's run up to the wicket was really like a slow stylized dance, and I am glad I had not written about it. He and Pachu were fierce rivals in the 1930s and 40s supporting rival teams but later, after Darashah shifted to Mysore, they became close friends and partners at bridge at the Cosmopolitan Club, Mysore. Pachu's invariable excuse when he came home late was, 'Safi wanted one more rubber.'

Luckily for me, my half-column came to an abrupt end. Several days before the visit of the C. F. Walter's team to Bangalore, I wrote to the editor of *Tainadu* asking him for a press pass. I thought I was entitled to one. I did not get a reply, and my reminders met with the same fate. On the morning of the match I called on the editor at his house. He came out and met me on the pavement abutting his house. In response to my query he told me calmly that he had given the press pass to someone else.

The Nawab Moin-ud-Dowlah Gold Cup Tournament was an important annual cricket event in Nizam's Hyderabad in the 1930s. According to Ramchandra Guha (1992):[1] . . . 'The Moin-ud-Dowlah Gold Cup has, year after year, brought the city the finest cricket talent in India, as well as elsewhere—for the great English opening pair of Hobbs and Sutcliffe appeared for the Maharajkumar of Vizianagaram's XI in the first year of the Cup, while Learie Constantine and Rohan Kanhai have graced the occasion since.' The 1934 Tournament included several important players, including the great West Indian all-rounder, Learie Constantine. I thought I would go and see the match, and my eldest brother Pachu was very supportive. I wrote to the editor of the *Daily Post* in Bangalore whether I could cover the match for the paper and he agreed. The *Daily Post* was a cantonment newsheet full of local trivia, races and the like. I suppose it served a local need. The editor sent me a letter saying that I was their representative and this ensured a privileged place for me in the press gallery. I went to Hyderabad by train from Guntakal, on the Nizam State Railway, arriving sometime in the night. I had a pleasant

[1] Ramachandra Guha, *Wickets in the East*, Oxford University Press, Delhi, 1992.

journey enjoying the company of a party of sociable fellow passengers who turned out to be, as I learnt the following morning, goldsmiths who were also thieves. The Hyderabad police had been tipped off about them. But luckily for me my host was a pillar of the local society, and he vouchsafed for me when the police visited him at midnight.

It was winter, and Hyderabad was cool and sunny, and the match was played in fine weather. Learie Constantine was the main attraction, of course, but there were also others, Mohammed Nissar, the paceman, the Yuvaraja of Patiala, Palia, and, I think, the Ali brothers, Nazir and Wazir. I remember Nissar, a giant of a man, returning after each spell of bowling to change his shirt and underwear. He sweated profusely. There was also Dilawar Hussain, wicket keeper, who made it a point to be friendly with the pressman. I sent my reports to the *Daily Post* which promptly published them.

Soon after returning to Mysore, I sent the editor an article on the England-Australia Test series, and in it I had mentioned that Harold Larwood, the spearhead of the English attack, and the man mainly responsible for subduing England's foe, Bradman, was 5′ 8″ tall. This seemed to annoy the editor no end, and he wrote a sarcastic letter asking me how I could make so silly an error. But I was certain that Larwood was not the six-footer that the editor thought he was. It was Bill Bowes of Yorkshire, another fast bowler, and one who played with his spectacles on, who was 6′ 6″ tall. But as far as the editor of the *Daily Post* was concerned, I was guilty of *lese-majesté*. The correspondence ended my relation with the paper.

I was also contributing a monthly letter to a sports journal from Madras, *The Field*, and I thought of interviewing the groundsman of the Bangalore Gymkhana's cricket grounds in South Parade, for one of my 'letters'. I met the groundsman, an Englishman, who was only too willing to be interviewed. He even gave me a photograph of his to go with the article. At my request the editor sent him a copy of the issue of *The Field* containing my article. The groundsman, whose name I have forgotten, did not like the article. At least, I got that impression. I had written that he looked like Mr Punch, and he probably did not like the comparison. He did indeed look like Mr Punch but had I been less tactless I would have refrained from pointing out the similarity. Around that time my connection with *The Field* also came to an end. The editor did not like my asking to be paid for my letters.

It is a matter of common knowledge that Bangalore is now an important centre for cricket, and boasts of a huge cricket stadium named after the most dedicated patron of cricket in the post-Independence years, the late Mr M. A. Chinnaswamy. Bangalore has produced several test cricketers of world standard: E. A. R. Prasanna, B. S. Chandrasekhar, G. R. Viswanath, S. M. H. Kirmani and Roger Binny. The present Indian Test team includes the paceman, J. Srinath, and the spinner, Anil Kumble, both from Karnataka. Brijesh Patel, the batsman who has played for the State several times in the 1980s, and the nephew of B. R. Patel, the all-rounder who used to be the mainstay of batting for the Central College against Maharajah's during the 1930s, has started a Cricket Academy in Bangalore with his friend and colleague, Imtiaz Ahmed, on the grounds of St Germain's School. Cricket, along with athletics, is serious business in Bangalore.

History

Bangalore is located on a plateau which is over 3,000 feet high with the 300 acres of the Indian Institute of Science occupying the highest part of the plateau. It has an equable climate, though its older inhabitants complain that the city is getting warmer with every bit of available space being built upon. Historically, however, it was Bangalore's elevation and climate which led to the British shifting their troops in 1809 from Srirangapatna to the city. Many of the big bungalows of the nineteenth century have fire-places, evidence of cold winters.

Bangalore seems to have been an inhabited area from first century AD. Roman coins have been found in Yeshwanthpur and the present HAL area. The Bangalore area was ruled by the Gangas for six centuries till the tenth century AD when it came under the Cholas. The name 'Bengaluru' occurs in a ninth century AD inscription in the Nageshwara temple in Begur, a village in the eastern part of present Bangalore. Kempe Gowda I, the ruler of Yelahanka, feudatory to the Vijaynagar rulers, built a mud fort around Bangalore in AD 1537. Kempe Gowda was a great builder of tanks and temples. Around 1637, Bangalore was conquered by the Bijapur Sultans, and Shahji Bhonsle, father of Shivaji was given Bangalore, along with a few other towns in Karnataka, as *jagir*. Shivaji spent about eight months in Karnataka, from April to December 1676, claiming his share of the paternal *jagir* from his stepbrother, Venkoji. It is very likely that Shivaji spent at least a part of that time in Bangalore. After fifty years of Bijapur rule, Bangalore was captured by the Mughals who held it for three years. Then the town came under Chikkadevaraja Wodeyar of Mysore (1673–1704) who built the four watch towers, at cardinal points marking, according to folklore, the boundaries of the city. As of today, the city's boundaries have gone far beyond the watch towers.

The fort built by Chikkadevaraja Wodeyar was greatly strengthened by Hyder Ali and Tippu Sultan who substituted granite for the original mud fort but only a small portion of the northern wall survives, facing the City Market.

It was Hyder Ali who planned, in the 1960s, a new garden in Bangalore, 40 acres in extent, named Lalbagh, on the model of the Moghul garden in Sira. Hyder Ali imported plants from Delhi, Lahore and Multan to beautify Lalbagh. Tippu Sultan further developed Lalbagh making it a repository for growing plants imported from Africa. After the fall of Tippu Sultan in 1799, Lalbagh passed into the hands of Major Waugh, a military botanist, who took a keen interest in developing the garden, introducing foreign plants. However, in 1819 Major Waugh presented Lalbagh to the Marquess of Hastings, and this resulted in the garden's being recognized as a branch of the Bengal Presidency Botanical Gardens.

On the British assumption of the Province of Mysore in 1831, Lalbagh came under the control of the Commissioner of Mysore, Sir Mark Cubbon, who held that position till 1861. The garden had its ups and downs till 1856 when it was made a government botanical garden.

During the twentieth century, Krishnaraja Wodeyar IV, Maharajah of Mysore, paid considerable attention to the development of Lalbagh. He appointed Mr Krumbigal, a German, as the government horticulturist, and Krumbigal developed not only Lalbagh but beautified the entire city, planting beautiful blossoming trees such as jacaranda, tabebuia argentia, cassia, gulmohar, varieties of acacia, and others to make sure that avenue trees were rarely without flowers. He was the author of the idea of 'serial blossoming'.

Lalbagh is now recognized as a national asset, and its flower-shows held in the Glass House on Independence and Republic Days (15 August and 26 January) attract a large number of visitors. In the neighbourhood of Lalbagh there exist nurserymen who have plied their trade for generations. They have played an important part in the beautification of domestic gardens in Bangalore. Incidentally, the Glass House is modelled after the Crystal Palace in London, and in recent years, the Congress Party has held important meetings in it.

BANGALORE AND MYSORE

During the pre-independence years, acute rivalry characterized the relations between Bangalore and Mysore, or to be more specific, between the denizens of the two cities. Until independence, Mysore was the political capital of the state, being the seat of the Maharajah of Mysore, Sri Krishnaraja Wodeyar IV, who ruled Mysore for nearly thirty years till his death in 1940. He was, besides being austere in his life-style, a great patron of the arts, crafts and learning. Mysore was (and continues to be) the headquarters of Mysore University.

Mysore was a beautiful city in the pre-independence years but is now losing much of its attractiveness due to rapid expansion and official neglect. Krishnaraja Wodeyar IV, and his able Dewan, Sir Mirza Ismail, both paid considerable attention to the development of the city, adding to its amenities and enhancing its beauty. Krishnaraja Wodeyar was a popular and highly respected ruler, and the lives of innumerable citizens were linked with the palace and its annual round of festivals, rituals, processions and durbars. People with land in nearby villages, and rural links nevertheless tried to obtain a foothold in the modern professions and trades and they formed an integral part of the city's elite.

Bangalore, even during the pre-independence years was not only much bigger than Mysore, but was a bustling centre of commercial and industrial activity, besides being the administrative capital of the state.

Physically speaking, the cantonment and city formed a continuum, but there was a political and also a cultural divide between the two. The ordinary citizen avoided the cantonment which he called *dandu*. To him the place was full of drunken and disorderly soldiers who were given to frequent outbursts of violence. They did, however, go on rampage on Boxing Day, 26 December, when they broke shop windows, picked fights with passers-by, and generally made themselves extremely unpleasant. Cautious elders in the city advised youngsters not to venture beyond the Queen's Statue in Cubbon Park. To the British, on the other hand, *pettah* meant natives living cheek by jowl in small houses on narrow winding streets. It was also dreaded as the place where epidemics such as cholera, small pox and plague were apt to break out during the hot summer months and spread to the cantonment.

Apart from the fear of the troops, the city people felt that they had to be generally careful in the cantonment. For instance, the Tamil traffic policeman might book a city cyclist on the slightest pretext or shout at him for no reason. Nevertheless, thousands of civilians lived in the cantonment and most of them earned their livelihood locally.

While the cantonment and the city were different from each other in many ways, there were also strong links binding the two. Many people who lived in the city worked in the cantonment, and vice versa. There were also several elite educational institutions in the cantonment, for instance, Bishop Cotton, Baldwin, St Joseph, and Good Shepherd Convent, to which the middle classes sent their children. Syed Bawker was well known for stitching woollen suits, and was patronized by the officials of the state government and prospective bridegrooms. Reuben Moses was a favourite for shoes while Barton and Velu were photographers to the rich and fashionable. Sports fans in the city visited the cantonment for watching cricket, football and hockey matches. The Bangalore Race Course drew punters not only from the city but from Bombay, Poona, Madras and Mysore. The cantonment cinema theatres were a magnet for the middle classes who had a yen for 'English' films which were really films produced by Hollywood. Apart from the immigrants from nearby states who lived by providing goods and services to the troops, a small minority of westernized and well-off Indians chose to live in the cantonment, mixing among themselves and with a few British officials, and were largely cut-off from their cultural roots.

While the rivalry between Bangalore and Mysore was real, it did not come in the way of good relations between people living in the two cities, which were both regarded as the pride of princely Mysore. The rivalry was a cause for friendly banter when they met, and only very rarely did partisanship become unpleasant as when a favoured team was meeting its rival in the final of a tournament. Years after the event, however, they would recall their clashes over a cup of coffee, or more rarely, a glass of beer.

THE CANTONMENT

The cantonment area developed into a self-contained township during the latter half of the nineteenth century, a phenomenon helped by the establishment, in the 1860s, of a rail link to Jolarpet. Bangalore and Madras came closer together, and through Madras, Bangalore became linked to the rest of India. One of the consequences of this linkage was the considerable increase in trade between Madras and Bangalore. It also attracted immigrants from Madras Presidency to Bangalore;

traders, contractors, artisans, labourers, domestic servants and others. The immigrants spoke a variety of languages, of which Tamil was the most prominent while Muslims spoke a variety of Urdu. The development of Bangalore since the 1860s resulted in a number of civilian officers making Bangalore their home. It was during the years 1864–8 that the magnificent Public Offices (Attara Kacheri) were built by Colonel Sankey, Chief Engineer, Government of Mysore of which Arcot Narayanaswamy Mudaliar was the contractor. (The tank which is named after Colonel Sankey once extended from the Indian Institute of Science to Mekhri Circle.) The Cubbon Park, one of the attractions of Bangalore, houses, besides the Attara Kacheri, the Sheshadri Iyer Memorial Hall (the Central Library), the State Archaeological Museum, and the Karnataka Government Insurance Department, all forming a fine architectural complex giving Cubbon Park its unique character. The policy of the army authorities to encourage local men to build houses for renting by British officers facilitated the emergence of a class of contractors who, over a period of time, became prosperous. Local moneylenders also prospered lending money to British officers. Indeed, all manner of traders, tailors, shoemakers, photographers, tobacconists, liquor-vendors, restaurateurs and others prospered catering to the multifarious needs of the troops, officers, rich civilians and others.

The rapid development of the cantonment provided an ideal ground for the spread and elaboration of the bungalow type of architecture. The word 'bungalow' is said to be derived from 'Bengal' where houses with two verandas in front, were popular. But it must be pointed out here that a front veranda (*jagali* in Kannada, and *tinnai* in Tamil) running along the width of the house, except for the place where the continuity is broken by a flight of steps to the interior, is a characteristic of South Indian residential architecture. The bungalow as it developed in the cantonment had covered verandas in the front and sides, making the interior airy and cool. Over the years the bungalow-type of architecture became elaborated in all possible ways: the biggest bungalows had wrought-iron gates supported on either side by elaborate gate-piers, a driveway leading from the gate to a central portico which provided shelter to a horse-drawn carriage. The bungalow had generally a sloping roof covered by red Mangalore tiles, and sometimes, also terraces protected by parapet walls. At the back were the quarters for the cook, gardener and coachman. The bungalow was set in a large garden with flowering shrubs, creepers and trees in front, a kitchen garden at the back, and fruit trees such as the mango, jack and tamarind growing in different parts of the compound. The wrought-iron gates, the gate-piers, the driveway and the portico, all proclaimed the status of the occupant.

While the higher levels of the middle classes and the rich lived in big bungalows, the lower middle classes lived in small bungalows with a small area for a few flowering shrubs, and one or two trees. One can still come across such dainty little bungalows in various parts of the cantonment. It is only where the municipal or other authority built houses for the very poor, that they resorted to dreary row-housing, like barracks.

It is necessary to emphasize that only some parts of the cantonment have wide roads. Bungalows set in spacious compounds with big trees and flowering shrubs are fast giving place to monotonous apartment-housing. The cantonment also contains long narrow lanes in which houses cling to each other, the neighbourhood being palpable, noisy and conflict-ridden. One has only to wander around the lanes leading to Russel Market to see this side of the area. Then there are parts which look as though they have been transplanted from a small Tamil town like Villupuram or Vellore. Houses have Tamil-style verandas in front, massive, carved wooden doors with parts daubed with turmeric or *kumkum* stripes. Inmates live very much like their cousins in Tamil Nadu. There are also slums on the outskirts of the cantonment like Pottery Town. The British could have planned a fine city when they moved their troops to Halasur but they did not seem to have been interested in doing so. They built quarters for the troops and amenities such as parade grounds, sports fields, churches, shops, markets, cinema houses, hospitals and schools around the quarters. But they do not seem to have bothered about making sure that the civilians who catered to the needs of the troops and officers lived in decent houses in a planned area. They allowed the cantonment to grow as it liked, and the result is the mess that we see today around the affluent parts.

No account of the cantonment is complete without a reference to Winston Churchill, who was a lieutenant in the 4th Hussars (Queen's Own) during the years 1896–9. He was a member of the United Services Club (the present Bangalore Club), and when he left Bangalore for good, he owed the club Rs 13 which was written off by the Committee of the United Services Club on 1 June 1899 as an 'irrecoverable sum'. Churchill was very fond of polo, and twice visited Meerut to take part in the big annual Inter-Regimental Tournament. During the second and final visit in 1899, the 4th Hussars won the tournament, Churchill playing with his right arm strapped tightly to his body to prevent further injury to his right shoulder which had been dislocated in 1896, when hopping from the boat onto the steps of the jetty when he landed in Bombay. Churchill was so fond of polo that he described it to his son Randolph as the 'Emperor of Games'. During his three years in Bangalore, he spent as much time away from the cantonment as possible, visiting England twice, and to participate in military action twice once in 1896, in the North–West Frontier, and the second time in 1898 in Khartoum in Egypt, in the war against the Mahdi's forces. Both experiences resulted in books: *The Story of the Malakand Field Force* (1896), *The River War* (1899). The books established his reputation as a writer, and as a man who kept his cool when facing considerable danger to himself. The books also brought him much publicity, and some money. Perhaps even more important, they gave him the confidence that he could earn a living by writing while pursuing his real passion, politics.

Even before coming to India Churchill was very clear in his mind that his future lay not in the army but in politics. He wanted money, and he wanted to be noticed by those who mattered in England. His participation in the battles in the North–West Frontier and Egypt were both aimed at promoting his long-term goals. He wrote to his mother constantly urging her to use her influence with those who mattered, including the Prince of Wales, to get him to the Frontier and to Egypt. He managed to get to Egypt in the teeth of Kitchner's opposition. It must also be said in his favour that he loved adventure, and was not scared of risking his life: quality and not quantity of life was what mattered, as he wrote to his mother. He believed that he was destined for great things, and during the years 1896–9, he told three people, in different continents, that he would one day become the Prime Minister of England.

In Bangalore, he lived in a bungalow on South Parade (the present Mahatma Gandhi Road) along with two of his colleagues, loving the roses in the garden, and collecting butterflies. He also fell in love with the beauty, Pamela Plowden, daughter of the British resident in Hyderabad, but the romance did not fructify into marriage. Pamela Plowden, later married Lord Lytton who eventually became the Viceroy of India. It is also true that when in India Churchill showed no interest whatever in the life of the Indians around him, or in the culture and history of the country. He was absorbed in reading Macaulay and Gibbon, and in the study of several volumes of the Annual Register, all in preparation for his entry into politics. India was only a great piece of real estate, ruled well and thoroughly by a small number of British officials and troops.

The political divide between the cantonment and the city ended with independence. The departure of British troops from India was followed by the exit of most foreigners who owned property there. A large number of Anglo–Indians felt insecure after the departure of the British, and they migrated to England or Australia. The cultural divide between the cantonment and the city is now a thing of the past with Bangalore becoming one large and ever-expanding urban sprawl.

Personalities   PERSONALITIES

Mokshagundam Visvesvaraya, usually referred to as Sir M. V., is generally recognized as the maker of modern Mysore. To this must be added the fact that during his official years in Bombay, he contributed to the development of every part of that sprawling Presidency, and subsequently, after retiring from both Bombay and Mysore, to the development of the entire country. But returning to his years in Mysore, he built the Krishnarajasagara Dam, and worked determinedly, and in the teeth of opposition from powerful interests, which were always ranged against him, to start such institutions as the Mysore University, the State Bank of Mysore, and industries under the government auspices for extracting sandalwood, making soaps, paper, and iron and steel. He initiated a compulsory insurance scheme for every government official, and founded the Kannada Sahitya Parishat, for the promotion of the language, and the Century Club for the recreation of officials. He was a nationalist, and the welfare and progress of the country was a deep and constant concern of his. His concern found expression in his book, *Reconstructing India* (London: 1920) and in *Planned Economy in India* (Bangalore: 1934). His book on planning was written before the Indian National Congress established a committee on planning under the Chairmanship of Pandit Nehru. He was a man of total integrity and refused to compromise his principles: he resigned from the *Dewanship* of Mysore as he was opposed to caste-based reservation for government jobs which the Maharajah was keen to introduce. To him merit and character were all-important.

During the years 1940–4, when I was studying for the Ph.D., I was a resident in the Bombay University Post-Graduate Hostel located on Queen's Road, and it was then my habit to take a walk in the evening on Marine Drive before returning to the hostel for dinner. During my walks, I came across, on a few occasions, three distinguished-looking elderly men walking together. They were Sardar Patel, in a *khadi kurta* and *dhoti*, Walchand Hirachand the industrialist, in a long, close-collared coat, *dhoti*, pumps, Marwari turban, and with a walking stick in one hand, and the oldest of the triumvirate, Sir M. V. in an impeccable silk suit, well-polished brown shoes, a felt hat in one hand, and walking stick in the other. I think that was the time when Walchand Hirachand and Sir M. V. were engaged in trying to set up a car factory in Bangalore, a project to which the British were opposed. But thanks to the exigencies of the war, an aircraft repair factory came into existence in Bangalore in 1940 instead of the car factory, with the collaboration of the Government of India, Mysore Government and Walchand Hirachand. And as everyone now knows, the Hindustan Aircraft Factory is today the main pillar of the Indian aircraft industry, serving defence as well as civilian needs. Sir M. V. took a keen interest in the progress of the factory, holding discussions frequently with the engineer in charge, M. N. Shah.

Sir M. V., strange as it may seem for a former chief engineer and *dewan* of Mysore, did not own a house in Bangalore. He rented one from the industrialist Manickavelu Mudaliar, a large bungalow named 'Uplands' on Palace Road, next to Balabrooie. He was a model tenant but that did not prevent him from receiving, one day, a lawyer's notice asking him to vacate the house when a mere word from the owner would have been enough. A very upset Sir M. V. started looking for a house which was within the jurisdiction of the House Rent Controller. Word got around, and Hanumanthaiah, the chief minister of Mysore, visited Sir M. V., and requested him with folded hands to occupy Cubbon House. Hanumanthaiah was a great admirer of Sir M. V., and he was very embarrassed to find the great man going to the House Rent Controller in search of a house to rent. Sir M. V. agreed to the chief minister's request but only after getting the chief engineer's estimate of the rent payable, and adding 10 per cent to the latter's estimate, to offset a possible bias in his favour. Sir M. V. stayed in the house till his end. After his death, during the 1970s, Cubbon House was razed to the ground, and the unsightly Visweswaraya towers now occupies its place. That such a historic structure as Cubbon House could be demolished without the matter first being discussed in public, is an eloquent comment on the power wielded by politicians and administrators, and their disregard for popular sentiments. Around the same time, attempts to demolish the classy Attara Kacheri and build a new High Court in its place was prevented, thanks to an agitation led by architecture students studying in Bangalore. It must be mentioned here that there is an urgent need for preparing a list of architecturally important buildings which should be declared as the heritage of the city and state, if not the country. The list should be published in the newspapers for the benefit of the public.

Bangalore is rightly regarded as a major centre of research in the sciences and technology. The roots of this go back to the existence of Central and Engineering colleges, the former being started in the 1860s, and the latter, much later, in the 1920s. They have been nurseries of scientists and engineers for a long time. The Indian Institute of Science (IISc.) is a centre of excellence for higher studies and research in the sciences and technology, it was started in 1911 thanks to the wisdom, foresight and patriotism of Sir Jamsetji N. Tata, and the support of the Mysore Government which donated 300 acres of prime land and an annual grant of money to support the Institute's research activities. A cluster of other similar institutions which came up later, and which continue to come up, have served to further enhance the city's importance. There are also a few big and fast-growing institutions with a direct bearing on practical application and they are, the National Aerospace Limited, the Indian Space Research Organization, and the Central Water and Power Research Institute. On the other side, high-tech industries such as the Indian Telephone Industries, Hindustan Aeronautics (HAL), Hindustan Machine Tools, Bharat Electronics and New Government Electric Factory, need support from research institutions for maintaining quality, lowering the cost of production, and innovation.

Sir C. V. Raman was the first Indian Director of the IISc., from 1933 to 1937 when he resigned from the directorship, but continued as professor of physics till 1948 when he retired. After retirement, he wanted to start a small institute with his life's savings (1988):[2] 'it so happened that he lost most of his savings in a 'south sea bubble' investment. He was sixty then and to anyone else it would have been an impossible situation. But Raman was undeterred. He went round the country and collected money.'

Adversity brought out not only the fighter in Raman but spurred his inventiveness. 'With the aid of a student with a chemistry background

[2] S. Ramaseshan and C. Ramachandra Rao, *C. V. Raman: A Pictorial Biography*, Bangalore, 1988.

he launched courageously into setting up a Welsbach mantle factory. Welsbach (1858–1959) discovered that a fabric soaked in thorium nitrate and cerium nitrate, both chemicals available in India, when heated glows with great brilliance. The products from Raman's factory sold well, and the dividends from this venture were substantial. In fact they were sufficient to support his Institute and keep it independent at a time when he decided, for good reasons, not to accept even marginal support from Government' (ibid.: 32).

During the 1940s, there was a businessman in Bangalore named Gopala Rao, and he used to accept deposits of money from people paying them a high interest rate. The interest sums were initially paid punctually, and word went round that investing money with Gopala Rao was a very profitable business. Large numbers of middle-class people invested their savings with Gopala Rao and were happy to receive interest on capital they had invested. Raman, who must have been an innocent in financial matters, also invested his savings with Gopala Rao. At that time, Gopala Rao's reputation was soaring, with everyone praising his financial wizardry. But one day the cheques failed to appear. The news spread, and there was a run on the deposits, but the creditors found that Gopala Rao had become bankrupt. When Raman discovered that he had lost his precious savings he is reported to have told Gopala Rao, 'you should have got the Nobel prize, not me'. R. K. Narayan's *The Financial Expert*, which some consider his finest novel, was inspired to some extent by the story of Gopala Rao.

Bangalore is closely linked with the development of modern Kannada literature, apart from being the headquarters of the Kannada Sahitya Parishat. The first novels in Kannada were translations from Bankim Chandra Chatterji's *Durgesha Nandini, Ananda Matha, Vishavriksha* etc., and the man responsible for them was Bindiganavile Venkatachar, a judge and Sanskrit scholar, who learnt Bengali. He wrote seventy-five books in all, of which sixty-five were novels. Venkatachar is now recognized as a pioneer of modern Kannada literature. In passing, it may be noted that Venkatachar's grand-nephew is Raja Ramanna, who headed the team which organized the nuclear implosion at Pokhran in Rajasthan in 1974. He is now the director of the National Institute of Advanced Studies, Bangalore.

There appears to be a consensus among scholars that the modern movement in Kannada literature began with the publication of the late Professor B. M. Srikantiah's *English Geethegalu* (1921). Srikantiah was a professor of English at Central College, and a highly respected scholar and teacher. He translated some English poems he thought highly of, into Kannada and this had a seminal effect on the growth of modern Kannada. He influenced a number of younger scholars and writers. Much later he wrote his epic play, *Ashwathaman*, in blank verse on the model of a Greek tragedy. Srikantiah, the initiator of the modern movement in Kannada literature, was a great lover of English. He is reported to have told his friends that if they cut open his heart they would find the word 'English' written on it.

Bangalore was the home of several other writers who made significant contributions to modern Kannada literature. Masti Venkatesha Iyengar, the father of the short story in Kannada, was a high official of Mysore State, and he won the Jnanapeeth award for his contributions to Kannada literature. (Karnataka has five Jnanapeeth awardees in all, the others being D. R. Bendre, K. V. Puttappa, Shivaram Karanth and V. K. Gokak.) D. V. Gundappa began his career as a journalist but he was also a Sanskrit scholar, a biographer, literary critic and poet, his last work being a long, philosophical poem, *Mankuthimana Kagga*. A. N. Krishna Rao, was a prolific writer of Kannada, and was perhaps the first to try to live entirely by writing. He was one of the founders of 'progressive' writing in Kannada. G. P. Rajaratnam, who began his career as a lecturer in Kannada in Mysore University, broke new ground by his charming poems about a poor drunkard, 'Endkudaka Ratna', then essayed into children's literature, and finally, ended up as a translator of Buddhist classics. M. R. Srinivasa Murthy was a government official and scholar, and wrote a fine biography of the twelfth-century Kannada mystic, reformer, and politician, Basaveshwara, founder of the Virashaiva movement. Srinivasa Murthy was also a memoirist, being the author of a fine account of his days as a government school inspector.

T. P. Kailasam (1884–1946) is best remembered for his plays satirizing the speech and ways of the urban middle classes of the inter-war years. Kailasam was born in a respectable middle class family in Bangalore. His father was a judge of the Mysore High Court. He studied at Presidency College, Madras, and later, at the Royal College of Science in London. He studied Geology, and after his return joined the Department of Geology of the State of Mysore. He worked there from 1915 to 1920 when he resigned. He then started writing plays which poked fun at the institutions and pretensions of the newly emerging middle classes. He used the actual language used by these classes which was a mixture of English and Kannada or Tamil. He had an intimate knowledge of dialectical differences and the carry-over of such differences in speaking Kannada. His satirical plays were warmly received while his serious plays in Kannada or English (*Bahishkara, Karna,* for example) were relatively ignored. After resigning his job, Kailasam adopted a Bohemian life-style, and was often steeped in poverty living off his friends and admirers. He was a chain-smoker, loved liquor, and was a witty conversationalist. His life-style, his gifts and his wit all went to make him a myth in his own lifetime. To know him was to be avant-garde, and a privilege. He had many imitators and admirers. In retrospect, his plays appear dated both by language and class but there is no doubt that Kailasam freed Kannada theatre from the strait-jacket of the traditional dramatic form. He also taught people to laugh at themselves.

One of Kailasam's admirers was the late R. Shivaram, a genuine 'people's doctor' who had a large number of very poor patients as well as many rich ones. He accepted whatever money the poor gave him, and occasionally, he paid for their medicines and even food. He had a rich sense of humour, and started, in the 1930s, a humorous fortnightly in Kannada, *Koravanji*. It provided a much-needed forum for humorists, established as well as budding. But unfortunately, the journal did not survive him.

Dr Shivaram played an important role in the founding of the Bangalore Medical College. A close friend of his, the late Dr M. V. Govindaswamy, developed the local mental hospital, of which he was the head right from the time of its location on Avenue Road to its present spacious grounds in Wilson Gardens. He was also responsible for the development of the All-India Institute of Mental Health which eventually became the National Institute of Mental Health and Neuro-Surgery (NIMHANS). The latter has made Bangalore a centre for the treatment of mental and neurological disorders, and thanks to NIMHANS, several voluntary organizations have come into being which care for the mentally stick and handicapped, and provide counselling for people in various stages of distress.

I have spoken earlier of the memoirs of M. R. Srinivasa Murthy. But perhaps the finest memoirs in Kannada are those of the late Navaratna Rama Rao, a distinguished official of Princely Mysore. Long after his retirement, at the prompting of his old friend and admirer, Masti Venkatesha Iyengar, Rama Rao wrote of his days as an Amildar (Tahsildar) of Yedatore and T. Narasipur *taluks* in Southern Mysore. His contributions to Masti's journal, *Jeevana*, were later collected in a book, with the title *Kelavu Nenapugalu*. Rama Rao's memoirs are written in Kannada as it was spoken when he was an official, and are hauntingly evocative of life in the two *taluks* he presided over. Rama Rao's masterpiece has gone unrecognized except by a few; it is a contribution not only to literature but to the cultural and social history of Mysore.

Rama Rao's great friend from his Central College days, during the closing years of the nineteenth century, was Chakravarti Rajagopalachari; lawyer, nationalist, friend of Gandhi, and the first Indian (and last) Governor-General of India. After Central College, the two friends went to Madras to study law, and thereafter their paths diverged. Rama Rao had to take up a job in Mysore whereas 'C. R.' went on to practise law, first in Salem, and then in Madras City. He was Gandhi's unobtrusive host in Madras in 1920, and subsequently, gave up his flourishing practice, to become a dissenting follower of Gandhi. C. R. was the first popularly elected chief minister of Madras in 1937 and after becoming the first Governor-General of India joined Nehru's Cabinet. Interestingly, both the future Prime Minister of England, Sir Winston Churchill, and the future Indian Governor-General of India, C. R. seem to have lived in Bangalore at about the same time. Of course, neither knew of the other's existence, the arch-imperialist and the symbol of the end of empire.

BANGALORE TODAY

Independence brought with it radical changes in Mysore State. It became an integral part of India politically with the Maharajah losing his powers and making way for a governor nominated by the President of India. Later, Mysore became part of a single Kannada-speaking state which included some parts of Madras and Bombay presidencies, parts of Hyderabad State, and the whole of Coorg. In the 1970s, during the chief ministership of Devaraj Urs, the state's name was changed to Karnataka.

Kengal Hanumanthaiah, who was the chief minister of Mysore in the early 1950s decided to build a secretariat building which would also house the legislature of the new state. The site chosen was the land opposite the Attara Kacheri. He wanted an impressive structure which would symbolize to ordinary people the transfer of the capital from Mysore to Bangalore; from the hereditary ruler to the elected representatives of the people. The new building was to be entirely of granite, a stone symbolic of Bangalore. Hundreds of masons were employed in the construction, and the building took about three years to be completed. Hanumanthaiah faced considerable opposition for wanting to build a 'white elephant' but he went ahead with his plans. Today Vidhana Soudha is regarded as an addition not only to the architecture of Bangalore but to that of the country. It is an impressive building dominating the landscape though it looks more like a palace than a secretariat. However, its resemblance to a palace may have been deliberate as it was associated in people's minds with power and majesty. That the Vidhana Soudha has majesty and even splendour none can deny.

Bangalore is unusual among Indian cities in the sense that it is a locus for both high-tech industries and advanced research in the sciences and technology. This happy mix of industry and research is a factor in its recent emergence as a world-class centre for computer software design, and also a magnet for foreign investment. 'Some 160 computer companies, most of them working on overseas software contracts, are located in Bangalore, including a score of multinationals—IBM, Hewlett-Packard and Bull among them. Some have joined forces with Indian high-tech companies such as Wipro and Tata Information Systems.'[3] Further, 'more than 5,000 computer specialists work in Bangalore and the city is the heart of a software export industry that has more than doubled in services in the past two years, topping 300 million.' The city is beginning to outstrip not only Singapore but Israel as a technology centre.

The present population of Bangalore is about 5 million but it is difficult to predict what the size of the city will be in AD 2001. The only hopeful sign is that Bangalore's growth did slow down in the decade 1981–91 as compared with the previous decades. This, however, is statistics, for old Bangaloreans do not see any reason for optimism about their city. In the last twenty years or so it has expanded at a dizzy pace in every direction, and old landmarks have disappeared, coconut groves, vineyards, guava and mango orchards, cut down to form mean layouts with even meaner streets. Tanks which were essential for maintaining the water table, growing food crops, vegetables and orchards, and attracting bird life, have been dried up for locating bus stations, playgrounds and residential colonies.

The pace of development has been such that municipal services are in danger of breaking down. While the government is making heroic efforts to pump water into the city from the Kaveri and other rivers there

---

[3] *Time*, 14 March 1994, p. 32.

is a limit to its ability to maintain supplies to every nook and corner of the fast-growing metropolis. Summer is the time when the resources of the BWSSB (Bangalore Water Supply and Sewerage Board) are strained to the utmost because of power breakdowns and voltage fluctuations making the task of pumping water from the reservoirs to all parts of the city most difficult. The Karnataka Electric Board (KEB) has become a by-word for inefficiency. Piles of stinking garbage adorning street corners, has become a common sight. Bangalore was once referred to as 'pensioners' paradise', 'air-conditioned city', 'garden city' and so on. Now cynical citizens refer to Bangalore as 'garbage city' and 'Ban-galore'.

Only very few existing roads are able to take the greatly increased traffic but even they will not be able to do it after a few years. Most roads in Bangalore are narrow and winding, and all are characterized by potholes. A few years ago a citizen with a sense of humour wrote to a local newspaper suggesting that the bigger and more enduring potholes should be named after the important members of the State cabinet.

The number of vehicles in Bangalore has increased from 20,000 in 1960 to 7,50,000 in 1994, and Bangalore is reputed to have the largest number of two-wheelers in the country, an acknowledgement of the criminal neglect of public transport in a country which swears by planning and socialism. During the peak hours the city roads are clogged with a bewildering variety of vehicles, buses belonging to the Bangalore Transport Service, and others owned by the industries and firms, lorries, petrol and water tankers, auto-rickshaws, two-wheelers and cycles. And everyone seems to regard the roads as a 'race track'. Speeding is universal, no one being hauled up for it. While private vehicles are required to pass an annual 'Emission Test', BTS buses and lorries are allowed to spew black, poisonous fumes onto the roads. Pollution has increased visibly during the last twenty years, and the recent decision of the police chief to provide masks for all traffic policemen in the city, is a sound if ominous one. In fact, it is desirable that all those living in Bangalore wear masks to protect themselves from pollution especially as Bangalore is known to be unfriendly to asthmatics. It is significant that in discussions regarding traffic management, the pedestrian's safety does not seem to occupy a central place. Paradoxically, the pedestrian runs a greater risk on the city's side streets than on the main highways. The former escape police supervision and all manner of vehicles from big buses to two-wheelers and cycles, speed along them heedless of the risk they pose to people. Walking at night is really perilous, as cycles, and often two-wheelers, are ridden without lights.

Pedestrians are denied even the use of pavements where such exist. . . . Paving pavements with granite slabs is common in Bangalore but it is hazardous to walk on pavements when, thanks to lack of maintenance, slabs jut out at all angles, becoming really stumbling-blocks to the unwary. Besides, they are being rapidly taken over by all sorts of people. The rich extend their gardens to include the pavements, and quite a few are even fencing them off. Builders use pavements for dumping all kinds of building material from sand to jelly stones and the materials lie there for months but no one seems to bother. Pavements also provide parking space, during working hours, for mobile eateries, cobblers' stands, cycle-repair shops, coconut sellers, fruit stalls and what have you. There are over 10,000 hawkers' vehicles in Bangalore.

There is a move now to restrict hawkers to certain areas but no one should be misled into thinking that this is aimed at providing some relief to pedestrians; but rather the hawkers are prevented from competing with traders who rent shops in shopping complexes and to see that they do not take over space earmarked for parking vehicles. Only a determined effort by the corporation officials to clear pavements of all obstacles and take other necessary steps will make them safe for pedestrians. The proposed changes in this direction of Brigade Road and Commercial Street are most welcome, if not necessary. But they require a strong political will to be implemented. But whether politicians will risk alienating influential traders in an election year remains to be seen.

In 1991–2, it was estimated that there were 545 slums in Bangalore. Slums proliferated with the rapid expansion of the city since independence. In the course of its expansion, the city has ingested peripheral villages which have become slums. The villagers had to take to new occupations, the richer becoming rentiers, transport operators etc., while the poor taking to petty trade and menial jobs in shops and firms. Old Bangalore also had other slums besides ingested villages and they not only continued but became worse with population increase. Poor immigrants from neighbouring states, in particular, Tamil Nadu, found jobs in the building industry and other areas of the unorganized sector, and either joined earlier slums or formed new ones. Finally, there were 'political' slums, which came into existence overnight: A 'leader' encouraged his followers—and voters–to settle on a stretch of vacant land, and material for the huts were supplied to the occupants along with party flags. It was the job of the leader to make sure that the occupants were not evicted, and later, were supplied with water, electricity, etc.

All political parties are interested in cornering the votes of slum-dwellers. The latter are only too aware of their value to politicians and they demand in return, to be confirmed in their ownership of the plots, get funds for constructing houses, and provision for electricity and water. Any attempt to move them to the outskirts meets with resistance on various grounds including the loss of jobs.

Another serious problem of Bangalore, and perhaps of other fast-growing cities as well, is the rapid shrinkage of lung space. Even areas set apart in the new layouts for schools, playgrounds 'civic amenities' etc., are often diverted to other uses with the connivance of officials and politicians. Indeed, the people are so disenchanted with the BDA (Bangalore Development Authority) that they associate it with corruption which includes losing inconvenient files, and phenomenal delay. Quite apart from the BDA, those in power do not seem to want to protect the environment of Bangalore, and their ideas of beautification of the city seem to be bizarre in the extreme. Two examples will make clear what I mean. The corporation officials of the city wanted to pull out the children's toy train from Cubbon Park and put in its place a musical fountain costing three crores of rupees. This harebrained idea has luckily been given up but the musical fountain will now appear in an island in Ulsoor Lake, which has been taken over by the military authorities for salvaging and beautification. My second example is the granting of a beautiful stretch of tree-covered land on the western shore of Sankey Tank for putting up a Children's Film Institute. Public agitation has delayed the idea from being translated into reality. What is disturbing, is the tendency to go on eating into green areas and tanks when it is known that there is a great need to preserve and extend lungspace and leave existing tanks untouched.

A few stretches of open land still exist in Bangalore but one wonders if there is any conscious intention to preserve them as open spaces. The two biggest stretches are the Bangalore Palace (about 460 acres) and the Roerich Estate (about 470 acres). If these two properties are acquired speedily by the government and utilized in such a way that the bulk of the land is kept green while a small portion is built up to pay for the upkeep of the rest, then pollution can be lessened and the city's beauty retained. But this requires strong political will. Further, many among those in power want to go in for populist schemes. For instance, there has been talk for over fifteen years about shifting the present Race Course to the outskirts of the city. Shifting the race course is indeed desirable but the land thus retrieved can be put to much better use than putting up an ugly Indian version of Disneyland.

One of the worst consequences of the hysterical expansion of Bangalore has been the destruction of its tanks. The undulating character of the Bangalore region favoured the formation and construction of tanks, and they were a valuable heritage of the people. Building a tank was a meritorious (*punya*) act as also planting avenue trees, and erecting granite platforms on roads for resting head-loads carried by people. In the Bangalore area, besides the head-load-rests (*talebhara*) there were also granite water-containers built at a convenient height for thirsty wayfarers to drink from.

The city and its neighbourhood had over 250 tanks (*kere*) prior to 1950 but their number is now reduced to eighty-five. But all tanks are threatened with extinction. Even such prominent tanks as Ulsoor, Hebbal, Madivala and Sankey may go dry unless measures are taken immediately to protect them. As already mentioned, Kempabudhi, once a fine tank, is now a foul swamp, and a source of mosquitoes and disease to those living nearby. The widespread tendency to let city sewage empty into the tanks has transformed them into foul-smelling breeders of mosquitoes. The spreading water hyacinth is choking the waters.

Bangalore has several fine temples, churches, mosques, and other religious structures such as Jain *basti, gurdwara, agiari* and so on. There is also an imposing Ramakrishna Mutt, and shrines exist for Shirdi Sai Baba and Ramana Maharshi. Some of the religious places are architecturally beautiful but greed, prosperity and modern technology are all enemies of such beauty. Religious organizations like to build commercial complexes on their spare land. The use of public address systems for broadcasting prayers, are not only increasing noise pollution in the city but making quiet-loving citizens hostile to religiosity. Glaring neon lights and liberal use of expensive marble detract from the sanctity of religious structures and stand out aggressively on the landscape.

One of the attractions of old Bangalore were the platforms built around fine *peepul* (Ficus religiosa) trees, and sometimes, intertwined with *neem* (margosa). Cobras in union, a popular fertility symbol were sculptured around the trunks of trees. These quiet shrines, monuments to our peasant heritage, are no longer left free. Ugly structures are coming up on the platforms disturbing the tranquillity which the tree-shrines stood for. Noise, microphones, crowds, neon lights and litter have become symbols of our pervasive mass culture.

There are, however, some hopeful signs, as in recent years a sharp increase in environmental awareness has given rise to large numbers of citizens demanding the continued existence of tanks in the city. The report of the distinguished official, N. Lakshmana Rau, on Bangalore's tanks and lakes, the fact that they have decreased in the last forty years from 250 to eighty-five, and stressing their importance for the city's ecology has provided a shot in the arm to environmentalists. The media has also shown a keen interest in environmental matters, and not a week passes without one or other environmental issue being highlighted. The authorities have transferred the task of restoration and management of Bangalore's tanks to the Forest Department, recalling a move made during Gundu Rao's chief ministership, transferring the task of greening Bangalore to an official from the same department. That experiment was a success and acknowledged as such. Luckily, the present Chief Conservator of Forests (CCF), Parameswarappa, has displayed considerable drive, energy and imagination in the move to save the tanks. He organized a children's rally recently to highlight the urgency of saving the Madivala tank. His department proposes to fence all the existing tanks and lakes, direct sewage away from them, remove the water hyacinth, grow trees on the shores, and even create small islands in the tanks with a view to attracting the birds that have deserted Bangalore. The lakes could also become breeding places for fish. Boating arrangements for children have also been planned. A trust is being formed to save Hebbal Tank. Industrial and business houses have shown an interest in doing their bit to keep Bangalore green and to save the tanks. The army wants to play its part in saving Bangalore's environment: it is undertaking the task of restoring Ulsoor Lake and creating a 20 acre park on a parade ground adjoining Mahatma Gandhi Road.

BANGALORE: AN OVERVIEW

It is obvious that Bangalore's various physical features, such as its elevation, climate, the beauty of its rolling countryside, its red earth, and its granite hillocks and rock outcrops, which contrast with the green of the cultivated fields, have all contributed to the place emerging as a major city of modern India. Its strategic importance was recognized even before the time of Kempe Gowda I, by the Gangas and Cholas. The two forts which were built round Bangalore and the erection of watch towers on cardinal points by Kempe Gowda II, all confirm the fact. The British moved their troops from Srirangapatna to Bangalore in 1809 because of Bangalore's climate and elevation. The establishment of the 'civil and military station' as the cantonment was called, was a major factor in the city's subsequent development. The nucleus of a modern city came into existence in the cantonment, and the fact that the British resident stayed in Bangalore, proclaimed its political importance. Bangalore also received special attention during the reign of Krishnaraja Wodeyar IV (1910–40), and his Dewans, M. V., and Sir Mirza Ismail. It was during this period that Bangalore came to be known as a 'pensioners' paradise', 'garden city' and 'air-conditioned city'.

After independence, Bangalore's choice as a capital of the state was only logical. Mysore had too many associations with the royal family to be the capital of a new state with an elected chief minister and a nominated governor. Finally, for an enlarged Karnataka, Bangalore was more central, and better linked with the major cities of the country.

Bangalore's climate, its cosmopolitan and western facade, its educational institutions, were all factors favouring the location of a few big industries in the 1950s. This in turn led to its recent emergence as a world centre for software research. Success breeds success, and the present chief minister is looking for another 5,000 acres of land for locating a second 'silicon valley'. Whitefield, Bangalore's once sleepy suburb and home for many Anglo–Indians, now houses a 'technology park' in collaboration with the Tatas and a few Singapore industries. More 'technology parks' are being created by the private sector on the outskirts of the city.

Bangalore is intellectually vibrant, a multitude of institutions of higher learning and research providing homes for scientists and other specialists in a variety of fields. A perusal of the lists of seminars, talks, discussions, plays, musical and other performances, exhibitions and religious events in the daily newspapers, will provide the curious reader with an idea of the city's deep interest in cultural and intellectual aspects of life.

From the point of view of providing medical relief, Bangalore has not only several hospitals and nursing homes where highly trained specialists function with the state-of-the-art equipment, but there are also nature cure centres which attract patients from all over the country. In the Kidwai Medical Centre of Oncology, Bangalore has a fine cancer hospital and mention has already been made of NIMHANS. In short, few cities in India can rival Bangalore for the excellence and variety of medical facilities it provides.

The media has a strong presence in the city and shows a keen interest in what is happening there and in its environs. Writers, artists, theatre persons, musicians, all find in Bangalore a beckoning if not a beguiling city. The violin shaped auditorium built in memory of the late T. Chowdaiah may look odd architecturally, but it symbolizes the city's friendliness to music and the performing arts. It is a zany but an appropriate symbol of the city's love of music and the other performing arts.

Games and athletics are central to Bangalore's existence. The city boasts of a huge if ungainly cricket stadium, a football stadium, the Kanteerava Stadium for athletics, and the Netaji Subhash Institute of Sports (Southern Region Sports Authority of India) near the Bangalore University campus. There are two golf courses in the city, a third one in neighbouring Kolar, and a likely fourth one near Devanahalli to be funded by NRIs. The proliferation of golf courses in Bangalore speaks of the kind of people who are flocking to the city from all over India. Playing golf is an increasingly popular status symbol for the high executives on the look out for other high executives and VIPs generally.

Gourmet cooking and eating is catching up in Bangalore, and the well-heeled like to experiment with new foods. Apart from cuisine from different parts of the country, Chinese food is very popular not only in Chinese restaurants and five-star hotels but even in the bigger vegetarian restaurants. The inhabitants of China will find it unusual if not shocking that their food should be the favourite of many who have not eaten even an egg. 'Club houses', and new restaurants are springing up on the outskirts of the city, each with its own individual features. Food is becoming a cult, and the citizens of Bangalore seem to be willing to pay fancy prices for eating exotic food served in 'snob' places.

Along with the sprouting of new eating places, including fast food stands, a pub culture has overtaken Bangalore. Draught beer is sold at these pubs along with snacks, and in the bigger ones, there is even music! Young men and women like to gather at these pubs, and conversation flows freely, noisily, tongues and minds lubricated by frothy draught beer.

The middle classes are prominent in the city, the entire range of the middle class in fact, from those who are very close to being rich to those who have just managed to enter the lowest level. This fact explains the infestation of the city's roads with two-wheelers and Marutis, and the unappeasable consumerism of its inhabitants.

The architectural face of Bangalore is changing fast. Bungalows and houses are being pulled down rapidly to make way for apartment-housing putting tremendous strain on the provision of utilities such as water, sewage and electricity, not to mention parking space and other incidentals. High rise buildings seem inevitable but it is essential that they are confined to the industrial areas. They should be prevented from spreading to the extensions, and it should be remembered that provision of infrastructural facilities for high rises is very expensive, and therefore need to be limited to commercial areas. If this does not happen, Bangalore is certain to go the way Bombay went.

It is necessary to emphasize in the context of the city's recent rapid expansion that Bangalore, or its core, is culturally a part of old Mysore State and Mysoreans were—and even now are—notorious for their laid-back attitude to things. They like to stay in their cities and when they are forced to stay away in pursuit of their careers, return home in the evening of their lives. Bangalore has a reputation for being a very cosmopolitan city and while this is certainly true, when old Bangaloreans get together they talk about the 'invasion' of their city by aggressive and brash outsiders. They are too polite, however, to mention this to the latter. It is also undeniable that there is resentment of the aggressiveness and push of the outsiders who are increasingly taking over the city. Such resentment is more palpable at the lower economic levels.

During the last twelve months or so, much concern has been expressed by the media and influential persons about the urgent need for planning Bangalore as a 'mega city'. A few hopeful developments have occurred in this direction. Commuter trains have been introduced from Mysore, Tumkur and Kolar to Bangalore. The broadgauging of the track to Bangalore and Mysore has reduced the distance between the two by an hour, and there is talk of electrification of the line, and also of plans to construct a four-lane express-way between the two cities. If all this is done, Mysore may emerge as a twin city to Bangalore, offering an equally good climate, and cheaper and better living conditions. There is also a need to develop Kolar, Tumkur and Channapatna as satellite towns. It is in the interest of Bangalore to call a halt to the hysterical expansion of the city, and that can only be done by planning for the region as a whole. It is vital to remember that success can kill a city too.

The Study of Disputes in an Indian Village

Within a few days of my arriving in Rampura village, I heard vague reports of a case of arson in which a poor man's straw-rick had been burnt down by a man from a neighbouring village. The better-off villagers each gave a head-load of straw to the injured man, and the result was that he obtained more straw than he had lost. The villagers did not give me the details of what had happened, and such facts as I obtained came my way a few months later when there occurred another case of arson. When a dispute occurs, people's memories are stimulated and precedents are quoted. Something like case law exists, though it is not systematized.

At about the same time, a widow brought a complaint against another woman who had accused her of leading an immoral life. I managed to secure a brief account of the incident but not in sufficient detail. It was clear that the villagers did not like giving information about the 'seamy' side of village life to an outsider. I felt that this was a challenge to me as a fieldworker. Besides, I must confess that like the villagers I found that a dispute broke the monotony of village life, and gave people something to talk about. The villagers were quick to see the humorous side of disputes.

Disputes also had a dramatic quality. Thus one afternoon a man walked into my veranda dragging a lamb's skin with him, hurled it before Nadu Gowda, a respected elder, saying, 'Mrs Siddamma's dog ate up my lamb. You must secure justice for me.' Or again, another afternoon, Mrs Khasu, a Muslim, was pouring forth a Niagara of words in Kannada as well as Urdu, while laying her case before the Headman. The assembled men were all enjoying her oratory—in fact, some of them had previously expressed a hope that I would get a chance to listen to her oratory before I left the village. (There was a 'master' of abuse in the village, a peasant woman, and a boy offered to steal her fowl so that I could record her abuse!)

A good many disputes have a public as well as a private side. The former would take place in the field or street or on a veranda, while the latter, inside the house. Only in a few 'partition' cases was I able to witness a private session. The fact of my being kept out of the private sessions spurred me to devise ways and means by which I could get to know what had happened in them.

Every society has its own preoccupations, and whatever the problem the fieldworker is pursuing, he cannot entirely ignore the former. It is only in a village or area which has been already studied sufficiently intensively that he can ignore the preoccupations of the people to concentrate on his own particular problem. I was insensibly led into paying some attention to disputes even though my main interest was the delineation of intercaste relations. I am afraid that the amount of time and energy I could spare for disputes was not at all enough. This was especially so when I had to keep track, as I had to occasionally, of two or three disputes each of which ran on for a few weeks.

Partition disputes generally tend to drag on. When the idea is first mooted, it is at the end of series of quarrels for which the women, especially those who have come in by marriages, are usually blamed. The elders who are approached to effect a division of the property among the coparceners usually advise them to stay together and keep their women in control. After a while quarrels break out again, and finally, the elders concede that it is better to divide than to quarrel perpetually. Then a second set of quarrels occur—how should the property be divided and who should get what? There are some conventions regarding this, but they do not prevent quarrels. After the property has been divided, one member feels that he has fared badly and he demands a redistribution. In such a case, adjustments are made with some difficulty and the document registered to ensure that similar demands are not made again. Another set of quarrels arises during the paddy-transplantation season when the bunds separating the flats are trimmed, and brothers, who are usually neighbours, accuse each other of encroachment. Right of way across a brother's field and right to irrigation water flowing through it, are other matters over which disputes occur. Such disputes go on for years. The partition of property among brothers does not promote amity and it is frequently found that adult brothers are not on speaking terms with each other. While the members of a lineage show solidarity among themselves in relation to other lineages, there are tensions. The narrower the lineage-span, the greater the tension. An exception to this rule is the elementary family when the siblings are still very young.

Besides the reluctance of the people to discuss the seamy side of their life before a respected outsider, there are other difficulties. Only some of the 'facts' of a dispute are accepted as such by all. And even the 'same' facts are fitted into different configurations by different people. The arbitrators as well as the neighbours and onlookers know the disputants intimately, and everyone has his own image of the character and personality of each disputant. This is a pre-existing image and the facts of the dispute are woven into it. But the image is not unchangeable.

Let me give an example: in a dispute between two Oilmen who were uterine brothers, the elder brother's wife, a strong personality and an attractive woman, was found walking in the direction of the river Kaveri at about 3 p.m. A farmer saw her and asked her where she was going and she replied that she was going to the river. She was so fed up that she wanted to drown herself in the river. When this was mentioned during the dispute, a few men laughed and said, 'Is she the type that commits suicide?' One of those who laughed was an arbitrator. Here the 'objective' fact is, the woman walking to the river and expressing her intention to drown herself. This is interpreted differently by different people. The danger is that interpretation and fact are so closely woven that if the sociologist is not continually on the alert, he is in danger of accepting some interpretations as facts.

These interpretations are not haphazard but are related to other factors. Thus, a decision of the village or caste council is often explained by saying that the Headman or another powerful arbitrator wanted to favour his kinsman or casteman or friend or client. In the case of 'The Potter and the Priest' the Headman was stated to have changed his decision overnight about the punishment to be meted out to two people accused of fornication because an agnatic kinsman of his, accused of attempted rape, was suddenly brought before him.[1] He could not pass a harsh sentence on one and a lenient one on the other. The interests of

---

[1] *Man in India*, 1959, 39 (3): 190–209.

a powerful man like the Headman spread everywhere and he is likely to remember his interests while judging cases. An arbitrator also has his prejudices. Thus Nadu Gowda, normally a fair man, disliked one Untouchable in particular, and this came out sharply whenever a matter concerning him came up for discussion. Friendships are common and occasionally cut across caste lines, and they influence the interpretation of events by witnesses as well as arbitrators. Finally, the solidarity of the dominant caste and the kind of local leadership which it has, are relevant facts in the dispensation of justice.

Where the defendant is a powerful leader of a large faction, the arbitrators tend to be lenient because the defendant is capable of defying them and thus endangering the entire fabric of village law and order. (I am assuming here that factions are not so deep that the village council no longer functions.) There are saws which elders quote: 'We floated the matter away' (winked at it), 'We let it slip through our fingers' (ignored inconvenient facts), and so on. One arbitrator mentioned how when he raised a point during the settlement of a dispute, the Headman's son winked at him to make him keep quiet. The poorer villagers are heard complaining about the corruption of arbitrators.

I must hasten to add here that this does not mean that the arbitrators can do just what they like. The ideal of justice (*nyāya, dharma*) is there, supported by moral and religious sanctions. The arbitrators cannot entirely and consistently ignore public opinion. There are also unwritten rules of evidence. In 'A Caste Dispute among the Washermen of Mysore', the defendant trapped the plaintiff by making him eat food handled by her, and also took care to see that a witness was present on the occasion.[2] This was one of the crucial facts in the case. As I mentioned earlier, one of the tasks of village councils is to determine what are the facts of the case. Evidence is insisted upon, and a distinction is made between direct and hearsay evidence. The reputation of a witness is important in evaluating the truth or otherwise of his statements. A person is sometimes made to swear to the truth of a statement in a temple. But this is an extreme measure.

The tutoring of witnesses seems to occur frequently and this makes the arbitrator's task all the more difficult. In some cases, tutoring is not necessary as the man has an interest in *suppressio veri* and *suggestio falsi*.

It is usual for a man to know only some of the events which have occurred, but he maintains that what he knows is not only true but is the whole truth. This was brought home to me when I was taking notes of

[2] *Eastern Anthropologist*, 1954, VII (3–4): 149–68.

the dispute between the Potter and the Priest. What I did then was to confront one informant with another's version. It is obvious that several versions are more likely to yield the truth than a single version.

Then there are men who have a vested interest in disputes. They try to further their interest which may be monetary gain, or a trip to town ostensibly to see a lawyer or official, and so further their sense of self-importance. The existence of such men is not only recognized, but they are credited with having even more influence than they actually do. (They also provide convenient scapegoats.) The words 'chitāvani' (instigation) and 'kitāpathi' (love of creating quarrels) are frequently heard in the village. My invaluable friend and assistant Kulle Gowda was active whenever a dispute occurred. His capacity for making mischief was widely recognized.

Once the sociologist has obtained an idea of the prevalent pattern of antagonisms in the village, he can use this knowledge for obtaining better information. Thus the friends of a man will provide one version of events while his enemies provide another version. And there are a number of marginal people who may provide a third version.

For a period of two years after leaving Rampura I was unable to so much as glance at my fieldnotes. When I finally came round to writing up a few disputes for a fieldwork class I experienced a certain amount of difficulty in achieving a completely coherent account. This was specially so with the partition disputes which usually ran for a few weeks and involved much acrimonious discussion. Some of my entries were vague or mutually inconsistent, and in the process of producing a coherent account for the dispute, I had to omit, change and reinterpret some parts of my notes. I mentioned this fact in my first published account of a dispute.[3]

Social anthropologists have in recent years stressed the fact that their descriptive monographs are a contribution to history. They claim that these monographs provide better data for future historians of primitive and peasant life in different parts of the world, than are available for any country and for any period in the past. This is no doubt true but it is essential to state that a social anthropologist's note books occasionally contain entries that are wrong, vague or partial. This is specially true of the data collected in the first few months. When he is writing up, the social anthropologist discards the entries which he knows or suspects to be wrong. But he rarely mentions that his clear and coherent accounts of various aspects of the life of the people he has studied are occasionally produced from notes which are far from clear

[3] 'A Joint Family Dispute in a Mysore Village', *Journal of the M.S. University of Baroda*, 1952, 1 (1): 7–31.

and consistent. These difficulties exist in all cases excepting where the fieldworker has periodically taken time off from the field to read and ponder over his entries and resolves his doubts and difficulties by discussing them with his informants. They are particularly prone to occur where the fieldworker is spending a year or less in the field and also when he is recording disputes which occur over several weeks. I am not concerned here with the other limitations of fieldnotes as historical documents, namely, the subjectivism imposed by the field-worker's interests, his limited energy and the degree of his conscientiousness. It is obvious that where the social anthropologist uses an interpreter, as he frequently does, the notes do not have the same value as when he has enough mastery over the language of the people he is studying.

Recent research has shown that even the genealogies recorded by an anthropologist do not always provide an accurate record of descent. This is especially so in segmentary societies where the genealogies regularly adjust themselves to the dynamics of the lineage system.[4] Even where there is a caste of genealogists whose business it is to record genealogies and bring them up to date periodically, they do not always provide an accurate record of descent at all levels.[5] Generally speaking, the remoter the past, the less reliable are the memories of informants. Even with regard to events which happened a year or two ago, informants' memories are not particularly reliable. But where a large number of people are involved, several can be questioned to obtain an account which is broadly true. And where documents exist, informants can be questioned on the basis of the documents. I used the first technique in gathering facts about a dispute which had occurred in October 1947 between Kere and Bihalli, and the second in my account for the Washerman dispute.

It was while collecting the facts of the dispute among Washermen that the idea occurred to me to look for documents referring to settlement of past disputes. I was told that caste and village headmen in the big villages had such documents. I had no luck, however, with the Peasant Headman of Hogur, the *hobli* to which Rampura belongs, but I fared better with the Peasant Headman of Kere, at a distance of three miles from Rampura. In the summer of 1952, I made several trips to him and finally obtained loan of over seventy documents, some of which referred to settlement of disputes which had occurred in Kere Hobli during the years 1900–40. The documents referred to a wide variety of

[4] E. E. Evans-Pritchard, 1940, *The Nuer,* Oxford, p. 246.
[5] See A. M. Shah and R. G. Shroff, 1959, 'A Caste of Genealogists and Mythographers—

matters, and I am convinced that where such documents exist, they are invaluable for the study of rural social history. My own analysis of the concept of the dominant caste owed much to these documents. I do know that such documents also exist elsewhere. The people with whom these documents exist do not take enough care to preserve them, and white ants, cockroaches and the monsoon are steadily diminishing the quantity of documents available to the anthropologist. These remarks also apply to village records lying in the *taluk* offices everywhere. Documents [such as these] have, somehow, failed to attract the attention of historians in spite of their obvious importance.

The systematic study of disputes in rural areas and their settlement by non-official *panchayats* constitute an important field of research. It is completely neglected at the present moment by sociologists as well as lawyers. The latter confine themselves to laws passed by the State and Central legislatures. Customary law as observed in the villages is not regarded as law even though it governs the lives of millions. Convenient myths exist to the effect that the introduction of British law destroyed the law and customs followed by the village *pnchayats*. Indian villagers are really 'bilegal' using both their traditional system as well as British-introduced law administered by the official courts situated in towns. I have been told of cases withdrawn from the latter to be settled before the unofficial *panchayats*. The study of the effects of introduction of British law on the indigenous system and on Indian society needs to be investigated by historians, anthropologists and lawyers.

The concentration on formal and written law has distorted the perspective of Indian lawyers and intellectuals. It has led to even pretending that the law enforced in the unofficial *panchayats* is not law.

I am convinced, however, that the study of the submerged legal system is extremely important and will be one of the things which will have to be undertaken if we plan to develop a much-neglected field of study, namely, the sociology of law and legal institutions. Such a study will also throw light on a historico-legal riddle, the relation between law as embodied in the sacred books of the Hindus and law as actually observed and obeyed by the bulk of the people living in villages. Finally, the study of this problem is not unrelated to the policy of devolution which finds much vocal support among modern India's leaders.

---

the Vahi Vancha Barots of Gujarat.' Milton Singer (ed.), *Traditional India: Structure and Change.* Philadelphia, pp. 40–70.

A Caste Dispute among the Washermen of Mysore

I

The dispute which I have described in the following pages, occurred among the members of the Washerman caste (Madivala Shetti or Agasa)[1] in Mandya and Mysore Districts of Karnataka State during the year 1946. It began formally on 20 May 1946, in Bihalli, at a wedding, when Maya of Bella, the plaintiff, charged the defendant, Shiva of Magga, with having given his niece Javni in marriage to Kala, the son of Kempi of Kotti, the sister of Arasi who had been outcasted about twelve years previously for having had sexual relations with a Holeya (Untouchable caste of Karnataka). (See Document III and the genealogical chart.)[2] Maya's charge needs to be explained! According to it, it was not Kempi, but her elder sister Arasi who was outcasted. The guilt extended to Kempi only by association or identification with Arasi. This is a crucial point and will be discussed later. The defendant Shiva was brought within the orbit of guilt because he gave his younger sister's daughter in marriage to Kempi's son, which again provides an instance of guilt by association. It is necessary to add here that normally it is the

---

[1] The common Kannada word for a Washerman is Agasa, which is a caste name, the more high-sounding Madivala Shetti, is only used in the rural area and that too not commonly. The term Shetti is a honorific title used at the end of either a caste or personal name by some artisan and trading castes such as Washerman, Potter or Trader. It is used on formal occasions, or in documents. In the present documents, the suffix, Shetti, after a personal name, is used somewhat erratically.

[2] Henceforward, capital D will be used for Document. The English version of the documents is given at the end of the text.

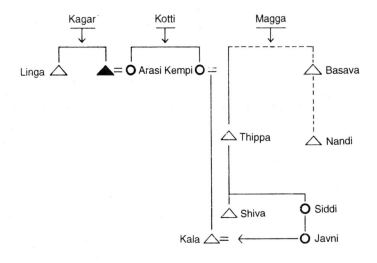

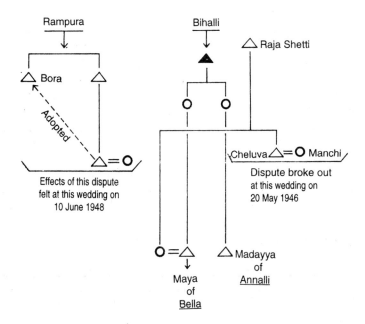

Note: Underlined names refer to villages.

parents who choose a partner for their son or daughter, and as between the two parents the father's responsibility is much greater than the mother's. It is only when the father is dead or very ill that the father's or mother's relatives, especially the former, have the responsibility of finding a spouse. In the above case it has to be presumed that Shiva's sister was either a widow or a divorcée, and that her husband's brothers had no influence upon her. Perhaps she had gone to live with her brother after her husband's death, or after divorcing her husband. This is the only explanation for Shiva's having the power of disposal over his niece.

The timing of the charge was significant. The elders of the Washerman caste from several neighbouring villages had gathered together for the wedding at Bihalli, and Maya gave utterance to his charge when the guests were about to sit for dinner. Maya was asked whether he could prove, or provide evidence (*rujuvatu*) for his charge. He gave an undertaking in writing (*muchaliké*) that he would do so (D III). In D I the defendant Shiva agreed to subject himself to such punishment as the members of his caste (*kulastharu*) thought fit, if Maya succeeded in proving his charge (*phiryād*) before witnesses to that document. It was reported that Shiva was made to leave the dinner pending the inquiry. This was an insult and the Bihalli hosts were annoyed with Maya for causing this unpleasantness at an occasion like a wedding.

D II is a letter written by the plaintiff on 1 June 1946 to an elder in Rampura informing the latter that in accordance with the decision arrived at the wedding, a meeting of elders to adjudicate the dispute had been fixed for Tuesday, 4 June 1946, at the Mādeshwāraswāmi temple in Gudi, a village about a mile from Rampura. (The time of the meeting was mentioned as 10 a.m.) The plaintiff informed the Rampura elder that the responsibility for producing the defendant before the panchayat was his (the elder's). It is interesting to note that the dates mentioned are according to the Gregorian calendar, and not the Hindu calendar which is still used for all ritual occasions.

The inquiry into the dispute began on Tuesday, 4 June 1946 at the temple[3] mentioned above, before a large body of assembled elders of the Washerman caste. One or two informants estimated that several hundred Washermen had gathered on that day. Bora of Rampura, one of the hosts, had cooked 35 *seer*[4] of rice for his friends and supporters

---

[3] It is probable that the meeting was actually held in the shade of the sacred peepal tree by the side of the temple.

[4] A *seer* measure is equal to about $2\frac{1}{2}$ lbs.

alone. Kempi, who was accused by Maya of having been outcasted, was made to serve food to these guests—this was a tactical move on the part of her friends, aimed at proving that everyone had social relations with Kempi and that she had not been thrown out of caste.

In D III Maya mentioned both the immediate and ultimate origins of the dispute. The immediate origin was at the wedding in Bihalli, and the ultimate origin was the outcasting of Arasi, the elder sister of Kempi. Maya stated that ever since Arasi's outcasting, no member of the Washerman caste had any social relations with her or her sister. (Social relations include inter-dining, marriage, and other forms of interaction which normally prevail among the members of a caste.) Maya challenged that if he was proved wrong he would pay whatever damages the elders thought fit. He actually used the word 'damage'—it was spelt *dāmij* in Kannada.

D IV is a statement of the defendant Shiva. It is written in a somewhat formal manner clearly imitative of the records of proceedings in urban courts of law—some of the participants, including Kulle Gowda of Rampura, were familiar with lawyers and law courts in the towns.

Shiva answered Maya's charge by stating that for eleven years since the outcasting of Arasi he had no contact with either her or Kempi. But about a year and a half ago Maya (the plaintiff) had himself gone to Shiva and told him, 'You must see that your younger sister's daughter is given in marriage to Kempi's son.' Shiva replied, 'I agree, as you have done me the honour of coming and asking me.' Sometime later Shiva and Kempi went to Bella to obtain the advice of Maya regarding the arrangements for the wedding. Maya replied that he had no time that day and that he would come another day. He also suggested that the wedding should be held a month later. Shiva and Kempi agreed to Maya's suggestion, but when, some days later, they went to invite Maya to the wedding, he said, 'The marriage is between the bride's people and the groom's people. I have nothing to do with it. I will not come.' The marriage was celebrated without Maya. Shiva added that all his relatives continued to have social relations with him and Kempi.

In brief, the line of defence adopted by Shiva was to make Maya responsible for his (the former's) having social relations with Kempi. He also stated that neither he nor Kempi had been outcasted.

It was possible, however, for Shiva to adopt a different line of defence: he could have separated the charges against Arasi and Kempi, and argued that the outcasting of the former did not extend to the latter. Perhaps Shiva felt it was safer to steer clear of the career of a strong personality like Kempi. But, as will become clear later, the charge against Arasi did get separated from the charge against Kempi in spite of Maya's attempt, although not explicit, to mix up the two, and to condemn Kempi by implication.

D V is Kempi's statement of her defence. It is evident that this was made after the witnesses for Maya had given their evidence. Kempi roundly declared that everything that had been said on behalf of Maya was false. Another statement of hers cut the ground under Maya's feet by separating the charges against her and those against her elder sister. She stated that for a long time there had been no social relationship between her and Arasi. She added that Maya and some witnesses on his behalf, such as Elehalli Lingappa and Boodnoor Mallayya, had been having social relations with her all along. Finally, like Shiva, she made Maya responsible for the marriage between her son and Shiva's niece. Her version of the wedding negotiations was substantially the same as Shiva's. There were minor discrepancies no doubt, but these were not picked on by the opposition to puncture the evidence of either Shiva or Kempi. Perhaps the discrepancies were not there in the statements as made but only in the written record. But the documents have to be taken, in spite of their great brevity, and obvious deficiencies in draftsmanship, as giving a fairly accurate account of what happened. The great evidential value ascribed to documents in rural India ensures that what is reduced to writing in the presence of several witnesses representing different 'parties', is essentially true. The possibility of deliberate cheating by a clever and corrupt scribe should not, however, be ruled out.

D VI is a statement by Boodnoor Mallayya, described by Kempi as a 'witness for Maya', but at the head of D VI it has been mentioned that he is a witness for Kempi! His evidence was quite crucial as is recognized in D XIV: it is mentioned there that it was on the strength of his evidence that the case against Shiva and Kempi fell through, and eventually, it led to a fine being levied on Maya. Mallayya's statement was regarded by the panchayat as providing a clear evidence that Maya had continued to have social relations with Kempi himself, which clearly disproved his allegations that she had been outcasted along with her sister, Arasi. Or, alternatively, if Kempi had really been outcasted, and Maya had eaten food touched by her, he too had been rendered impure.

Mallayya told the panchayat that some time previously he and Maya had occasion to return to Bella from Bihalli *via* Kotti, Kempi's village. Maya took Mallayya to Kempi's house—this was Mallayya's first visit to her house. After a little talk, Kempi told the guests that she had some steamed cakes bought for them from the shop, and that she would make some coffee. She requested the guests to wait till the coffee was made.

When Kempi went in to make coffee, Maya and Mallayya went towards the village pond to perform ablutions. I was, however, told by some informants that during the period of Kempi's absence in the kitchen, Maya came to learn—it is not known how—that Shiva and Kempi have become lovers. This made Maya very angry indeed and he left the house at once without partaking of Kempi's hospitality.

Kempi must have suspected that something had gone wrong when she found that her guests had suddenly disappeared without informing her. But, clever woman that she was, she carried the food on her head to the two men, taking care to be accompanied by a man of the Okkaliga (Peasant) caste, a different and higher one than the Washerman, to act, if and when necessary, as a witness. Kempi's actions point to premeditation on her part, and but for it she would not have been able to out-manoeuvre Maya.

To Kempi's and the Okkaliga's queries as to why they had left so suddenly and without informing anyone, Mallayya replied that they wanted to perform ablutions. After a while the two guests ate the food brought by Kempi in the presence of the Okkaliga. The entire incident suggests that Kempi was able to anticipate Maya's reaction when he learnt that Shiva had become her lover.

Mallayya was followed by Annalli Madayya (D VII) who began his evidence by declaring that he was Maya's (classificatory) brother. His evidence confirmed Mallayya's: he said that he had been having social relations with Kempi for the past five years and that he and Maya had occasionally dined together at Kempi's house. He also deposed that there was harmony among them all until the incident at the wedding. He had seen Washermen from Bihalli and other villages partaking of the dinner served at the wedding of Kempi's son and Shiva's niece.

A point which is worth commenting upon is that in D XIV Malayya's evidence is referred to, but not Annalli Madayya's, in spite of the latter being the classificatory brother of Maya. Whether this is merely an omission, one of several, or whether Mallayya's evidence was given greater weight because of the presence of an impartial third party viz., the Okkaliga companion, it is not clear.

D VIII is a brief statement by one Rudra of Settalli saying that he had been having social relations with Kempi for the past six months and was unaware of anything else in the case. This statement, along with Ds VI and VII, aimed at proving that Kempi did have social relations with her castefolk. From which it followed that the ban against Arasi did not extend to Kempi.

D IX only confirms the evidence of the three earlier documents. In it Kempayya of Bella declared that while everything he knew about Arasi was direct and first-hand, what he knew about Kempi was only hearsay. He added that he was eighty years of age. I was told by informants that Kempayya's evidence carried considerable weight because of his advanced age and reputation for honesty. His clear separation of direct *record* from hearsay (*dubāri*) evidence was also appreciated. D XIV does not, however, contain any reference to Kempayya's evidence.

Ds X–XII are all statements by witness for the plantiff, Maya. DX is a statement by Kyatayya, an elder of the Washerman caste in Kotti, Kempi's village. He alleged that sometime ago the Washerman elders of Kotti had received the information that Kempi had resumed social relations with her outcaste sister, Arasi, after having broken them when the latter was expelled from caste. The elders sent for Kempi who was, according to Kyatayya, in a defiant mood. She is alleged to have told the elders that she preferred her sister to her caste. A ban was then imposed on her. Since then no one, with the exception of Shiva, had any social relations with Kempi.

Ds XI and XII are both statements of Linga, the younger brother of Arasi's dead husband. In D XI, he provided evidence in support of the allegation that Kempi did maintain social relations with her elder sister and in D XII, he adduced evidence on the ultimate source of the present dispute viz., the outcasting of Arasi for having had sexual relations with an Untouchable.

Linga stated that he and Arasi occupied two partitioned halves of a single house—when a partition takes place all joint family property, immovable as well as movable, is divided, and quite frequently, a single house is divided by walls into two, three or more parts according to the number of sharers. In such a case each partitioned household gets to know a good deal of what goes on in the other households. It is necessary to make clear here that Linga began by stressing the advantages of his position for observing the conduct of his dead brother's widow. He stated that whenever Kempi visited Arasi, the two had dinner together. He reported the matter to the panchayat who then issued a rule (*vidhi*) to the effect that none may have social relations with Kempi. In D XII

Linga deposed that about twelve years ago he reported to the elders of his caste the fact that his elder brother's widow had sexual relations with an Untouchable. He caught the pair red-handed. The elders took a statement from Arasi before 'releasing her from caste', i.e. outcasting her. Since then all social relations with her were suspended.

In D XIII, a parallel cousin of Shiva gave evidence against the latter. According to him, Kempi had approached the elders of the Washerman caste in the previous year in Magga, with a request that they should help her to secure Annalli Madayya's daughter for her son. Shiva's father reported that Kempi maintained social relations with her outcaste sister, and she was made to leave the panchayat immediately. Shiva was asked whether he maintained social relations with Kempi to which he replied in the affirmative.

It may be pointed out that pollution is the means by which guilt spreads. Pollution may be described as social contagion. Whoever comes in contact with the guilty party also becomes guilty. Marriage, sex and dining constitute contact always, and in certain situations, contact may have a wider connotation.

D XIII has appended to it the signatures of five Washerman elders in addition to that of Shiva. In D XIII (a), they declare that they have seen certain things with their own eyes and reflected with their minds on what they have seen, and they have come to the conclusion that *both* Arasi and Kempi stood expelled from caste.

D XIV states the verdict of the assembled Washerman elders and others. Kulle Gowda of Rampura, who at that time held the purely titular and high-sounding office of Village Organizer, was present as the document in question eloquently testifies. The reference to the Nadu Gowdas who are officials of the traditional social structure in this part of Mysore State, and who come from all the high castes in the area, illustrates how the decision of a caste court is supported by officials representing the entire society. Caste cannot exist by itself—it must take note of the village and of the wider territorial units.

In D XIV, Maya is described as admitting to eating cakes and drinking coffee given by Kempi. This was witnessed by Boodnoor Mallayya. Maya was fined the traditional sum of 12 *hanas* (Rs 2), and the money was paid into the temple of Madeshwara. It is explicitly stated that the verdict was read out to the assembled elders who gave their approval. It is not, however, stated in the document that Kagare Linga (Ds XI and XII) was fined for giving false evidence (*suḷḷu sākshi*).

II

A few facts which I was able to collect about the dispute and some leading personalities in it may not be out of place here. It must be mentioned that these facts were collected in Rampura in 1948 and 1952, two and six years respectively, after the dispute had occurred.

Kempi had the reputation of being both a virago and a loose woman. Even while the dispute was in progress she threatened to beat Maya with sandals—a great insult indeed, involving both the aggressor and the victim in a temporary loss of caste—and she said that she was prepared to spend Rs 2,000 on the ceremony of purification and readmission to caste (*kulashuddi*). The ceremony involved, among other things, giving dinner to the castefolk.

Kempi's father seems to have had no sons. After his older daughter, Arasi, had married into Kagare village, he had his second daughter, Kempi, married in the *manevālathana* way. In this form, the son-in-law leaves his natal kin-group to join his conjugal kin-group, and the children born of the marriage are regarded as the children of the wife's natal group. Kempi had a son by her husband, and sometime later she became the mistress of Hori, a Peasant of Kotti village. Kempi's husband heard of this liaison, and he beat her. She complained to her lover who promptly took her away, and gave her shelter in the house of an Oilman (*Gaṇiga*). Kempi left her husband and son to join her lover. Though the two lived together, Hori did not eat food cooked by his mistress because he belonged to a higher caste. He cooked his own food. Kempi had a daughter by her lover, and two or three years later, Hori died. Her husband had predeceased her lover. She went back to her son who was about sixteen years old at that time. Maya became her lover soon after and he took an interest in the marriage of her son. Maya, an important elder of the Washerman caste in Bella, went to Shiva, his wife's sisters' husband,[5] and asked Shiva to see that his younger sister's daughter Javni was given in marriage to Kempi's son Kala. A little later Maya, to his chagrin, discovered that Shiva had become Kempi's lover. His annoyance when he made the discovery was so great that he refused to attend the wedding which had been arranged at his initiative. He then tried to get Shiva thrown out of caste for having social relations with Kempi, an outcaste—the very framing of the charge shows what a clever litigant Maya was. But, unfortunately for him,

---

[5] This relationship is not shown in the chart. I regret that I was not able to obtain the complete genealogies of all the parties to the dispute.

Kempi was more than a match for him. She anticipated his moves and trapped him successfully. It is surprising that Maya fell into the trap. Either he allowed his desire for vengeance to get the better of his sense of evidence, or he was confident of his ability to produce witnesses who would prove his charge against Shiva and Kempi.

I was told that Maya had paid Rs 100 to the members of the Washerman's caste-panchayat at Hogur. I do not know whether this is different from the bribe that was alleged to have been given to the five members who appended their signatures to D XIII. If it is the same, it is difficult to understand some of the facts mentioned below, assuming of course that they are true.

I was told by Bora of Rampura that as a result of this dispute, Keshava, the leader of the Washerman caste-panchayat at Hogur, was removed from his office for having accepted a bribe. (There is a problem here: Keshava's name does not occur among the five who signed D XIII.)

Bora's reliability as an informant should not be exaggerated, but I do know that he is not a *persona grata* with the Washerman elders of Hogur. In 1948, two years after the dispute had ended, a few days before the wedding of Bora's son to a girl from Kollegal, the Hogur elders wrote a letter to the girl's parents saying that Bora had lost caste as a result of having eaten food cooked by Kempi.[6] They advised the girl's parents not to give their daughter to Bora's son. Bora was agitated by this, and he took the documents of the dispute to show to his would-be-affines. The latter advised him that he should file a suit for defamation in a court of law against the elders of Hogur. Here was an attempt to use the legal system introduced by the British to strengthen caste mores.

III

The subject of the dispute relates, in the last analysis, to the operation of the moral sanctions of caste. Maya tried to have Shiva outcasted because the latter had social relations with Kempi, whose sister had been outcasted twelve years earlier for having had sexual relations with an Untouchable. The sanction of outcasting is an extremely powerful one, especially in its more severe form which does not envisage a return to caste under any circumstance. In the milder form the offender is permitted to return after the lapse of a certain period, after he has performed the required expiatory rites and given his caste members a

---

[6] Bora's younger brother's son, whom he had adopted.

dinner and paid a fine. For instance, the offence of which Arasi had been found guilty was one which did not normally permit of readmission. On the other hand, dining, not deliberate, of course, with an outcaste, would not lead to the diner being outcasted for good (see D XIII).

Traditionally, caste was able to exert great pressure on a member: even one who had defied it for a decade or two would try to return to the fold when he wanted to get his son or daughter married. Kempi, after a life of defiance, approached the elders of her caste when she wanted to get her son married (D XIII). Without the support of one's caste it is not possible even today for a person to obtain a spouse: I am not referring here to the high caste, westernized groups living in the cities but to the millions living in the villages.

While a woman of a high caste would be outcasted for having sex relations with an Untouchable, a high caste man would not normally be thrown out of caste for having a *liaison* with an Untouchable woman. In the former case the panchayat would say that a mud pot defiled by a dog's touch must be thrown away, whereas in the latter they would say that a brass pot touched by a dog should not be thrown away but purified. Women are expected to observe a much sterner code of conduct than men.

Relations between members of different castes, and frequently enough, between members of the same caste, are governed by the concept of pollution. When all the members of a sub-caste in an area have social relations with each other, it implies that there is no pollution. When a member has been punished for an offence, having any relations with him, even drinking water from a tumbler touched by him results in pollution. Strictly speaking, there is no need for a deliberate act of punishment by the caste-panchayat—both the wrong-doer and castefolk consider that indulgence in a prohibited relationship results automatically in impurity. Readmission to caste occurs only after the necessary expiatory rites are performed.

In this dispute the Washermen of several villages were involved. In D III, Maya issued a challenge that he would produce evidence of Shiva's guilt before all the leaders of the various caste-panchayats (*ellā gadiya kulada yajamānaru*); and again in D IV, it is said that the Washermen of Mandya and Mysore Districts were present to settle the dispute. Several hundred Washermen are reported to have gathered together at the Madeshwara temple on that memorable occasion referred to earlier. This should provide some idea of the spread of caste ties—that too for a numerically insignificant caste like the Washerman—and the strength and vigour of caste as an institution.

Representatives of other castes too were present: it is stated that Maya paid his fine before the assembled Nadu Gowdas. The elders of a village or region frequently belong to different castes and recognize that each sub-caste has a sphere of action in which they do not interfere unless asked to do so. On the other hand, caste and village normally support each other.

IV

The effective unit of the caste system is not an all-India category like the Brahmin or Kshatriya, but a small local group such as the Kannada-speaking Washermen living in a number of adjoining villages. In other words, it is a small, homogeneous and well-knit group spreading over the villages of a small area. Usually the members of a caste in an area are all related to each other either as cognates or affines. The wide-spread prevalence of cross-cousin marriage frequently duplicates the kind of kinship bond prevailing between persons. So when a dispute breaks out, it disturbs the harmony of social relations among a closely-knit body of people. Existing cleavages deepen, new ones occur, and alliances are formed between individuals and groups. In the dispute discussed above, Shiva and his father were on opposite sides. Maya's mother's sister's son, Annalli Madayya, gave evidence against Maya. Maya and Shiva were themselves related as *shadgas* viz., husbands of sisters. In short, existing configurations of relationships break down while a new one takes time to form. In the meanwhile there is conflict and confusion.

It is seen that caste disputes pervade the sphere of kinship. Even intimate relationships such as those of father and son, brother and brother, and brother and sister, are breached. Kempi was asked to suspend her relations with her elder sister Arasi. In D X, she is reported as having said that she wanted her elder sister, not her castefolk. Whether this was true or not, it gives an insight into the nature of the conflicts produced by a dispute in a small local group the members of which are related to each other by a variety of ties. In such a case one generally obeys his caste, perhaps after an unsuccessful effort at defiance. As long as marriage has to take place within one's caste, the caste elders hold the trumps in their hands. And the sanction of boycott in a small face-to-face community is a very powerful weapon.

As has been said earlier, the procedure adopted in caste courts or panchayats is markedly influenced by the procedure obtaining in urban courts of law. In every village there are a few individuals who have journeyed many times to the law courts either on their own or on behalf of their kinsfolk or friends. Sometimes they act as touts for urban lawyers. They have a vested interest in disputes, and do not miss a chance to enlarge any existing differences. Village courts imitate only to a very limited extent the procedures of government law courts. In fact, not infrequently, documents which are parts of rural disputes carry the signature of irrelevant or wrong persons. For instance, there was no reason why D I should have carried Shiva's signature, or D IV, Maya's. Besides, the draftsman usually contributes his own errors and oddities usually in an effort to impress other villagers with his familiarity with lawyers an law courts. He introduces bombastic, technical terms and phrases, frequently wrongly spelt.

Where the procedure, however, differs radically from that of the urban law courts is in the choice of place for conducting the proceedings. In ordinary disputes, any odd veranda (*jagali*) before a house will do. I have heard an elder, sitting in his veranda, sharply emending a loose-tongued woman, party to a dispute, that she was in a *nyāya-sthāna* (place of justice, court). But when a serious dispute, involving important people and several villages, is to be settled, the meeting is usually held before a temple. Every person begins and frequently ends his statement, by a reference to his 'soul as witness' (*ātma sākshi*), of 'god as witness' (*Ishwara sākshi*). He says that he is making the statement on oath (*pramāna*). A false statement under these circumstances is supposed to bring on the head of the guilty person, or on a member of his family, some disaster which is the result of divine wrath. But this does not mean that witnesses are always truthful—in the dispute first discussed, Kagare Linga was fined three *hanas* for giving false evidence. The tutoring of witnesses is quite common.

The assembly of caste-elders is referred to as *Kulaswami* or 'lord caste'. It is treated with respect bordering upon reverence. A person prostrates before the assembled elders before being readmitted to caste.

Occasions such as weddings when a number of castefolk come together seem to be chosen for bringing a complaint formally to the attention of the caste-assembly. Maya's behaviour, described in D III, may be said to be typical. When the wedding guests were about to sit for dinner, he announced that Shiva, himself one of the guests, had no right to be in the assembly as he had social relations with the outcaste Kempi. And he refused to sit for dinner till Shiva was sent out of the hall. Some of the members present must have demanded evidence for what he was saying, and consequently he gave an undertaking in writing that he would prove his charge. The date and place of the meeting were agreed upon on that occasion alone.

It is probable that the case was settled in one sitting. Maya stated his charge formally (D III) and Shiva replied to him (D IV). As the crucial issue in this case was whether Kempi had been outcasted along with her sister, she was asked to make a statement (D V). It is very likely that witnesses for Maya were called before witnesses for Shiva, but the statements of the latter have been recorded before those of the former. Kagare Linga made two statements (DX and DXI), the first one referring to Kempi's having social relations with her outcaste sister, and the second, to the ultimate source of the dispute, the outcasting of Arasi. The slightest doubt regarding the latter—or rather the failure to establish it as an indubitable legal fact—would have completely destroyed the case against Shiva. A perusal of the documents shows that the elders knew what really were the crucial issues in the dispute, and they were able to proceed straight to them in spite of a vast mass of obtruding and irrelevant data. In the present dispute, for instance, the question is, 'Is Shiva guilty or not of having had social relations with Kempi who is alleged to have been outcasted along with her sister Arasi?' The correct answer of this question involves finding out first of all whether Arasi had been thrown out of caste, secondly, whether Kempi had been expelled for continuing to have social relations with her sister, and finally, if the answer to the second question is 'yes', the further question arises, 'Did Shiva have social relations with Kempi?' Arasi was no doubt outcasted, but there was no evidence to prove that her sister too had come under the ban. On the contrary, there was evidence to show that she had social relations with the plaintiff. Shiva did not, therefore, commit any offence when he gave his niece in marriage to Kempi's son.

'Did such-and-such an event actually occur?' is a question frequently asked by a panchayat. How to establish the truth of an allegation before the panchayat? *Sākshi* or witness, *rujuvātu* or evidence, and *muchhalike* or written statement, are terms one frequently hears in the rural parts of Mysore. A panchayat will not accept that a particular event occurred unless evidence is provided for its occurrence, and what is evidence? Evidence can be of several kinds, according to the degree of reliability. But all evidence has this in common—it needs a witness. The character of the witness is a highly important fact—if he is a man of straw his words will not have value. A man of substance, possessing land and money, and with a reputation for piety and integrity, will sway the judges considerably. If, in addition, he is an elder, then the opposing party will have a difficult time controverting his evidence. As mentioned earlier, my informants thought that the evidence of Kempayya, the old man from Bella, was extremely important. He was known to be a man of integrity and he was eighty years of age. He made only a very brief statement saying that he knew everything about Arasi whereas he had no direct evidence at all about Kempi. The panchayat distinguishes between direct and hearsay evidence. The latter does not have much value. This helps to explain why a shrewd woman like Kempi took a man of a different and superior (also dominant) caste with her to witness Maya's eating of food handled by her. The Peasant witness was not called, but Boodnoor Mallayya's statement (D VI) was not contested by Maya.

There is also a difference between written and oral evidence. The former has more value than the latter. It is universal for joint family property to be partitioned before a few elders and the terms to be reduced to writing, but registering the deed is not so common. That a registered deed has even greater value than a merely unregistered one is recognized by rural folk. The weight attached to documents is enormous even when the draftsman's acquaintance with the language is only elementary.

Normally the weight of evidence tells. In spite of the fact that Maya was a powerful man, and in spite of the alleged bribing of the judges, the decision was given in favour of Shiva. Maya was fined, and so was Kagare Linga, the latter for false evidence. The amounts of the fines are small, but what is important in punishment is not the financial loss inflicted but the loss of face.

THE DOCUMENTS

A Brief Description of the Documents

DOCUMENT I: The defendant agrees to abide by the decision of the caste assembly in the matter of the dispute.

DOCUMENT II: A letter written by the plaintiff informing one of the parties of the date and place of the meetings.

DOCUMENT III: Plaintiff's statement.

DOCUMENT IV: Defendant's statement.

DOCUMENT V: Kempi's statement.

DOCUMENTS: VI, VII, VIII and IX are statements by witnesses for Kempi, and ultimately, for the defendant.

DOCUMENTS: X, XI, XII, XIII (a) are statements on behalf of Maya, the plantiff.

DOCUMENT XIV: The court's decision.

DOCUMENT I

Agreement entered into on 20.5.1996 at the wedding of Cheluva s/o Raja Shetti of Bihalli, Hogur Hobli, Sangama Taluk. In the presence of the witnesses who have gathered here, I, Shiva s/o Thippa of Megga, agree willingly to pay whatever fine or other punishment my castefolk (*kulas-tharu*) may decide on, should the charge (*phiryād*) levelled against me by Maya s/o Bogayya of Bella, be proved true before witnesses.

Signed by SHIVA

Witnesses

(1) Ramu	(7) Harigolu Kempa
(2) Hogur Keshava	(8) Boodnoor Mallayya
(3) Kapi Nanja	(9) Rampura Bora
(4) Annalli Madayya	(10) Bettalli Veera
(5) Maghu Kempa	(11) Bihalli Kempa
(6) Settalli Rudra	(12) Kagare Linga

Document drafted by Kuri Malla.

[Washermen from fifteen villages are mentioned in the above document.]

DOCUMENT II

On 1 June 1946, Maya wrote the following letter to Puttayya of Rampura: It was decided at Bihalli to arrange a meeting of castefolk a fortnight from 20 May. Accordingly, a meeting will be held on Tuesday, 4 June, in Gudi near the temple of Sri Madeshwara. Please come to the meeting at 10 a.m.

Signed by MAYA

N.B. It is your responsibility to bring the defendant (*aparādhi*) Shiva s/o Thippa. Please bring him to the meeting at the time mentioned above.

[Temples are favourite places for the settlement of disputes. It is believed that people are less prone to perjury before a temple than elsewhere. Occasionally one of the parties may be asked to swear to the truth of a statement, and the settlement of a dispute is marked by *puja* being performed to the chief deity.

The Madeshwara temple at Gudi is a favourite place for settling disputes. In this case it was also the most convenient place, situated as it is in the centre of the villages involved in the dispute.]

DOCUMENT III

[A meeting was held on Tuesday, 4 June 1946 [7]]

Maya's statement before the meeting: I went to my brother-in-law's [Cheluva's] wedding at Bihalli on 20 May 1946. As soon as the *dhāre* was over, I mentioned [to the guests] that Shiva s/o Thippa of Magga has begun a relationship (*nentasthana*) with the house of Kempi of Kotti, sister of Arasi, who was outcasted for having sexual relations with an Untouchable (*holabālike*). I was asked to prove (*rujuvātu*) my allegation, and I agreed in writing (*muchhalike*) to do so. I undertook to provide the evidence (*kaiphayat*) of relevant witnesses at an assembly of all the headmen of the caste-courts (*gaḍi*) of Madivalas to meet at the Madeshwara temple, 4 June 1946. About twelve years ago, after the decision against Arasi had been given, no one was normally having any relation (*bāḷike*) with either Arasi or her younger sister Kempi. Food cooked by them was not eaten, nor were they allowed to dine with caste-folk. If my statements are proved untrue, I am willing to pay such damages (*dāmij*) as you think fit. I have narrated the facts as they are before castefolk.

Signed by MAYA

Witness: Ramu

[1. *Dhāre*: Sanskritic ritual at which the bride is given as a gift to the bridegroom. Also referred to as *kanyādana*.
2. Note the use of *dāmij* in the document.]

DOCUMENT IV

There was a meeting of the Madivala Shettis of Mandya and Mysore District at the temple of Madeshwara in Gudi in Hogur Hobli, to inquire into the following dispute:

Plaintiff (*phiryādi*), Maya—Defendant (*aparādhi*), Shiva.

Defendant's statement: With my soul as my witness (*ātma sākshi*) I state firmly before the deity Parameshwara, and before the assembled

[7] All statements in square brackets are my own. They do not occur in the documents.

caste-elders (*kulaswāmi*, literally, 'lord caste') that for eleven years (after Arasi's outcasting in 1934) I did not eat food cooked by Kempi, or have any other relation with her. About one-and-a-half-years ago the plaintiff came to me and said, 'you must persuade your younger sister to give her daughter to Kempi's son'. I replied, 'I agree as you have done me the honour of coming and asking me'. Sometime later Kempi and I went to Bella in order to obtain the defendant's advice about arrangements for the wedding. The plaintiff told us, 'I have no time today. I will come another day. Have the *lagna* (wedding) fixed for next month, not for this month'. We fixed up the date of the marriage according to the plaintiff's instructions. Some days later Kempi and I went to the plaintiff's house to invite him to the wedding. He answered, 'The marriage is between the bride's people and the groom's people. I have no connection with it. I will not come to the wedding'. We celebrated the marriage. We continue to have all types of social relationship with our relatives. I have stated the facts as they are before the caste-elders.

Signed by MAYA AND SHIVA

[1. It is likely that all statements by witnesses were made and recorded on 4 June 1946.

2. I learnt only in 1952 that Maya and Shiva had married sisters. I am not sure whether they were full or classificatory sisters.

3. Maya is addressed as *yajamān* (master or leader). I learnt in 1952 that before this dispute took place Maya was the leader of the Washermen in Bella and a few surrounding villages. The respectful way in which he is addressed by Shiva, and the readiness with which the latter agreed to give his sister's daughter to Kempi's son are indicative of Maya's importance. The attempts by Kempi and Shiva to ensure the presence of Maya at the wedding further strengthened this view.

4. Strictly speaking *lagna* means the time when the bride is ritually handed over to the groom. It is determined by the astrologer. In a loose sense it also means wedding.

5. It is not easy to understand why Maya signed this document; nor Shiva's signing Document XIII.]

DOCUMENT V

[The following statement by Kempi seems to have been actually made after the statements of witnesses of Maya.]

I, Kempi, make the following statement before castefolk, with Iswara as witness: ever since the outcasting of my elder sister, there has been

no social intercourse between her and me. All that has been said on behalf of the plaintiff is untrue. Maya, and witnesses on his behalf, Elehalli
Lingappa and Boodnoor Mailayya, have been having social intercourse
with me all along. Over a year ago I asked Maya to secure a girl for my
son. He sent for Shiva of Magga, and told the latter, 'Arrange for your
younger sister Siddi's daughter to be given (to Kempi's son)'. Shiva
agreed. Subsequently, he and I discussed the arrangements for the
wedding and then went to Bella to consult Yajamān Maya. He said, 'I
am not free today. Fix up the marriage in the month of Gouri (i.e. festival
of Gouri, wife of God Shiva)'. When we went to him on the wedding day
to invite him he said, 'I will come for the *dhāre* ritual'. But he did not
come. I have stated the true facts before castefolk.

Signed by K<small>EMPI</small>

[1. There is a little difference between Shiva's and Kempi's versions of what Maya said to them when they went to invite him for the
wedding. See D IV.

2. Maya's position was high enough to send for Shiva and ask him
to arrange for his niece to be given in marriage to Kempi's son.]

DOCUMENT VI

Statement of Malla Shetti s/o Boodnoor Doddayya on behalf of Kempi:
The plaintiff, headman, Maya, and I were returning from Bihalli to
Bella *via* Kotti village, and Maya took me to Kempi's house in Kotti.
Until then I had not gone to Kempi's house, nor had I dined there. After
we had talked for a while Kempi said 'I have had some steamed cakes
(*kadubu*) bought for you. I will make some coffee. Please stay here till
I get the coffee ready.' Then we went towards the pond to answer calls
of nature. In the meanwhile Kempi came to us, accompanied by a man
of the Okkaliga caste, bringing with her steamed cakes, butter, jaggery
and coffee. She sat her companion under a banyan tree, and asked us,
'Why did you leave? You ought to have eaten at my place before
leaving'. Kempi's companion asked, 'Why were you trying to go away
without eating the food offered to you?' I replied, 'We would not have
gone away without eating. We came here to answer calls of nature'.
Then I said (to Maya), 'They have brought food with them'. We ate the
food sitting on the edge of the pond. Maya did not tell me anything about
Kempi. I have stated the facts as they are before the caste-elders. I
swear (I am telling the truth).

Signed by M<small>ALLA</small> S<small>HETTI</small>

DOCUMENT VII

Statement of Annalli Madayya s/o Linga Shetti:

I am the plaintiff's mother's younger sister's son, and I have been having social relations with Kempi for the last five years. On her side she has been visiting our house occasionally. My elder brother (classificatory) Maya and I have both sat together (*saha pankti*, literally, same line) at Kempi's house, and eaten meals cooked by her. We have all been living in harmony (*eki bhāva*, literally, feeling of oneness). I do not know anything else. I have also seen Bihalli people and others eating in the wedding house.

Signed by MADAYYA

DOCUMENT VIII

Statement of Rudra s/o Rudra (Snr.):

For the last six months I have been having social relations with Kempi. I do not know anything else.

Signed by RUDRA

DOCUMENT IX

Statement of Kempayya s/o Kalayya of Bella:

I know everything (directly) about Arasi but about Kempi all that I know is hearsay (*dubāri*) and not direct (the actual expression used is 'not based on record'). I am about eighty years of age. I am telling the truth before castefolk.

Signed by KEMPAYYA

DOCUMENT X

[Kyatayya, whose evidence is given below, appears to be an elder of the Washerman caste in Kotti, Kempi's village.]

We learnt that Kempi had resumed relations with her elder sister after having severed them for some time. We sent for her and questioned her. She replied, 'I want my elder sister, I do not want you'. We then made a rule [*kattu*] that our caste people should not dine at Kempi's house. About a year ago, Shiva s/o Thippa of Magga, gave his younger sister's daughter in marriage to Kempi's son. Neither we, nor people related to us, have had social relations with Kempi. I make this statement with my soul as my witness.

Signed by KYATAYYA

DOCUMENT XI

[Documents XI and XII are both statements by Kagare Lingayya.]

I swear by God to tell the truth before castefolk. My house and Arasi's are but two halves of a single house. I used to observe that whenever Kempi visited her elder sister, she ate food with Arasi. But none of us went to Arasi's house. When the elders of the Washerman caste in Kotti told us, 'As Kempi is eating food cooked by Arasi, none of you may have social relations with Kempi', we decided to obey them. I am telling the truth before my caste-elders with my soul as my witness.

Signed by LINGAYYA

DOCUMENT XII

Arasi and I belong to the same group. That is, she is my *attigé* (elder brother's wife). About twelve years ago I saw with my own eyes my sister-in-law sleeping with an Untouchable (Holeya), and I reported the matter to the caste-elders. The elders took a statement from her and released her from caste. Since then we have not had social relations with Arasi. Even now neither we, nor our relatives have any social relations with her.

DOCUMENT XIII

Statement of Nandi s/o Basava of Magga:

I state on oath what I know before castefolk. About a year ago Kempi came to us to request us, in the presence of castefolk, to obtain the daughter of Annalli Madayya in marriage to her son. Thippa, my uncle (*Doddappa*, father's elder brother or mother's elder sister's husband), said, 'Kempi is having social intercourse with her elder sister who was outcasted for having slept with an Untouchable'. When we heard this, we made Kempi leave the caste-assembly. Then we learnt that our uncle's son Shiva was having social relations with Kempi. We questioned Shiva and he told us, 'I dine at Kempi's house'. Then we laid down a ban that Shiva may not have any social relations with us till he had performed expiatory rites.[8] I have narrated the truth before castefolk.

Signed by SIDDA SHETTI

(The signatures of the following five men appear below Shiva's.)

1. Borayya s/o Borayya (Snr.) of Doddakere village in Maddur Taluk.
2. Adayya s/o Adayya (Snr.) of Elehalli.
3. Chennayya s/o Chennayya (Snr.) of Saralu villave in Mandya Taluk.

[8] The actual term used is *kulasiddi* which is a corruption of *kulashuddi*, i.e., caste purification. The member outcasted regains his caste, and the ritual is performed by a priest before the assembled castefolk.

4. Kariya s/o Kariya (Snr.) of Kere.
5. Siddappa s/o Siddappa (Snr.) of Oddur.

DOCUMENT XIII(a)

We the (above mentioned) five men have seen certain things with our own eyes and reflected with our minds on what we have seen, and we have concluded, like some others who have given evidence before, that both Arasi and Kempi have been expelled from caste. This we state on oath.

DOCUMENT XIV

This dispute (*nyāya*) was decided at Sri Madeshwaraswami temple in the presence of Rampura Village Organizer, Sri Kulle Gowdaru. Maya admitted to having eaten the steamed cakes and coffee given by Kempi. Boodnoor Mallayya witnessed the above act. As to Shiva's guilt, no evidence was forthcoming. Maya paid a (traditional) fine of twelve *hanas* into the temple before the elders of the *nādu* (*nādu gowdaru*).

The dispute was settled on 4 June 1946 in the presence of Sri Kulle Gowdaru who read out the statement of Maya to the assembled elders of the Madivala Shetti caste. The elders approved of the verdict.

[1. Kulle Gowda was one of the arbitrators in Rampura. See my 'A Joint Family Dispute in a Mysore Village', for the part played by him in that dispute.

2. The sum paid by Maya is a traditional sum, and it is customary to pay the fine into a temple.

Kagare Lingayya (see Documents XI and XII) was fined three *hanas* (a hana = 2 paise) for giving false evidence. His evidence may be the source of another dispute.

3. The term *nadu gowda* in the singular refers to a hereditary office held by a peasant elder, which enables him to settle caste disputes among members of his caste. In the plural, and in a looser sense, it refers to the important elders of the area.]

A Joint Family Dispute in a Mysore Village

I shall in this essay try and give an account of a partition dispute which took place in Rampura village during my stay there in the year 1948. I am treating the dispute primarily as a 'field incident'. I want to show how it gradually became less mystifying to me though even towards the end I felt that I had knowledge of only a segment of the total social reality which was the dispute; I want to show how, in the course of its development, the dispute gave birth to a number of minor disputes; and finally, I want to show the kind of evidence that is available to the fieldworker—a considerable part of it is hearsay, and it frequently consists of interpretations and evaluations of one person's words, actions, motives and personality, by another. The sociologist has in his turn to evaluate this kind of evidence and draw his conclusions from it.

I have presented here most of the information collected by me about the dispute. I have done it for several reasons, one of them being my desire to show the frequent change of point of view of the parties to the dispute and their protagonists. It is necessary to stress that there are always certain clear-sighted individuals in the village who are able to keep their interests in view all the time and they try to use every incident to further such interests. For instance, Kulle Gowda, who was one of the arbitrators, tried to use the dispute to work off a grudge he had against the village doctor. I have seen Kulle Gowda use the most unlikely situations to further his interests. While Kulle Gowda was an unusual kind of man, the use of situations to further particular interests of individuals went on all the time.

The total absence of privacy, and the fact that I was only spending about ten months in the village prevented me from attempting to write up systematically the notes I had jotted down everyday; and after leaving the village, preoccupation with other material prevented me from paying attention to the Rampura material till September 1950. When I went through my notes of this dispute with a view to writing it up, I discovered that several of the entries were only partially intelligible to me. This is not an unusual experience for a fieldworker, and I mention it only to make clear that I have had to reinterpret some of my own entries. This will give readers some idea of the distance between them and the actual events, many of which were first of all interpreted by the parties to the dispute and their protagonists. These were then recorded by me, always in haste, and not always totally accurately. This was the kind of raw data that was at my disposal for presenting an account of this dispute.

Studying Rampura is in some respects different from studying a primitive society without written history and writing—the peasants resort to a scribe whenever they want something to be recorded. Besides, the sociologist who studies an Indian village is not able to publish all the material he has collected as some of it might be plainly defamatory, while some other material, while not defamatory, might embarrass or give pain to many people. Even the device of altering the name of the village and of the chief participants, which has been adopted here, does not release all the material for publication.

The basic kin-group in Rampura was the joint family, though the elementary family was a close rival to it especially among the poorer people. But many of those elementary families had been formed a few years previously by the splitting of their parent joint families. This is only my impression, however. Where the elementary family is the basic kin-group, it frequently includes besides a man, his wife and children, an elderly parent or widowed sister of the man, or a relative of the wife.

The joint as well as elementary family may be looked upon as a traditional form. A joint family normally splits into a few elementary families in course of time, and an elementary family develops into a joint family when the sons marry and bring their wives home. But in some cases a family stays joint for a few generations because of the amount of land it owns, or its business interests, or its strong sense of family tradition and loyalty, or all these combined.

The joint family in Rampura is patrilineal and patrilocal. It consists of the descendants, in the male line, of a common ancestor, and their wives, sons, married as well as unmarried daughters. Sometimes after her marriage a girl leaves her natal home and becomes a member of her husband's joint family. The widow of a deceased member usually stays with her conjugal joint family except in the event of her remarriage.

The joint family is a corporate, property-owning, co-residential and commensal group. Every male member has a share in its property by virtue of birth in it, but he becomes entitled to sue for division only after he becomes a major. Such a member is called coparcener, and a joint family is a coparcenary.

The feeding and clothing of members, as well as their marriage and funeral expenses are met out of the joint family's income. All the male members work under the head of the joint family, who may be father or paternal uncle or eldest brother of the other members. The women work under the wife of the male head of the household though when the latter's mother is alive and active, she is the leader.

The partition dispute described here occurred in the joint family of the late Sadhu I. The male head of the joint family was Sadhu II, son of Sadhu I, and the female head, Kempamma, mother of Sadhu II and widow of Sadhu I. The joint family was made up of Kempamma, Sadhu II and his wife and children, Kempayya and his wife and daughter, Honnayya II, the minor son of the late Honnayya I, Kenchayya and his wife, and finally, Kiri, the youngest and unmarried brother of Sadhu II. The widow of Honnayya I had remarried and was living with her husband in Hotte, a village a few miles away from Rampura. Before the partition took place all the members lived in one house on the income from the ancestral estate.

As the genealogical tree shows, the brothers of Sadhu I were all alive when the dispute occurred, and each of them was the head of a separate joint family. They all lived on the same street, and had to co-operate with each other on certain occasions like marriage and death though in the years preceding the dispute, differences had developed among the members of the lineage. I witnessed two disputes between these joint families during my stay in Rampura in 1948.

The joint families of the late Sadhu I and his brothers were all part of a still wider agnatic kin-group which was referred to as *annalammike*,

A JOINT FAMILY DISPUTE IN A MYSORE VILLAGE

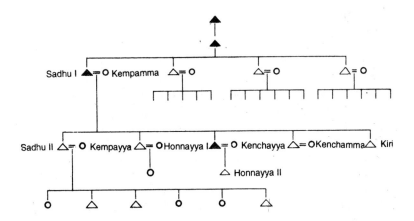

which may be transliterated as 'elder-brother—younger-brotherhood',
and translated as 'brotherhood'. This brotherhood comprised thirteen
joint families and included the wealthy and powerful joint family of the
Patel or Headman of the village. The Headman was the most important
man in Rampura, and by virtue of his office, wealth, the reputation of his
lineage, and his personality, was the leader of the brotherhood. The
brotherhood was not, however, the biggest brotherhood among the
Peasants (Okkaligas) of Rampura. There was another brotherhood consisting of over thirty households, and considerable rivalry characterized
the relationship between the two brotherhoods. Open conflict between
them was, however, prevented by the great friendship which prevailed
between the Headman and the chief of the other group, Nadu Gowda.

The brotherhood was an exogamous group. Whenever there was a
birth or death in one of the houses of the brotherhood, all the members
of it were affected by pollution for a certain number of days. They were
also bound by devotion to a common *mane devaru* or 'house-deity'
whom everyone within the brotherhood jointly propitiated periodically.
The possession of a common house-deity was an index of agnatic relationship, and difference as to house-deity usually indicated an absence

of such a relationship. Incidentally, the cult of the house-deity was found in southern Karnataka (formerly Mysore) state among Hindu castes.

The dispute in Sadhu's joint family was the first big dispute I witnessed in the village, and I came across it fortuitously on the night of Thursday, 10 March 1948. After dinner, I walked across to the Headman's veranda for a chat—every house in Rampura had one or two open verandas in the front, where strangers were received and friends sat down for gossip, and on which people slept at night, especially during the hot season. The verandas were well-known centres for gossip.

The Headman, his younger son Lakshmana, and Uddaiah, the eldest son of a former servant (and an agnatic kinsman), were sitting on the veranda while the disputants, five men and an old woman, were sitting in the middle of the street. (Those having a decidedly lower status than the Headman never sat near him, or on the same veranda). The faces of the disputants were not clearly distinguishable in the dark—the only light there was, came from the flickering flame of an earthen lamp which was in a niche high up in the front wall of the house. The disputants were arguing loudly and vigorously, constantly interrupting each other, and occasionally, interrupting Uddaiah, Lakshmana, and even the Headman himself.

I could follow the disputants only in bits and pieces. This was not because of any linguistic difficulty, but because they were speaking very fast and their talk was full of references to persons and incidents of which I knew nothing. The only thing I grasped clearly was that it was a joint family quarrel. I sat till 10 p.m. on the veranda and then returned home making a mental note to question Lakshmana or Uddaiah about the dispute the following morning. I learnt later that the disputants had argued before the Headman till midnight, after which a few of them had moved on to the immense log in the street in front of my house and continued arguing till well past 1 a.m.

In my first contact with the first big dispute I had witnessed, I had only heard a great deal of talk, and identified one of the parties (Kempayya, younger brother of Sadhu II). Everything else was a mystery.

Friday, 11 March 1948. Three of main characters in the previous evening's dispute came to my veranda in the morning. Lakshmana and Uddaiah, two of the three arbitrators, came about the same time, and Kempayya joined us later. I was sufficiently friendly with Lakshmana to ask him directly for an account of the previous evening's dispute. I also knew him sufficiently well to realize that his account would be far from 'objective'. Quite apart from his personal likes and dislikes, the fact of his membership of the Headman's joint family was bound to colour his approach to every village event. As already stated, the Headman's joint family was large and powerful, and its interests were all-pervasive. All the members of the Headman's joint family were remarkably loyal to it, and tried to further its interests in every context. *This fact should be remembered throughout.* Having uttered this necessary caution, I shall give Lakshmana's version of the events, and when I have any comments of my own, I will make them in square brackets.

Quarrels had occurred before in Sadhu's household and they had gone to arbitrators asking for advice. But of late, the quarrels were becoming very frequent.

The arbitrators normally counsel patience to those wanting partition. Village elders know the advantages of staying joint and the disadvantages of partition. For instance, when a family stays joint one earthen lamp suffices for the entire house. But when partition takes place, each commensal unit needs a lamp to itself. A man who is ill can stay in bed even during the transplantation season if he is member of a joint family, whereas he cannot do this if he has separated from his brothers, unless he has other relatives or servants to attend to his fields. Finally, partition frees the younger members from the healthy restraint of the elders. [Under the joint family system it is the head of the house who takes all the responsibility while the junior members do nothing but obey him in every matter. Not infrequently one comes across men over forty, occasionally grand-fathers, who look to the head of the joint family for every important decision.]

The girls who come into a joint family by marriage are the ones who are, in the last analysis, held responsible for the partition.[1] They do not like to be subordinate to their mother-in-law and to the wives of the husband's elder brothers. The brothers are after all sons of the same mother and even if they quarrel, they come together again. But their wives drive a wedge between them.

A man comes home tired and hungry from the fields in the evening. He wants a meal and then he wants to go to bed. But the women in the house will have quarrelled during the day and will be ready with their complaints when the men return. The house then has to become a court at sundown.

Lakshmana returned to the dispute after making the above general observations on the joint family. He said that Kenchayya was very fond of his young and pretty wife, Kenchamma. He also 'gave his ear' [listened] to her. [Both these are considered as not very desirable qualities in a young man. A man ought not

---

[1] This view is widely held by the peasants of Rampura and elsewhere. This is demonstrated later in the chapter.

to listen to his wife, but to his parents and elder brothers. It is unseemly to exhibit one's affection for one's wife, while it is proper, even laudable, to profess a great loyalty to one's parents and brother.] Kenchamma did not do her share of domestic duties properly—for instance, she did not thoroughly clean the house-front every morning, and she was able to flout the authority of her mother-in-law, because of her husband's support. Kempamma was annoyed with Kenchamma's defiance of her orders, and so, one day, she beat her daughter-in-law with a broom. [Beating with a broom or sandal, or spitting on a person, render the latter impure. It is also considered a very low form of punishment.] Kenchayya was very annoyed with his mother over this, and some say that he started demanding the partition only after the above incident.

Kenchayya had demanded immediate partition on the previous night. His elder brothers were opposed to this—if a partition had to occur at all, they wanted it to occur only after another house had been built on the vacant site belonging to the joint family in the new extension in the village, and after the marriage of Kiri, the youngest brother, had been performed.

The *panchayatdars* or arbitrators regarded both these suggestions as reasonable. Sadhu's joint family was at that time living in a somewhat small house, built during Sadhu I's time, and if partition came into force at once, the house would have to be divided into four or five units by means of bamboo partitions. This was extremely inconvenient, and instead of making things easier, it would have made life more difficult for everyone. They would be getting in each other's way all the time, and quarrelling incessantly.

The arbitrators advised Kenchayya to wait till another house had been built, and Kenchayya agreed to the suggestion, but insisted that it should be built within a year. To do this, the brothers would have to borrow money, an idea to which Sadhu II and Kempayya were both opposed. The latter said that given three or four years they would be able to build another house without having to borrow. [It is quite likely that they were trying to stall Kenchayya.]

Kiri's marriage too was an important matter. It is the responsibility of the head of a joint family to perform the marriages of all members who are of marriageable age. Kiri was 23 years old, and it was felt by all that his marriage was overdue. [Sadhu and his brothers had bought some land in 1945–6, and this probably came in the way of Kiri's marriage being performed. Among the Okkaligas of Rampura, marriage was much more expensive for the groom's people than it was for the bride's people. Kiri's marriage would have cost his joint family about Rs 1,000 or more.[2]]

If the partition took place before Kiri's marriage, Kiri would have to remain with his mother or one of his brothers. Otherwise he would have no one to cook for him. It was also widely held that a young man who came into money would

---

[2] Kiri was allotted only Rs 700 for his wedding expenses in the partition deed, but this does not represent what the wedding would have actually cost his joint family had they performed it.

not be particularly wise or discreet, and marriage was regarded as an insurance against 'unwisdom' and indiscretion. [The idea that a young man could not be trusted to spend his money wisely was consistent with the dependence of the younger members on the head of the joint family in all important matters.]

I have mentioned earlier that both Uddaiah and Lakshmana visited me in the morning, and that, sometime after their arrival, Kempayya joined us. Kempayya listened to Lakshmana's version of the dispute. He only interrupted Lakshmana once to say that the arbitrators should have to force Kenchayya to remain united with his brothers. [Later Kempayya told me that the Headman and his sons were favouring Kenchayya at the expense of the others. This kind of feeling is common in a dispute, irrespective of the fact that the feeling may have no foundation in fact..] Uddaiah retorted that the three brothers could remain united if they liked and throw Kenchayya out. Kempayya thought over this remark and agreed that it could be done. [Incidentally, parties to the dispute constantly change their minds. This is either due to second thoughts replacing first ones, or due to the influence of friends. A few people are to be found in every village who take an interest in disputes *qua* disputes, do their utmost to bring about and promote them, and occasionally, even profit by them. Even those who have no such strong interest in disputes, see the homorous and entertaining aspects of a dispute and advice and information are freely offered.]

Kempayya left us, and Lakshmana told me that he did not agree with Kempayya that only Kenchayya wanted partition. According to him, everyone wanted partition, but only Kenchayya openly said so. Lakshmana stated further that Kempayya not only wanted partition, but wanted to become the guardian of the minor boy, Honnayya II. Guardianship has certain advantages: Honnayya's share of the land would be available at a nominal annual rent in grain; and besides, Honnayya's labour would also be available. Honnayya II was then just ten years of age, and a boy of ten is very useful—he can milk cows and buffaloes, graze them, plough land, and in addition, do a number of odd jobs about the house and farm.

Last night Kenchayya had proposed that Honnayya's share of the lands should be released to a tenant at eight *khandagas* (*a khandaga* = 180 seers) per annum. Eight *khandagas* are a high rent. He also proposed that the money obtained by selling the grain should be deposited with the Headman till Honnayya came of age. Kempayya rejected this suggestion. [Kenchayya's suggestion would have made him more popular with the Headman and his sons.]

As everyone had the feeling that Kenchayya was the one who wanted to break up the family, the Headman offered to take Kenchayya as his servant in place of Kempayya. Kempayya, as one of the servants of the Headman, spent most of the day, from about 6 a.m. till about 10 p.m., working for his master. At night he slept on the veranda of my house and not in his own house. If Kenchayya replaced Kempayya, he would be more or less effectively withdrawn from his brothers, though his wife, who was believed to be the ultimate source of the trouble, would be staying with them. [Kempayya was considered to be a shirker, and Kenchayya, a good workman, by the members of the Headman's joint family. Also Kempayya had the reputation of being too sly: two years ago he had successfully defied the Headman in the matter of the buying of a certain piece of land. The solution offered by the Headman it should be noted would have not only benefited Sadhu's family, but also that of the Headman.]

I have also the impression that some of the moves made by Kenchayya were calculated to place himself in the good books of the Headman while doing damage to his brothers.

The next entry about this partition in my notebooks is dated 15 March. I will summarize it here.

Kempayya seemed to think that his request that the partition be postponed by about two years was a very reasonable one. It would have enabled the joint family to clear the existing debts as well as build another house. Kempayya would have liked the Headman to force Kenchayya to remain united with his brothers, and he seemed disappointed that he did not do this. He also seemed to think that the Headman had agreed to Kenchayya's suggestion that Honnayya the minor should be allowed to choose his tenant. Kempayya feared that the boy would then go and live with his mother in her village, and that she would choose some stranger as a tenant, thus depriving one of the brothers of the tenancy. [Kempayya's fears proved to be without foundation: the Headman later insisted that Sadhu II should be the guardian of the minor as well as the tenant of his land.]

Kempayya was narrating his grievances to Uddaiah and Kulle Gowda—the latter was one of the cleverest men in the village and was helping me in the collection of information. He was also well-known for using every situation to his advantage. When Kempayya told him that he felt that the Headman ought to have been firmer with the recalcitrant Kenchayya, Kulle Gowda replied that the village doctor was at the bottom of all this trouble. The Doctor was an employee of the Mysore District Board, and he was liable to be transferred from one village to another. He was not a native of Rampura. Kulle Gowda and the Doctor had a quarrel when the village ceremonially observed mourning on the eleventh day of the assassination of Mahatma Gandhi [on 30 January 1948], and Kulle Gowda was anxious to get even with the Doctor. Kulle Gowda's attempt to make the Doctor the villain of the piece seemed very far-fetched to me but what surprised me was that Kempayya seemed to swallow it completely.

A few days later Kempayya informed me that Kenchayya's wife was a relative of the Headman's mother. Kempayya seemed to imply that this was why the Headman was listening to Kenchayya. [This was, it is necessary to stress, only Kempayya's impression.] The Headman's mother was an elderly matriarch, held in great respect by the Headman and his offspring. It emerged from my subsequent inquiries that the Headman had arranged Kenchamma's marriage with Kenchayya, and that the girl was living for four or five years in his (Headman's) house before her marriage, as domestic help. It should be remembered that Kenchamma's inability to get on with her mother-in-law was immediately responsible for the partition.

The next entry after 15 March is dated 2 May. The interval of six weeks is not easy to explain especially as a few important events did occur like the division of the lands, house, site, assets, and some movable property. The Headman and a few *panchayatdars* effected the division among the members of Sadhu's joint family. The terms of the division were, no doubt, going to be reduced to writing, but the Headman advised against the registration of the partition deed as that would mean expense, and make the terms of the deed inviolable. Mutual readjustments would then become impossible.

The brothers appeared dissatisfied with the way the land had been divided by the *panchayatdars*. They expressed their dissatisfaction to Kulle Gowda and suggested that he should redivide the land—a request which pleased him greatly as he was being called in to solve something which the Headman and other elders had not been able to solve. Sitting on my veranda he suggested a division on different lines. (Kulle Gowda, each of the brothers, and one or two others who were present, carried in their minds a picture of the lands the joint family owned.) Kulle Gowda's division seemed to meet with the approval of all, though it should not be surprising if they later discovered flaws in it. Kulle Gowda also advised registration of the deed. He expatiated on the disadvantages of non-registration. The deed would lay itself open to repudiation by any of the brothers subsequently. He quoted the example of Molle Gowda and brothers who had divided a year ago, but had failed to register the document. The brothers were now coming to blows on the fields, each wanting someone else's land.

The senior paternal uncle of Sadhu II who was present agreed with Kulle Gowda. He mentioned how when he and his brothers [including the late Sadhu I] partitioned their lands, they refused to register on the present Headman's father's advice. A year after the partition, however, the younger brothers said they wanted the shares of the elder brothers. As the latter were good people [he was paying a compliment to himself] they gave in to the demand of the younger brothers.

Kulle Gowda was happy that an uncle of the brothers had supported him. He assured the brothers that he would see that the registration went through smoothly. [Kulle Gowda was interested in the registration—it meant one or two trips to town for him. The brothers would have to bear the expenses of these trips, and besides, Kulle Gowda would be able to charge them other expenses, real or imaginary—the clerk had to be paid a certain sum for doing the work quickly not creating problems, and so on.]

The incident narrated by the senior paternal uncle of Sadhu II brought out an important point viz., that when a dispute occurs, there are frequent references to precedents, which not only make the law clear, but perpetuate tradition and history.

The cattle, pots and pans, etc., had been divided a few nights previously under the supervision of Lakshmana and the senior paternal uncle. In none of the three partitions which occurred in the village during my stay was I able to witness the actual division of movables. This was probably due to the fact that the brothers who were dividing them wanted to hide their poverty from me, and also because they did not like a stranger to be a witness to their disagreements over the division of assets.

I have in my possession two partition deeds, one dated 8 May, and the other, 10 May. The former is incomplete, and it was abandoned in favour of the latter. A translation of only the second document is given below, though some important differences between the first and second are mentioned. Both of them were drawn up by Kulle Gowda, who might be called the chief scribe of Rampura, an occupation which gave him a little money, some power, and knowledge of the affairs of many, all three of which he valued highly. It is probable that in drawing up the document, Kulle Gowda had, as his model, a partition deed drawn up by a town lawyer. Kulle Gowda was very familiar with Mysore city, and he was more urbanized in his outlook than a great many in Rampura.

On this day, 10th May 1948, we the descendants of the late Sadhu I, viz., Sadhu II (about 40 years old), Kempayya (about 35), Honnayya II (about 10), son of the late Honnayya I, Kenchayya (about 31), and finally, Kiri (about 23), have partitioned our property, and the terms of the partition (*pālu pārikattu*) are given below. Before the *panchāyatdars* and before our mother Kempamma, we have divided equally our immovable property (*sthira āsthi*), and our assets and liabilities (*lēni dēni*). The shares of each one of us is separately liable for paying the assessment (*kandāya*) on his share of the land to the Government.

We have earlier divided the movable property (*chara svattugalu*) before our mother and *panchāyatdars* 2, and none of us has any complaints (*takarāru*) about the division.

As the fifth brother is as yet unmarried, Rs 700 have been given to him out of our assets for his wedding expenses. As Sadhu II's daughter has reached marriageable age, we give him Rs 150 for the expenses of her wedding. We give our mother Rs 218 (cash). As long as she is alive, each of us undertake to contribute to her maintenance 15 *kolagas* (a *kolaga* is a large paddy-measure equal to 9 seers) of paddy per year, measured in a nine-seer *kolaga* made in the Government Jail.[3] Each of us also undertakes to pay her Rs 5 per year. Besides, she is entitled to pluck as much as she needs of greens, lentils and vegetables on the lands of anyone of us. None may stop her.

Sadhu II has been appointed guardian of the minor Honnayya II. The boy is quite fit (*lagattu*) for work. Sadhu II should make him work, and in return for his labour, give him food and clothing, and pay the assessment on his share of the land as well. In addition, Sadhu must pay Honnayya an annual rent of five *khandagas*[4] of paddy. This is the amount decided by the panchayat. Sadhu should sell the rent-paddy every year and deposit the money with the Headman. If any *panchayatdar* asks him at any time to produce the accounts, he should do so. If he does not, his share (*hissé*) of land will be held liable for the sum due.

As our lands are adjacent, each has the right of passage on the lands of all the others, and also to receive water from the lands of all those above his own. (The country is undulating, and rice is cultivated in terraces at different levels.) The house in which we all live at present belongs henceforward only to Kempayya, Honnayya II and Kiri. To Sadhu II and Kenchayya we give the vacant site and Rs 1,000 (both to be equally divided between them.) As Kenchayya will have no house to stay in after the partition comes into force, we agree to allow him to stay for three months in our house during which time he is required to complete the building of his house. If, in future, any one of us, either out of his own volition or at the instigation of others, claims the share allotted to another, such a claim will not only be not conceded, but he will have to pay a fine of Rs 100. We have at present with us a pair of bullocks valued at Rs 275, cart valued at Rs 250, a sugarcane press valued at Rs 200, and the panchayat has agreed that Kempayya should have the press, and Kiri, the bullocks and cart. Consequently, Rs 200 shall be deducted from Kempayya's share of assets, and Rs 475 from Kiri's. Sadhu II, Honnayya's guardian, has taken over the assets as well as the liabilities of the minor.

We have earlier borrowed Rs 1,000 from the Headman. All the five of us are responsible for repaying the debt together with the interest due on the principal

---

[3] The measures manufactured in the Government Jail were supposed to be accurate. Peasants were very particular about the measures used, as cheating during measuring was common, and assumed a variety of forms.

[4] A *Khandaga* was equal to 180 *seers* of paddy, and each *seer* equal to about $2^{1}/_{2}$ lbs.

sum. Whoever fails to pay, his share of the land will be liable for the amount of the debt.

Our twelve-pillared, tiled house in Rampura village in Hogur Hobli, Sangama Taluk, bounded on the north and south by streets, on the west by—'s house and on the east by—'s house, has been divided as follows: the area of five *ankanas* in the southern part of the house, from east to west, to Kempayya, an equal area in the northern part to Kiri, and the middle area to Honnayya II. The eastern veranda (*hasaru*) belongs jointly to Kiri and Honnayya, while the veranda-room in the west belongs to Kempayya.

There were two schedules at the end of the document, one giving the assets, mostly loans, allotted to each, and the other, the amount of wet (*tari*) and dry (*khushki*) lands. They are combined into one schedule below:

Sr. No.		Share of assets (in Rs)	Share of Land			Remarks
			Wet	Dry	Total	
I	Sdhu II	844	1–7	0–24	1–31	
II	Kempayya	143	ditto	ditto	ditto	
III	Kenchayya	843	ditto	ditto	ditto	
IV	Kiri	569	1–9	ditto	1–33	
V	Honnayya II	246	1–7	ditto	1–31	
VI	Kempamma mother	218	—	—	—	

There are some differences between the two versions of the document which call for comment.

In the first version Kempamma, Sadhu II's mother, was made the minor's guardian and Sadhu was given only the tenancy of the minor's land, though at a rent (five *khandagas*) which was much less than that which an outsider would have had to pay. Sadhu was asked to pay the rent to his mother who was made responsible for paying the assessment on the minor's land to the Government. She was required to hold the sums received in trust for the minor till he reached majority.

The guardianship of the minor was throughout a bone of contention. Sadhu's brothers seemed to have expressed a preference for their mother as a guardian, but the Headman firmly vetoed the idea and nominated Sadhu as a guardian instead. (It is likely that Kempamma was dissatisfied with the Headman's decision.)

Again, in the first version the ancestral house was divided between Kiri, Kenchayya and Honnayya II, while Kempayya and Sadhu II were asked to build houses on the vacant site. In the final version, on the other hand, Sadhu and Kenchayya were asked to move out of the ancestral house. This was because originally the younger men elected to stay in the house, but when it was decided that those going out of the ancestral house would be given Rs 500 each, to build a new house, Kenchayya decided to move out. When a partition takes place, a younger member has the choice of a share or benefit before an older member—the principle of seniority is reversed.

There are also differences in the details of drafting the deed which need not be gone into here. I will now comment on some of the features of the final deed.

The mother was given Rs 218 cash while the others were given loan documents. This was because of her sex and age—the realization of a loan was frequently a difficult matter. The mother was also given an amount of paddy which more than met her needs. Each sharer had to give her Rs 5 per year. Finally, she was given the right of collecting vegetables and lentils from the fields of all her children. (In another partition the Headman said, 'Women value such rights'). It was also decided that Kempamma was going to live with her eldest son after partition. Care was taken to see that the mother was looked after properly; an attitude of deep respect and regard prevailed towards her.

In the first version, Rs 750, and in the final, Rs 700, were set apart for Kiri's wedding expenses. It may be recalled here that many would have welcomed the partition to be postponed till after the wedding had been performed. Rs 150, were also allotted for the wedding of Sadhu's daughter. As already mentioned, among Okkaligas (Peasants) a son's marriage costs more money than a daughter's, and also, Kiri's marriage was a more direct charge on the joint family's funds than Sadhu's daughter's.

I regret to state that I did not inquire sufficiently deeply into the financial status of Sadhu's joint family. That is why I am unable to comprehend clearly the schedule at the end of the deed. Sadhu received Rs 844 presumably because the joint family owed him Rs 500 for quitting the ancestral house, and Rs 150 towards the expenses of his daughter's wedding. In addition, Sadhu took over the assets as well as the liabilities of Honnayya II.

I do not understand why Kenchayya was allotted Rs 843. It was true that he was also moving out of the ancestral house, but he did not have a daughter to marry off. Kempayya received the smallest amount as he was given the sugarcane press. Kiri seemed to benefit the most: besides the cart and bullocks, he received 2 extra *kuntas* (an acre is equal to 40 *kuntas*) of land,[5] and Rs 569. This was presumably because of the Rs 700 which the joint family owed him for his wedding expenses.

I am certain that the schedule had been drawn up after a thorough discussion of every item in it. There were some discrepancies, however, which I am unable to explain. But I am certain that none of the brothers would have quietly accepted what he regarded as an injustice.

11 May, Sadhu II called on me in the morning, and I had a talk with him about the partition. He complained to me that when the paddy in the granary was being divided among the brothers nobody mentioned that he should be given a little more than the others as he was the father of many children. (The expression *makkalondiga* or 'man with children' means that the man has many mouths to feed, and consequently was entitled to greater consideration from the others.) Sadhu II thought that he was entitled to receive more paddy than the other sharers.

Sadhu had complaints against both Kempayya and Kenchayya. 'Kempayya', he said, 'both pinches the baby as well as rocks the cradle'. He talked reasonably in public while covertly he caused a great deal of trouble.

Kenchayya had been keen on partition all along. He listened to his wife and took part in the women's quarrels; and while the partition was in progress he was throughout being advised by Uddaiah, one of the arbitrators. (Uddaiah seemed to be a sower of the seeds of discord.) Kenchayya caused a great deal of trouble by frequently changing his mind during the partition.

Sadhu II told me also the story of the late Honnayya I's efforts to enforce partition while their father Sadhu I was alive. Honnayya I demanded partition from his father only to be bluntly told that there would be no partition till all the sons had grown up and were married. He was also told that he was at liberty to leave the house and fend for himself. Honnayya left his paternal house in wrath, and joined his wife in her village, Hotte. Sometime later he fell seriously ill, and when he was dying, he sent for Sadhu II, his eldest brother, and not for his father. He requested Sadhu II, to look after his infant son Honnayya II, and to regard the boy as his own son. Sadhu II gave his word of honour that he would do so.

The boy continued to remain with his mother even after the death of Honnayya I. Sometime later, Honnayya's widow remarried, and Sadhu II thought of bringing the boy to Rampura. He thought of this partly because Kempayya, who had been married for several years, was without any children. [Subsequently, however, Kempayya's wife gave birth to a baby girl who was two years old at the time of the partition.] Both Kempayya and Kempamma

---

[5] It is likely these *kuntas* had been allotted to Sadhu II in the first instance, and Kiri was refusing to pay for them.

Honnayya I's leaving the parental roof and going to his wife's village highlights a feature of the kinship system of the Okkaligas of Mysore. Marriages forge ties not only between the bride and the groom but also between their respective kin-groups. In a patrilocal community, the girl leaves her natal kin-group to join her conjugal kin-group sometime after marriage. Marriage weakened a girl's ties with her natal kin-group, making her a member of her husband's kin-group. But what was not clearly recognized was that marriage, to some extent, also weakened a man's ties with his natal kingroup. (An astute elder of Rampura once told me that when a marriage took place it was not only a girl who was lost to her parents, but to some extent, the boy also, to his parents.) A man's ties with his brothers were markedly juridical, they were a matter of rights and duties. Conflicts were common even after partition. A man's relations with his affinal kindred, on the other hand, were marked by exchange of gifts and feasts. Sadhu II was given a hen by his wife's people, and later, they promised him bamboos for his house. He said that his wife's people were 'good people'.

Conflict between the mother-in-law and daughter-in-law was ubiquitous. Residence in the same house, and the fact that in the first few years of marriage, the mother-in-law was in some respects a more important relative than even the husband, increased the tension considerably. Kempamma beat Kenchamma with a broom; and later she complained that Sadhu II's wife was ill-treating Honnayya II.

It was common for the people of Rampura to say that the women who came into a joint family on marriage were responsible for its splitting. There was a substantial amount of truth in this statement. The brothers had many interests and experiences in common, and fraternal solidarity was always stressed in speech, and held up as an ideal. But the women who came into the joint family were strangers to each other, and they found the loyalty of a man to his brothers, sisters, and parents, very irksome, to say the least. Usually, the woman who came into the joint family by marriage was interested in making her husband break away from his brothers. It was part of her struggle for autonomy not only from her husband's brothers but from her mother-in-law as well.

Mother-in-law and daughter-in-law quarrelled, a woman and her husband's brother's wife quarrelled, and finally, a woman and her husband's sister quarrelled. But this did not mean that the relation between the brothers was always one of harmony. In fact, the conventional explanation that the women who came into the family ultimately broke it may be regarded as a convenient myth, the function of which was to protect another myth which was fraternal solidarity. There are great tensions between brothers—there is economic rivalry, the younger brothers are expected to be subordinate to the eldest in every trivial detail of daily life which irks them, and so on. As long as brothers stayed united, the social personalities of younger brothers did not develop fully. The younger brothers were husbands and fathers, and heads of elementary families. But as members of the joint family they were subordinate to the eldest brother. The headship of an elementary family and membership of a joint family were in some respects incompatible. That was why the chances of a joint family breaking up became greater after the marriage of all brothers. It was only where the joint family had a substantial amount of land or solid trading interests, or a great sense of family tradition, or when it was spread over a wide area that it continued to remain joint even after the brothers had become heads of elementary families. The management of huge properties required the cooperation of a number of people and this gave new opportunities to the joint family. The joint family also aided, if not necessitated, the expansion of family commerce: tensions between brothers or cousins diminished considerably when they did not share the same house.

The Potter and the Priest

CHARACTERS IN THE DISPUTE NARRATED BELOW

1. Peasant KARAGU.
2. Peasant KEMPU, elder brother of 1.
3. Peasant MOLLE MARI, agnatic cousin of 1 and 2.
4. Lingayat BASAPPA.
5. Shepherd CHIKKAVA alias JAVARAYI.
6. Potter NINGA.
7. Lingayat PUTTA, agnatic cousin of 4.
8. Oilman MADA.
9. Potter SUBBA, brother of 6 and seasonal labourer in the house of 7.
10. The VILLAGE ACCOUNTANT, a Brahmin.
11. Peasant JAPI, agnatic cousin of 1 and 2, and brother of 3.
12. Lingayat THAMMA, elder brother of 7 and head of the joint family.
13. Trader SAPPA has kept a grocery and cloth shop.
14. Peasant YANTRA, operator of the biggest rice mill in Rampura.
15. Peasant SWAMY, elder brother of 1 and 2.
16. Peasant NADU GOWDA, father of 1, 2 and 15.
17. Peasant HEADMAN of the village.
18. Peasant MILLAYYA, member of the same lineage as 15, and owner of the biggest rice mill in Rampura.

This paper was read at a seminar in the Department of Anthropology in the University of Chicago in the last week of May 1957. The award of a Fellowship by the Rockefeller Foundation for the academic year 1956–7 enabled me to spend the greater part of the year working on my Rampura material.

19. Peasant LAKSHMANA, 17's second son.
20. Lingayat MAHANT, a lawyer, elder brother of 4.
21. Lingayat SANNAPPA, elder brother of 20, and Food Depot Clerk in 18's mill.
22. Toddyman SENDI.
23. Peasant KULLE GOWDA, a busybody.
24. Lingayat KANNUR, a bachelor.
25. Peasant KARASI, a widow.
26. Peasant CHAMAYYA, CHIKKADEVA, and CHELUVA, complainants.
27. Peasant DADDA, son of KARI HONNU, agnatic kinsman of the Headman.
28. Smith SUBBA's wife.

The dispute which I am about to describe occurred in the summer of 1952 when I was doing a second spell of fieldwork in Rampura, a village in the south-eastern part of Karnataka in South India. The earlier spell was ten months long in 1948, and the second trip was undertaken to cover certain gaps in the data. One of the subjects to which I wanted to pay some attention was the mode of settling disputes in the village.

I present the present case more or less as it is in my notebooks as I want to convey an idea of how the dispute gradually unfolded itself to me. Each informant gave his version of the dispute, which not only added to the information which I had obtained from the others, but also modified and sometimes contracted it in some places. In doing so he revealed a new dimension to the dispute. It is hardly necessary for me to add that the version which emerges finally in this paper is only an approximation to the truth—closer probably to what actually took place than the earlier versions but still not *the* truth.

During my stay in Rampura in 1948, I was lucky enough to win the friendship of some of the influential young men in the village and when I returned in 1952, I told them that I wanted to understand how disputes were settled in the village and they agreed to be my mentors. In the course of hearing a dispute, one of my friends would turn to me and say, 'Come on, you give us your verdict'. This had the embarrassing effect of suddenly switching the attention from the disputants to me, and if I was foolhardy enough to accept the challenge and say something, my friends proceeded to dissect in public the implications of my verdict. They had no difficulty in showing what a great ignoramus I was, much to the amusement of the assembled crowd. This became a kind of sideshow but I thought that I had to put up with it if I wanted to progress in my understanding of dispute settlement.

The main characters in this dispute are Ninga and Putta. The former was a Kumbara or Potter by caste but he did not pursue the traditional occupation of his caste. He owned very little land and he was the brother of Subba who was an agricultural servant in Putta's house. Putta was a Lingayat, a Shaivite non-Brahmin sectarian caste. Since the Lingayats had been recruited from a number of non-Brahmin castes, each Lingayat was found to be following the traditional occupation of the caste to which he belonged before it came within the Lingayat fold. Some Lingayats were, however, priests. In Putta's agnatic lineage vested the hereditary priesthood of the temple of Madeshwara in Gudi village which was only a mile away from Rampura. The priestly lineage lived in Rampura, and cultivated the lands with which the Madeshwara temple was endowed. The lineage was considered well off by village standards. The deity Madeshwara commanded a large following among villagers in this region.

I shall start the narration with an extract from my diary.

I went to Karagu's grocery shop. Karagu is an Okkaliga or Peasant by caste. I found sitting there, besides Karagu, his elder brother Kempu, their agnatic cousin Molle Mari, Lingayat Basappa, agnatic cousin of Putta, and Shepherd Chikkava alias Javarayi. They were engaged in an animated discussion. Kempu told me that there was an interesting dispute which he would describe to me and he would like me to give my verdict on it. Kempu gave me a brief account of the dispute.

Potter Ninga had lent Rs 100 to Putta, younger brother of Thammayya. Ninga himself owed money to Oilman Mada and was about to clear it, when Putta took the money from him saying that he, Putta needed it urgently. Putta left for Mysore saying that he would be returning by the following morning, by the Lalita Bus. But Putta did not return as promised. The following evening Potter Ninga sat in a teashop abusing Putta. Shepherd Chikkava was also in the teashop at that time. The Potter said, 'May I sleep with the Priest's wife. May I sleep with his mother'. Then he said something even more serious. 'I am going to beat him with my sandals, and I am going to beat him till five pairs of sandals wear out'. [Leather defiles and if a man is beaten with sandals he loses his caste. He may be readmitted only after he has undergone an elaborate and expensive ritual or purification.]

Chikkava was annoyed at the Potter abusing the Priest in so foul a manner. He got up to leave the teashop, and said, as he was leaving, 'Stop abusing. Remember that man is your guru'. [The Potter's and Priest's families had been friends for a long time, and at the time the dispute occurred, Ninga's elder brother Subba was working as a seasonal labourer in Putta's house. The Potters were in a sense the clients of the Priests. As the patron family were Priests, Putta was called Ninga's guru. While Subba and some others were clients of the Priests, Ninga was a kind of client of Peasant Kulle Gowda.]

Someone went and informed Putta's brother and agnatic cousins about what had occurred in the teashop. The Priests then went in a body to the teashop to beat up the Potter. But the Potter had managed to leave the teashop in the nick of time by a back door, and hid himself from the Priests for a while. Basappa, addressing Kempu, said, You Peasants will have to decide this case. We shall see how you settle it. We Lingayats are very few here'. [The Peasants were the dominant caste in the Rampura region. In Rampura they were a little less than 50 per cent of the total strength of the village, and were wealthier than all the other castes put together. Disputes were referred to the Peasant elders by everyone and not merely by Peasants. The two most powerful Peasant elders were the village Headman or Patel, and Nadu Gowda, Kempu's father. It is relevant to point out in this connection that in the local hierarchy of castes, Lingayats were ritually higher than Peasants. But because the Peasants were numerically the largest caste, and were wealthy, everyone including Brahmins and Lingayats were secularly subordinate to them.]

The case was then discussed by us. Karagu said that if the dispute was allowed to take a legalistic turn, it would make matters worse. He was for seeing the dispute in its proper perspective and for solving it soon. Otherwise, it was likely to be blown up into a big thing. He also said that as the Priest was the richer party—'fat bottom' to quote him—there was a tendency to take his side against the poor man. [Until then I had regarded Karagu as a placid person and I was surprised to find him so excited over this matter.] When Basappa said that even Shepherd Chikkava was angered by the abuse which the Potter had poured forth, Karagu countered, 'Perhaps Chikkava owes money to the Potter'.

Then Kempu playfully put the matter up to me for a decision. I rose to the bait. I said, 'It is a very simple case. It can be settled in a minute'.

Kempu: 'Come on then. Give us your verdict'.

Srinivas: 'Both the parties are in the wrong here. The Priest failed to keep his promise while the Potter used grave abuse. The first should be fined Rs 5 and the second Rs 25.'

There was a chorus of approval. Molle Mari stated that this was exactly his decision the previous day.

I was called upon to state my reasons for such a verdict. While I conceded that the Potter had enough provocation, the mention of sandals was a serious matter indeed and he ought to be fined heavily. [Perhaps there would have been no case if 'sandals' had not been mentioned.]

Kempu, however, pointed out that a creditor has to be patient. He must expect the debtor to procrastinate repayment. For instance, he had lent Rs 50 to X over a year ago, and he had not been paid either principal or interest. Karagu answered his elder brother: 'The Potter is a poor man and he is not used to lending. Your arguments would have held good if he were wealthy.'

[In 1948, Basappa and his brothers had formally partitioned their property including the hereditary right to the priesthood of the Madeshwara temple. During the course of partition relations had been strained between the brothers. But in the face of this attack by the Potter not only did Basappa unite with his brothers but the two branches of the lineage came together. In fact, it was even regarded as an insult to the entire caste of Lingayats in Rampura.]

Basappa said that had he met the Potter that day he would have beaten him thoroughly. Even now, when he thought of it, his stomach burned like a lime-kiln. He said, in his anger, that the matter would have to be referred to the elders of the Lingayat caste, and they would come and decide. Everyone deprecated this idea. The Lingayat elders would probably throw Putta out of caste. The Potter might reconcile himself to the loss of Rs 100 for the pleasure of seeing the Priest outcasted. Basappa replied, 'It does not matter. We shall take the matter to the caste elders'. It was obvious that he was highly incensed.

I asked Basappa, 'How can your caste elders have jurisdiction over the Potter? They can only bind you, but not the Potter. You will have to go to the Peasants in Rampura for justice'. Karagu: 'Don't allow this matter to become big. It is best to settle it here (in Rampura). If you press it too far, things may go against you'.

The Village Accountant chipped in, 'If you bring in outsiders, local people may refuse to give evidence'. One of the ways in which elders force the truth out of parties and witnesses is to ask them to swear in a temple as to the truth of their statement. Such a step is, however, serious, and the elders use it only as a last resort. But while they are able to put most villagers on oath, the elders of a caste can only put members of their own caste on oath. The others refuse to be put on oath.

I said, 'The matter could be closed by taking a small fine—say a rupee—from the Potter.'

Basappa: 'If the fine is too small, it will encourage everyone to indulge in abuse. The fine should be so heavy that he will remember it for the rest of his life'.

Basappa then cited the caste of Kannur, a Lingayat bachelor, and Karasi, a young peasant widow. The two were discovered co-habiting, late one night, by a group of Peasant youths. They reported the matter to the village elders who promptly fined Kannur Rs 50. (The case is described at the end). Basappa seemed to think that the dispute was promptly settled, and Kannur was fined heavily because he was a Lingayat, and he had the audacity to sleep with a Peasant girl.

Later that evening I ran into Japi, a young Peasant and a member of the same lineage as Kempu and Karagu, when I brought up the dispute in my talk with him. I told him that Karagu had been very sympathetic to the Potter and was against the Priest. Japi said that Karagu was ignorant of the real facts of the case. He then proceeded to give me his version of the dispute which revealed complications of which I was ignorant.

As I have mentioned earlier, Ninga's elder brother is an agricultural servant in the Priest's house. Subba's wages, amounting to about Rs 100, had not been paid. Subba was telling his close friends that he wanted to leave the service of Thammayya. When the latter was away in Ganjam village to buy a tree,[1] Subba requested Putta to pay his wages. Oilman Mada was demanding the repayment of the money he had lent Subba. Would Putta please pay? Putta gave Subba a hundred rupee note which Subba passed on to his younger brother Ninga to be returned to the creditor. Ninga went to Sappa's shop to get the note changed. As the note was being changed, Yantra, the operator of the rice mill, came into the shop, and requested Ninga for a loan of Rs 50. He said he would return the money, without fail, on the following morning. The shopkeeper told Yantra, 'If you are born to your father you will stick to your word'. Ninga lent him Rs 50, and then went to the teashop and had a large tea.

Very soon after he had paid Rs 100 to Subba, Putta came to learn that Subba was contemplating a change of masters. Putta realized that he had been tricked. He knew that his elder brother Thammayya would be very angry with him when he learnt about what had happened during his brief absence from Rampura. Putta decided to try and take back the money he had paid to Subba. He went to Subba and said he needed Rs 100 urgently. He would repay it on the following morning. Together they went to the shopkeeper and recovered the note. [For the sake of greater clarity I should mention now that Subba had borrowed the money from Oilman Mada with his younger brother Ninga as his surety.]

The following morning I met Karagu and we talked about many things including the dispute. I told Karagu that I thought he was being partial to the Potter. Karagu replied, 'He is a poor man. Why should Putta have borrowed money from him? He is in the wrong to begin with'.

A villager who was present told Karagu, 'Ninga is weeping. You should see that he gets the money soon. Putta will be tempted not to return the money to the Potter. Ninga will be forced to complain to the Headman and Nadu Gowda.'

A few minutes later Ninga met me and I asked him, 'Why on earth did you drag in sandals?' He seemed unrepentant. 'I shall say it again before the elders'.

I must have had some doubts regarding the truth of Japi's version because I discussed it with Kempu and his elder brother Swamy. They said that Japi and Putta were friends, and Japi was naturally giving a version which favoured his friend.

---

[1] It had been decided to have a new Juggernaut made for the annual festival of the deity Madeshwara. Thammayya was busy touring neighbouring villages trying to buy a suitable tree for timber for the Juggernaut.

I have now to make a brief digression.

In the summer of 1952, there was a serious split in the largest Peasant lineage in Rampura. Kempu's father Nadu Gowda was the traditional leader of this lineage. Nadu Gowda was wealthy by village standards, but the richest man in the lineage was, however, Millayya. In 1951 the Headman and Nadu Gowda both encouraged Millayya to start a mill to hull, clean and polish paddy, and a smaller one to grind rice flour. Millayya invested a considerable sum of money and started a big mill. A few weeks after the mill had started working, Kempu urged his father to install a mill of their own. Kempu was encouraged by the Headman's son, Lakshmana, in this enterprise. Millayya and his brothers were upset by this. They petitioned to the Government not to grant a licence for starting a second mill in Rampura. But Kempu, aided by Lakshmana, succeeded in securing a licence, and another mill was installed. It was smaller than Millaya's and it was made in Japan. Millayya's group carried on propaganda against Nadu Gowda's mill.

While all this was happening, Putta's agnatic cousin Mahant, a lawyer in a neighbouring town, had obtained a licence to install a paddy-huller. Sannappa, Mahant's elder brother, was at that time employed by the Government of Mysore as a Food Depot Clerk and he was friendly with Millayya. His office was in the mill itself, and he spent a great deal of his time in his office. He, Yantra, the mechanic of the mill, Japi and Putta were all working together in connection with the installation of a huller.[2]

Swamy and Kempu saw Millayya's hand in the huller. They believed that Millayya was encouraging the installation of the huller in order to take trade away from them. I remember Kempu telling me, in a different context, that he was annoyed that a fellow-casteman (Peasant) was injuring them and helping a Lingayat.

Yet another version was forthcoming from Sendi: Subba urged Thammayya to pay him his wages, and just before he left for Ganjam he told Putta, 'Give Subba four pallas of paddy'. (One palla is equal to 100 seers, and a seer is equal to a little over 2 lbs.) Putta replied, 'How can we pay him his wages when he still owes us three months of labour?' Thammaya said, 'He will do it. Where will he go? He is with us. Give him the paddy.'

The paddy was measured and given. Subba sold the paddy for Rs 108. Subba and Ninga together took the money to Oilman Mada's house. But Mada was not at home. As they came out of the house they met Yantra who asked for a loan

[2] In 1948, Japi installed a huller, with crude oil for fuel, in his house. He sold it, however, before Millayya and Nadu Gowda installed rice mills powered with electricity.

of Rs 50. After some discussion, the brothers agreed to lend the money to Yantra. They went to Sappa's shop to get the note changed. Sappa did not have change for Rs 100. He had only Rs 50 which he gave Yantra. Putta owed Yantra Rs 25, and the latter requested the former for the return of the loan before the following morning. Putta replied that he himself needed Rs 100 urgently. He requested Ninga to lend him Rs 100. He assured Ninga that he would secure the return of the loan-deed from Oilman Mada, and that no interest would be charged on the loan as from that day. Ninga handed the hundred-rupee note to Putta. Putta then left for Mysore without telling anyone. (This assumes that the hundred-rupee note remained with Ninga even after Sappa paid Rs 50 to Yantra.)

On the following morning, Oilman Mada asked Subba for the return of the loan. Subba took him to his younger brother. Ninga narrated to him what had happened on the previous day. Oilman Mada said Putta had not seen him at all. Ninga looked everywhere for Putta. It was only then that Ninga learnt that Putta had gone to Mysore the previous evening.

I told Sendi that I had already listened to three versions of the case and I wondered whether there was not a fourth. He said that his was the true version, and if he was proved to be lying he would pay me any damages that I cared to stipulate.

Both Swamy and Kempu were inclined to accept the latest version as true. They wondered whether the clerk Sannappa and his brothers had got together to get Ninga punished because Ninga was a close friend and follower of Kulle Gowda, who was the Food Depot Clerk before Sannappa, and from whom Sannappa had taken over. Kulle Gowda, angry at having to give way to Sannappa, had carried on propaganda against the latter. (I mentioned this here to illustrate how occasionally two big people fought each other through their clients or followers. Also the events which occur are given different interpretations in terms of previous relations among the various actors in the drama.)

Swamy said, 'I now see why Ninga abused Putta.'

I asked, 'Isn't there a tradition of friendship between the Priest's lineage and the Potter's.'

Kempu said, 'There is. They will come together again'!

Kempu then said that the elders would abuse Basava. Poor man cannot escape abuse. They would also pull up Putta and make him return Rs 100.

I said, 'But Basappa seemed furious yesterday'.

Kempu said, 'They are furious before you and me. Do you think they will be furious before the Headman and Nadu Gowda?'

The Case of Kannur and Karasi, Daughter of Devi

It has already been mentioned that in the course of the discussion, Basappa referred to the case of Kannur and Karasi. Sometime before the occurrence of the dispute between the Potter and the Priest, Kannur, a Lingayat bachelor, was adjudged guilty of having had sexual relations with Karasi, a young Peasant widow. He was fined Rs 50, and she Rs 25, by the village elders.

I obtained a brief account of the case as it was quoted as a precedent. Since the events which are referred to below occurred several months previously, I do not know how accurate the account is. There were no documents against which I could have checked the version which I obtained. But I have no doubt, whatever, that it is at least broadly true.

Kannur was seen visiting Karasi's house by three Peasant youths, Chamayya, Chikka Deva and Cheluva. The complainants, it is alleged, were jealous as they had been snubbed by the girl in their efforts to get friendly with her. Kannur knew that the complainants wanted to catch him in *flagrante delicto*, and report him to the elders. He insulted the complainants saying. 'What can these Peasant youths do?' [He actually said, 'What can they pluck?' an expression which literally means that they are free to pluck his pubic hairs. The expression generally means that the speaker has utter contempt for his opponents.]

One night, sometime after midnight, Kannur was seen coming out of Karasi's house. Kempu said that Kannur was caught 30 yards away from the house. The complainants took him to the Headman. The latter sent for Swamy as his father Nadu Gowda was away on a pilgrimage to Banaras. But Swamy refused to go. Kannur was fined Rs 50 and Karasi Rs 25. Karasi was told that she ought to get remarried soon, and to someone in another village. Two or three days after the incident she left Rampura for her elder sister's village where she spent two or three months. She was then married in the *Kuḍāvaḷi* form (an abbreviated form for widows and divorcees). The Headman seemed to take a serious view of the incident. He told Kannur that he would be tied to a pillar in the Mari temple till the fine was paid. He was made to sit in the veranda of the temple. His fellow-casteman Thammayya paid the fine and freed him. Karasi had to leave her gold necklace with the Headman to be redeemed only after the fine had been paid.

Karasi's mother was known to be one of the masters of abuse in Rampura. This was a skill in which a few women excelled, and for which they were feared, disliked, and also admired, in the village. When the incident narrated above occurred, she was out of Rampura and was expected to return on the following morning. The complainants told the Headman, 'When Karasi's mother returns she will abuse us all. Karasi should see to it that we are not abused: If we are, she should be fined Rs 100.'

The mother returned on the following morning, and in spite of the warning issued by the Headman, she started abusing everyone involved in the previous night's incident. The complainants reported the matter to the Headman who, again, sent for all the elders in the village—Peasants, Millayya, Lakkayya, and Kempu (representing Nadu Gowda), and Lingayats, Thammayya and Sannappa. Rama, the Headman's eldest son was also present.

It was on this occasion that Kempu was irritated by the aggression and righteousness of the complainants, in particular that of Chikka Deva. Kempu knew that Chikka Deva's mother had slept with everyone including the Untouchables. He wanted to say, 'If there are holes in the pancakes everyone makes, there are holes in our pan'. (This remark has the same meaning as the Biblical one referring to the beam in one's own eye.) Ramu guessed that Kempu wanted to interfere on behalf of the respondents. So he winked to Kempu and Kempu took the hint and kept quiet.

Kempu boasted that he could have had the case against Kannur dismissed by asking the simple question, 'Was Kannur really caught red-handed?'.

I asked, 'Couldn't Kannur himself have asked that question?'

'No. They would then have made him take the oath'. Whereas if any arbitrator had raised the question, the case would have been dismissed for lack of evidence. One supposes that the friends of the respondent could have raised this point; but it was up to the arbitrators to decide whether to put a man on oath or not. A hostile arbitrator would not resist the temptation to use all the weapons at his disposal.

According to Basappa, on the second day, the Headman wanted to settle the case leniently and without much fuss as he had to take up another case in which an agnatic kinsman of his was involved as respondent. Dadda [son of Kari Honna] was accused of trying to sleep with Smith Subba's wife. The latter was walking near the Basava Pond when Dadda met her. It was not clear whether Dadda tried to rape her. Smith Subba's wife ran to the Headman and complained to him about Dadda's conduct. In his desire to see that Dadda was not punished severely, the Headman let off Karasi lightly.

Dadda's case was more serious than Kannur's as in the former, the husband was alive and Dadda's attentions were unwelcome. Finally, while in Kannur's case, the complainants were in no way related to either party, in Dadda's case, it was the victim herself who had complained. But the Headman merely abused Dadda and let it go at that.

GENERAL REMARKS

Kempu and Swamy then said a few things about justice in village courts. Kempu stressed the distinction between a Government Law Court in the city and a court of village elders. The former is able to decide an issue entirely on its merits, while a village court has to look to the wealth and following of the disputants. If one of the disputants is capable of building a 'party' against the elders then the law is not strictly enforced. One has to allow 'the string to sag (*saḍila biḍabēku*)' for otherwise it will snap. Sometimes, facts have to be ignored. 'Let the facts slip through one's fingers' (*beraḷu sandiyalli biḍabēku*). An issue is sometime 'floated away' (*tēlisi bittēvu*), i.e. let off lightly.

One of the essentials in an elder is *jabardasti*, i.e. a capacity to inspire fear in the disputants. If the parties are not afraid of the arbitrators, then there can be no justice. And one thing everyone was agreed upon was that the poor always got abuse from the arbitrators.

An example was given to show that where a man had a large following in the village he could defy the arbitrators. Eight or ten years prior to 1952, three close kinsmen of Nadu Gowda and Molle Gowda (father of Mari, Japi and Kempayya) stole paddy from a field just before the harvest. The culprits were fined heavily by the two elders. About the same time Shepherd Chenna, tenant of the Headman, stole horsegram leaves (fodder) from J.L. Sab's fields. Sab caught him red-handed and took him to the Headman. As Chenna was his favourite tenant, the Headman merely abused him and sent him away.

This made Molle Gowda very angry with the Headman, for, while he and Nadu Gowda had fined close kinsmen very heavily, the Headman had let go a mere tenant. He vowed to teach the Headman a lesson.

There was a village rule to the effect that during the paddy harvest, the shops which sell edibles, beedis and matches to the labourers were not to be stationed in the fields but inside the village site. This rule was enforced in order to prevent the theft of paddy. Molle Gowda asked his followers to put up shops everywhere in the fields. He did this to challenge the Headman to try and punish one of the offenders. The Headman realized that Molle Gowda's lineage, consisting of over thirty houses of Peasants, were with him in this matter, and kept quiet.

DISCUSSION OF THE CASE

The dispute may be said to have a caste origin. While the Potter's expressing a wish to sleep with the Priest's wife and mother was certainly a serious abuse, threatening to beat him with sandals, was an even more serious one. While the abuse, 'May I sleep with your wife or mother?' is occasionally heard in rural areas, the other abuse, 'I shall beat you with sandals' is rare.

The seriousness of beating with sandals arose from the fact that leather defiled, and sandals came into contact with all kinds of dirt lying on the road. When Basappa threatened to take the matter to his caste elders, his friends warned him that it would probably result in Putta having to pay a fine and undergo the expensive ritual of purification. Putta was a priest and in an important temple at that, and the Potter's threat to beat him with sandals was likely to be interpreted by the caste elders as being equivalent to the act itself. I may mention here that a feature of village ethics which I had difficulty in comprehending was that when a case of sexual union between members of different castes was reported, the elder and more conservative members thought as much of the resultant pollution as of the immorality of the act itself.

The dispute revealed the strength of caste as a principle of social affiliation, and it followed from this that village society was divided into as many layers as there were castes. The Peasant elders of Rampura of whom the Headman was, and still continues to be, the leader, acted with exemplary promptness in the case of Kannur and Karasi, and fined the former heavily, and made him stay in the veranda of the Mari temple till the fine was paid. Basappa, a Lingayat, felt that all this was due to the fact that a Lingayat boy had slept with a Peasant girl. Bassappa's agnatic cousin Thammayya, one of the village elders before whom Kannur and Karasi were tried, himself paid the fine because a man was expected to go to the aid of his casteman. Generally, the members of a caste living in a village were related by agnatic or affinal links. A casteman was also, frequently, a kinsman. He was also a kith.

The Peasant youths who apprehended Kannur were probably angry because a Peasant girl had chosen to confer her favours on a Lingayat youth in preference to themselves. Kannur expressed his contempt for the Peasant youths in such a way that it was also a challenge to their caste and to their manhood. This was probably why the Headman levied a heavy fine.

The harshness of the first day's verdict contrasted with the lenience of that of the second day's; Karasi's mother was not punished in spite of the threat of a heavy fine. Basappa attributed this to the fact that in the case which came up after Karasi's, the accused was an agnatic kinsman of the Headman. The kinsman was let off with abuse.

Kempu espied Millayya's hand in the Priest's attempt to obtain a licence for a paddy-huller and he interpreted it in caste terms. A more immediate idiom would have been the ties of lineage, and when I heard Kempu using the caste idiom, I thought it was due to Kempu's recent increased contact with towns. Lingayat–Peasant rivalry is a feature of urban Mysore, and Kempu was seeing village relations in urban terms. I mention this because nowadays urban influences reach the more accessible villages principally through youths who visit the towns frequently.

The Peasants were the dominant caste in Rampura—and also in the two paddy-growing districts of Mysore and Mandya—and some of the implications of their dominance were made clear in this dispute. The Lingayats were regarded as ritually superior to the Peasants, but as the latter were numerically preponderant and economically powerful, all the other castes including the Brahmins, were dependent upon them. This meant that the picture of caste hierarchy implicit in the all-India concept of *varna* did not have much meaning in the village, except in specified contexts. The economic and political power at the disposal of each of the castes varied from village to village and, therefore, each multi-caste village represented to some extent a unique instance of caste hierarchy. The dominance of a caste occasionally extended over a whole district or region, giving rise to a uniform hierarchical pattern over the entire area. But even in such a situation, there were differences from village to village.

Caste, however, was not the only principle of social affiliation. The village was another such affiliation, and it was based on the common interests which people inhabiting a restricted piece of territory possessed. Their common interests cut across caste. When Basappa mentioned that he wanted to take the dispute to the Lingayat elders, everyone was against the idea. The general opinion was in favour of the settlement of the dispute within the village. The dangers of taking it out of the village were pointed out. The court of village elders was a more friendly court, and more likely to take a lenient view of the case than a remote court of caste elders. What was even more significant, the elders of a caste would be helpless if they did not have the support and co-operation of the elders of the locally dominant caste. Only the latter were able to ensure the presence and co-operation of all the parties to a dispute—they had physical force at their disposal, they could enforce a boycott of the non-co-operator, and they could also bring economic sanctions to bear on him. The elders of any caste had to cultivate friendly relations with the elders of the village which in turn meant the elders of

THE POTTER AND THE PRIEST

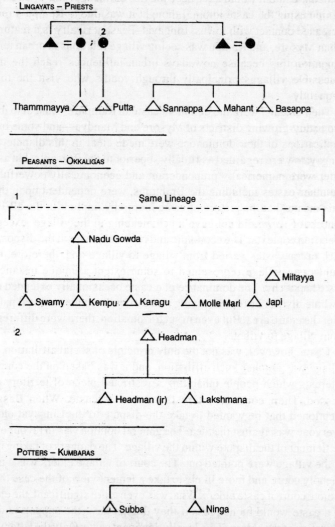

the locally dominant caste. Seen this way, caste and village were complementary and not conflicting but a clash between the two could occur.

Besides caste and village, the angatic lineage, joint family and elementary family were the other elements of the social order. During

1948, Basappa was active in demanding partition from his brothers and on that occasion he made common cause with an agnatic cousin.

One explanation why the Priests wanted the case against Ninga to be treated seriously was that it afforded them an opportunity to wreck their vengeance against Ninga's friend and councellor, Kulle Gowda; Ninga had previously spent a few years as a farm labourer in Kulle Gowda's house. Occasionally a fight between two poor persons led to two more powerful persons entering the fight on either side. The poor persons then became pawns in a fight that was really between their powerful supporters. In the recent history of the village, it seems to have been frequent for patrons to fight each other through their respective clients.

Where a village was deeply factionalized, the overall authority of the elders was weak, and the leaders of each faction settled disputes between members of that faction. The village elders were not then able to enforce their decision on a faction which refused to submit itself to them. In such a situation village law resembled international law.

The ties binding individuals were multiplex and enduring. That was why Kempu was confident that the Potter and the Priest would come together again. Social relationships in rural areas were not specialized and temporary as in urban areas.

The Changing Village

Looking back, I find that I was lucky to have lived in Rampura at a crucial period in its history. In 1948, it still retained enough continuity with the past while the potential was building up for radical change. The biggest landowners, who had acquired considerable sums of money during the war years, were looking out for new opportunities for investment in the 1950s. Unlike their fathers and grandfathers they did not want to buy up more and more land.

When I revisited the village in the summer of 1952 it had already taken a few steps in the new direction and there was promise of further change. There were two rice mills, two buses and a 'complete' middle school. (It was an 'incomplete' middle school in 1948 and village child-ren who wanted to take the Lower Secondary examination had to go to another village, or get private tuition.) A school building was being built and plans were ready for constructing a hospital. The number of buses on the Mysore–Hogur road had increased and many village youths were studying in Mysore in high schools or colleges. The richer men in Rampura were finding it necessary to visit Mysore frequently. It looked as though the day was not far off when Rampura would be a dormitory of Mysore.

In 1948, I had occasionally come across a housewife carrying, on a flat piece of cowdung cake, a few live embers which she had obtained from a neighbour's house. It was usual for neighbours to take live embers from each other. Starting a fire from scratch was a slow business especially as kerosene was scarce and expensive. Taking embers from another also had a symbolic significance: it meant that both the giver and taker were in relationship with each other and with others. When a man was guilty of a serious offence against local morals and customs he was ostracized by the village leaders who proclaimed by beat of drum that no one was to have a relationship with him. He was denied the privilege of taking live embers (*benki* fire) and hot water (*bisiniru*) from the others. Taking live embers from neighbours had become much less frequent in 1952.

I have stated earlier that the preparation of food, of which cooking was a part, meant much drudgery for the housewife; with the staple grain, *ragi* for instance, it had to be ground into flour for cooking and this was monotonous and time-consuming with the stone quern then in use. Rice, which was next only in importance to *ragi* as a staple, was not an easy grain either. It had to be dehusked and this was done with a primitive pestle and mortar. A hole of suitable size scooped out of a block of granite served for mortar and this was imbedded in the floor while a four-foot-long stout wooden pole with an ironband at either end, served for pestle. Two women worked the pestle, each alternating with the other in perfect coordination, while a third minded the mortar. Scattered grain had to be pushed back, husked grain taken out, and new grain fed in. All the three did their jobs while singing a traditional 'pounding song'.

There was also the more complicated *kotna* combining a mixture of the principles of the pestle and mortar and see-saw. The *kotna* was accommodated in a long veranda or hall, and it was worked entirely by women. A pestle was fixed to one end of a ten-foot beam which formed an angle of about fifteen degrees with the floor. Below the pestle was the usual stone mortar imbedded in the floor. The beam was balanced on a two-feet-high post fixed to the ground. The free end of the beam was treaded alternately by two women, which caused the pestle to go up and then come down with force to hit the grain in the mortar. The women, who were treading the *kotna*, hung on to ropes suspended from beams supporting the roof. Another woman minded the mortar.

Only small quantities of paddy could be dehusked by the *kotna*. It was painfully slow, and the proportion of broken grain (*nuchchu*) was greater than in a huller let alone a proper mill. Only those who wanted small quantities of paddy to be dehusked used the *kotna*. During the War years, landowners who had small quantities of paddy for milling or who for various reasons did not want to go to a mill, took their paddy to the *kotna*. In 1948 Rampura had only two or three *kotnas*.

It was usual for landowners in Rampura to have their paddy milled in Hogur, which, as I have stated earlier, was the capital of the *hobli*, and both Hogur and Rampura lay in T Narasipur *taluk*. Landowners avoided the mills in Kere, even though it was as near as Hogur, for Kere lay across the district boundary. It was difficult enough to have one's rice milled in the same *taluk*. It did not even occur to the villagers to think of crossing the district to get anything official done except when they had to go to the Secretariat in Bangalore.

Japi, one of the young men of God's House lineage, was responsible for putting the quern and *kotna* out of commission. Towards the end of April, he bought a second-hand huller and flour-mill and had them installed in a walled-off portion of his living room. His decision to invest his resources in a huller and flour-mill called for daring as well as foresight, especially in view of the many confident forecasts of failure from several villagers. He was only a middle-range landowner and he did not have much cash to invest. But he did not subscribe to the local belief that village women would rather grind their *ragi* at home than take it to the flour mill, and that landowners would not, under any circumstances, take their paddy to a huller. Village women seemed to welcome the opportunity to escape the drudgery of spending long hours rotating the stone quern, and also, those who wanted their paddy milled urgently took it to the huller instead of *kotna*. Besides, no government permit was needed for hulling paddy. This was a loophole in the regulations governing the milling of rice, helpful both to those with small quantities of paddy and to black-marketeers. The prices obtaining in the black market were so high that landowners did not mind the relative inefficiency and slowness of the huller.

Japi took me home a day or two before the formal inauguration of his enterprise; he had walled off a section of his long living room to house the machines, and he gave me an account of the trouble he had in getting them to Rampura and having them installed. He put on the switch and after a few preliminary and uncertain noises, the huller thudded into activity, and I felt as though the floor and the walls were shaking in sympathy. A few neighbours came in to see what was happening, and their faces broke into broad grins at the machine's coming to life. I was glad that I was not one of Japi's neighbours: the noise and the shaking would have been too much. But to the villagers the machine was a novelty and a very useful one at that. Japi had changed the lives of village women by removing a perennial source of drudgery. He was also responsible for the disappearance from the village of *ragi*-grinding folksongs, and of songs sung while women dehusked paddy over the indigenous husker (*kotna*). Japi was also cautious and knew when to pull out. In 1952, some time after Milayya's mill had come into existence and before Nadu Gowda had started his own, he sold his machines to an entrepreneur in another village. 'And for a profit', he grinned.

Before World War I, the principal means of transport was the ubiquitous bullock-cart. Grain, goods and human beings were usually transported in open carts drawn by pairs of bullocks. It was a slow mode of travel—the bullocks travelled at three or four miles an hour while the occupants sat hunched up inside enduring acute discomfort. The discomfort became torture when the journey was long and the roads were uneven, rutted and embedded with stones. Sometimes the men got out of the cart and walked to stretch their legs for a while.

In 1948, inter-village roads were in a wretched state. Even bullock carts could only use them with difficulty, and frequently even that only in the dry season. But in spite of the difficulties, bullock cart travel was popular during the dry months following the rice harvest. As I have said earlier, this was the season for weddings, festivals of village deities, pilgrimages, journeys to cattle fairs, etc. The journeys were welcome breaks from the dull and back-breaking routine, and took the villagers into the world outside. It was still a world dominated by rural concerns but urban forces were penetrating them increasingly.

The first buses began plying in the Rampura region in the 1920s. Not every entrepreneur who invested in buses prospered and this was particularly true of the pioneers. But bus travel became increasingly popular during World War II. Higher prices for agricultural produce put money into the villagers' pockets, and the villagers' contacts with urban areas increased significantly. The wartime buses were invariably crowded. Since petrol was scarce, charcoal gas was used as fuel, and breakdowns were common. Wartime transport conditions continued to prevail till 1950 or so.

But the situation changed rapidly between my first and second field-trips. When I returned to the village in 1952, I saw gleaming new buses, bigger than the ones they had replaced, plying the same routes. Several big landowners in the area had become owners of the new buses and lorries, and in a few villages, several men had come together to start 'cooperative bus services'. These activities were evidence of the villagers' ability to take risks, especially when it is remembered that the declared policy of the government then was to 'nationalize' road transport. Important and remunerative routes had already been nationalized, and the routes allotted to the 'private sector' were new, unproven and circuitous, and the roads, horrible. The government knew that it could not afford to antagonize totally the rural landowners on whom it depended heavily for votes, and allowing them to ply along some routes, and granting them licences for rice mills and other small industries, were the repayment.

The new enterprises not only taught new skills and changed the pattern of life of those involved in them but also their outlook in significant ways. They learnt the art of cultivating politicians and officials, and became familiar with governmental procedures. Running buses called for new organizational skills and accounting procedures, and dealing with lower officials whose palms needed greasing regularly. The richer village youth did not want to look after ancestral farms but enter the new and challenging world of trade, commerce and industry. The more educated youths dreamed of becoming members of the State legislature, and even ministers in the cabinet. In short, they had come a long way from the world of their fathers and grandfathers. The entrepreneurs gave jobs to their kinsfolk, castefolk and fellow-villagers, and this had the effect of drawing more people to them.

As I said earlier, the first man to own a cycle in Rampura was my friend Kulle Gowda. That was in the early thirties, and in 1948, there were three or four cycles, in varying stages of decay. This situation had changed in 1952 when Yantra, the mechanic who operated Millayya's mill, kept a shop where several new cycles were available for hiring by the hour. Several years later, the richest villagers were buying cars and motor-cycles. One of them wrote to me in Delhi to help him buy a motor-cycle at the capital as the products of the factory in Mysore had been booked for a few years. Another village youth once saw me walking on a road in Mysore city and insisted on driving me home in his car.

In 1948, there were five sewing machines in the village, and they were owned by two traders, and one Fisherman, one Toddyman and one Muslim. Tailoring as an occupation did not involve loss of status presumably because it meant working with a machine and required new skills. (In neighbouring Kere, a Brahmin chaplain derived the bulk of his income from tailoring.) Another interesting feature of tailoring was that men tailors did not regard it as beneath their status to make blouses for women. In other words, tailoring cut across differentiation based on caste and sex, and in addition, it made manual labour, when accompanied by new skills and machines, respectable. It brought the men tailors into new relationships with women who were not their kin or caste. The chaplain-tailor of Kere, for instance, ran a 'chit-fund' in which most of the participants were his customers. His scheme prospered greatly for a while but only to collapse later, robbing many women of their hard-earned savings. The entrepreneur had to flee the village and settle in another.

Among the several changes which had occurred between 1948 and 1952 was the availability of electric power. It not only powered the two mills in the village but provided lighting to several homes. The latter also had radios. I saw transistors only in the sixties with college-going youths who had returned home for the holidays.

I have referred to the villagers' request to the visiting minister to make available to them, on a hire system, a tractor and bulldozer, owned by the government. Four years after the request was made a government-owned bulldozer was levelling six acres of land on the headman's farm. This piece was too high to be reached by the feeder canals but the bulldozer was able to remove enough soil to make it irrigable. The bulldozer stayed on the headman's farm for a few weeks as it needed frequent repair, and it made an impact on the villagers in the same way as Japi's huller. To see the monster machine pull down huge trees and cut through blocks of earth was an experience which they would not easily forget. Modern technology did indeed perform miracles and human labour appeared pitiful in contrast.

There was also progress in public health. Rampura had been included in the Hogur health unit, and one of the consequences of the inclusion was the periodical spraying of street gutters and walls with DDT. Plans were also afoot for the construction of a hospital.

ECONOMIC CHANGE

There were two sources of irrigation before the extension of the CDS Canal in the 1860s, one being the Big Tank, and the other being the Ramaswamy Canal, which hugged the river Kaveri. Both the sources irrigated only a little more than 200 acres of low-lying land while the considerable quantity of land irrigated by the CDS (as it was referred to by the younger villagers) lay at higher levels. Again, though it was only an administrative matter, the land irrigated by the Ramaswamy Canal lay within the jurisdiction of Hogur and not Rampura.

Naturally, a greater quantity of land was under the dry crops in the pre-CDS days. The crops grown were millets such as *jowar* and *ragi*, the various pulses, and oilseeds such as sesame and castor. Dry crops were totally dependent upon the monsoon rains, which were notorious for their unpredictability, and people in dry villages were both poverty-stricken and backward. This was well known.

The extension of the Canal, and the consequent shift to the cultivation of rice resulted in a severe epidemic of malaria.[1] The original village of Rampura was located to the south of the Big Tank, in the bottom of a trough as it were, while the extension of the CDS Canal looped around the top of the rise in the land, irrigating all the land below it. Only the present village site of Rampura and the land around it did not come under any canal.

The decision to move the village to its present site was taken in the wake of the epidemic, the actual shift taking place in 1874. The deputy commissioner of Mysore district was an Englishman, and he located the village site on the top of the rise, to the west of the canal as it skirted the village before turning sharply east and making a beeline for Gudda. The villagers took all their belongings including their deities (excepting Basava) to the new site. The deities Rama, Sita, Lakshmana and Hanuman were accommodated in a small house till they were moved into the present beautiful temple.

Any attempt to explain the failure to move the Basava temple on the ground that it was too solid a construction, does not carry much weight, as the Rama temple, also of stone, was moved. Indeed, the dressed granite slabs were first dismantled to be used in the construction of the new temple.

In 1948, several villagers contrasted their present prosperity with the poverty of the inter-war years, 1918–39. As described earlier, rice merchants from Mysore visited the village at every harvest and took away nearly half the produce to be adjusted towards the interest due to them. This was true of everyone including the biggest landowners. This state of affairs forced the leaders to introduce certain reforms such as cutting down by one the number of feasts to be given when village girls got married and the banning of gambling. In an effort to promote harmony and economy in one village they permitted the dropping of the complex ritual of the distribution of the 'big betel' (*dodda vilya*) at weddings on the bride's father agreeing to pay Rs 8.25 to the *panchayat*.

[1] Malaria in epidemic form similarly affected Mandya district in the 1930s when it came under the Visvesvaraya canal system. The water stagnating in the fields, canals and feeders was a potent source of the disease, and only the anti-malarial drugs of the forties, and DDT helped to wipe it out. The economic prosperity and political importance of Mandya dates from the forties.

The ritual invariably gave rise to bitter disputes: a guest's right to represent his village did not go unchallenged while to have it rejected amounted to loss of face before equals and betters. Tempers got frayed, each tried to outshout the other, and walking out of the assembly was not unknown. Matters of protocol were not taken lightly in the village. The prudent welcomed paying Rs 8.25 to escape an explosive and expensive ritual.

One of the important results of World War II was to bring about a greater integration of village economy and life with the national. A poignant instance of this was the sudden loss suffered by the sugarcane growers as the result of a steep fall in jaggery price.

Further, the surplus paddy of the villagers was taken away by the government at rates determined by it, and growers could only have the paddy remaining with them milled against permits. They had to buy the *ragi* they ate from local shops against ration cards. And so on.

Before World War II, villagers in Mysore generally preferred handling coins to paper money. In fact, ordinary villagers were not willing to accept high denomination notes. Even coins were examined carefully before being accepted. A proferred rupee coin, for instance, was first flipped into the air, and only when the recipient was satisfied with the music of the silver hitting the ground, did he accept it. Frequently the older and better-off villagers stashed away hoards of silver rupees, and those who could, converted their cash into gold.

But these habits began changing during the war years. Villagers had to accept paper money as there was an acute shortage of metal. The silver content of the rupee decreased fast and flipping rupee-coins disappeared as a habit. Villagers sneered at the government's parlous financial position saying, 'They have no silver or gold but only paper.'

The Kannada term for coin is *nanya* but the villagers used it on occasion as a synonym for culture of refinement (*najooku*). They were convinced that refinement had come to them with the irrigation canals. In contrast, people in 'dry' villages were still without *najooku* and *nanya*. Their style of life and speech were crude.

POLITICAL CHANGE

I referred earlier to the increasing penetration of rural areas by officials since the beginning of this century. This occurred side by side with the development of communications. The government was becoming more pervasive and also assumed new duties and responsibilities for the well-being of the people.

Independence, and the subsequent introduction of adult franchise, marked a radical change in the villagers' attitude towards officials. The previous obsequiousness and fear which characterized earlier behaviour was replaced by a sense of self-confidence if not power. This was especially true of the richer, more urbanized and younger villagers. The lower officials in particular felt the impact of new attitudes.

Independence and popular rule increased the power of politicians who tried to influence the decision of administrators to promote their interests.[2] For instance, honest officials who failed to oblige them attempts were made to transfer while those who obliged them were given benefits in turn. They wanted contracts, licences and permits to be given to their relatives, clients, friends and caste-fellows. During the fifties Kannada journals and newspapers were full of references to the activities of 'Congress *pudharis*'. A *pudhari* was a broker or middleman in politics, a man who had cultivated the men in power and interceded on behalf of those in whom he was interested. He obliged both those whose cause he sponsored and the politicians whose aid he sought. And like all brokers he expected to benefit from his intercessions. And he did. The term *pudhari* was pejorative and people, especially villagers, complained about the activities of *pudharis*. They donned the uniform of white homespun dhoti, *jubba* and Nehru waistcoat and wandered from village to government offices and ministers' and legislators' homes, taking with them their *protégés*.

The visit of the State's finance minister to Rampura in 1948 was a landmark, literally speaking, in that it was the first time that so high a dignitary had walked its streets. According to the older villagers, the highest official previously to visit the village was the deputy commissioner, the official head of a district. The minister's visit meant much work for the villagers. It was preceded by the visits of lower officials who demanded that village streets be cleared of logs, carts, stores of fuel, bricks, etc. They also wanted the street gutters to be cleaned, and the insides of houses to appear neat and tidy. (There was the possibility that a 'popular' minister might take it into his head to visit a village house: the ministers had a keen nose for publicity.) The officials wanted the streets to be sprinkled with water a few hours before the dignitary's

---

[2] Writing in the popular Kannada newspaper *Prajavani* in the fifties, A. N. Rama Rao summarized the changes which had taken place in the position of the *amildar* (official in charge of a *taluk*), saying: 'Then the lord (*dhani*) of the *taluk*, now, recipient of favours (*runi*) from low political touts'.

arrival so that the convoy would not be choked with village dust. (They ignored the fact that the rest of his journey was going to be dusty in any case.) They saw to it that two welcome arches were erected on the Mysore–Hogur road, one by the Harijans and the other by everybody else. (It was customary for Harijans to erect a welcome arch and the officials encouraged them to put up one on this occasion too. But it later turned out that the minister expressed his anger at the 'separatist' tendencies displayed by Rampura Harijans, and the Muslims who wanted additional facilities for the Urdu school.)

During the first few years of Independence villagers became so used to visits by ministers that they affected indifference. Being hard-headed men they asked the question, 'What good have these visits done to us?' They contrasted the old days when the deputy-commissioner, the 'lord' (*dhani*) of the district, had the power to help them with the contemporary situation when ministers kept coming but nothing happened. A minister's visit threw the village off its usual routine and meant some expense and ceremony in addition. It also gave a chance to local malcontents to have access to high officials and even the minister. While the elite liked to hobnob with the high and the mighty, they wanted the privilege to be denied to the poor, and to their opponents.

During the summer of 1952 I remember having a brief discussion with Tammu, the smart young man who was helping Millayya run his mill. The papers had reported Mr Hanumanthaiah, then chief minister, as saying that ability and qualifications had to be the sole grounds for recruitment to jobs in the government, and not the caste from which the applicants came. I thought that Mr Hanumanthaiah had made a wise and courageous statement but Tammu pointed out that the voters who had elected him wanted applicants to be recruited from the backward sections of the society. Mr Hanumanthaiah's desire to appoint men on 'British principles' would not succeed. Tammu's comment perhaps revealed a keener sense of grassroots political realities than mine, and Tammu was typical of the politicized village youth. The latter had grasped the fact that the voters' interests had to be respected by their elected representatives. They were also aware that they could influence their representatives to bring pressure on officials to give favourable decisions. They had a sense of power which they liked to display. The villager was no longer scared of officials but was learning to flex his political muscles. The time-honoured rules of the political game were beginning to change.

Independence and adult franchise also brought new ideas and aspirations to the villagers. I shall illustrate my statement by referring to certain changes which occurred in Lakshmana's style of life, and to one of my brief encounters in Kere.

I have already commented upon Lakshmana's shrewdness and political ambitions. He once expressed to me his deep regret at his lack of education: if only he had been a graduate he could have done so much. He was sharply critical of his younger brother Bharata, who, after getting a BA, had settled down to a quiet, low-level job in the government. Lakshmana felt that Bharata should have gone into politics. (There was an unstated assumption among the politicized village youth that a BA was indispensable for a ministership. I remember a bus journey in the summer of 1952 when a Kere man was reading out from a newspaper the list of newly-appointed ministers in Mr Hanumanthaiah's cabinet, and as he read, he graded them on the basis of their being graduates or 'double graduates', the latter being those who had secured a law degree after their BA or BSc. Small town legal practice gave ample leisure for political activity.)

Certain changes occurred gradually, almost insensibly, in Lakshmana's clothes and hair style. That symbol of Sanskritic orthodoxy, the tuft at the crown of the head, was the first to be sacrificed at the altar of politics, and Lakshmana grew a crop. (I do not know what his father and grandmother had to say to this.) He bought a green Nehru jacket flecked with white, and wore it above his shirt when he was visiting Mysore or some other town to meet officials, politicians and others. He wrote a few letters to the Kannada papers in which he called himself vice-president of the *taluk's* ryots' (cultivators) association. (I had not heard of his election or nomination to that august office.) He held a meeting of the ryots of the *taluk* and invited a budding and well-connected lawyer-politician from Mysore to take the chair. Lakshmana took great pains to have an elaborate lunch cooked for the influential guest and other invitees. (There was a fish course, from fish caught in the rice-fields on the previous day, and chicken curry, besides, of course, rice and vegetables.) But the meeting did not go as he had wanted it to. At an early stage in the proceedings two members of the audience from different villages got into a heated argument which threatened to explode into a fight. The energies of the organizers had to be diverted to bringing about peace between the angry debaters. This incident perhaps taught Lakshmana that the path to power was not roses all the way. He did not give up trying to win influential friends but he conducted his activities in a lower key.

During the latter half of 1948 Lakshmana began to be increasingly absent from the village. He was seen either getting on or off a bus, and the villagers did not fail to notice it. Previous to his developing political interests he had told me, and perhaps one or two others, that he wanted to live in the farm house quietly, away from the noise and dust of the village, and close to the river Kaveri. Lakshmana was a good supervisor and he may have genuinely wanted to stay in the farm house but at that time there were rumours that he had differences with the other members of his joint family. There may have been opposition to his shifting to the farm house from others in the household, including his wife. It was at this juncture that he became deeply interested in politics.

When I returned to Rampura in 1952, I found that the new activities of his household gave Lakshmana ample opportunities to travel. Running bus lines was no easy matter and needed unremitting attention on several fronts; the taxes and cesses to be paid, inspections by brake inspectors and other officials, dealing with policemen and law courts, getting spare parts, supervising the activities of bus drivers and conductors, maintaining accounts and so on. There were also houses in Mandya from which rent had to be collected, and finally, there was the cinema theatre in Mysore which the family had bought. In addition, Lakshmana retained some contact with the Ryots' Association.

I knew a village leader in Kere who had studied up to the SSLC and developed political ambitions. He was a man of violent antagonisms, and headed a faction. He wanted to become a legislator and tried to secure a Congress ticket in 1952. But Kere had several graduates who had been in the freedom struggle and one of them was given the ticket. My friend contested as an independent and lost to the Congressman. But he refused to be discouraged—he was tough and persevering. He owned a rice mill and was wealthy and had some local influence. One blistering afternoon I walked from Rampura to his mill in Kere and asked him if he could kindly let me borrow some documents which I wanted. He was then attired in freshly-laundered *khadi*, and his white Gandhi cap was placed at a jaunty angle. He was about to get into his new, gleaming Ambassador car to go to Bangalore. Mr Hanumanthaiah, the Chief Minister, was celebrating Sathyanarayana Puja and my friend had been invited. I could not help thinking then of Max Weber who had stressed the otherworldly, 'soteriological' character of Hinduism!

On another afternoon, I met a few boys in my friend's large household and I asked one of them what he wanted to be when he grew up. One of the boys was slow to open up but I persisted. He gave way finally: 'I want to become a minister'. As soon as he had uttered these words, my host rushed to him and pinched him on both the cheeks in delight. It was only then that I discovered that the boy was my host's only son while the other boys were his brother's. The son was going to fulfil the father's ambitions.

In Rampura in 1948, inter-caste relations were on the whole co-operative if not friendly. This was facilitated by the fact that Peasants greatly outnumbered all the other castes, and also owned the bulk of the arable land. And the headman and Nadu Gowda working in close cooperation provided unified leadership. The non-Peasants, including the Muslims, depended upon the leaders to give them a fair deal.

But with the introduction of adult franchise and of the electoral principle into panchayats and other local self-governing institutions, tensions between the castes increased sharply. In the summer of 1952 the Headman was angry with the Harijans for not voting for the candidate whom he wanted elected. And in Kere, my friend, the Peasant leader, was defeated at the election to the State legislature, and he asked the members of a Brahmin household to quit the village on their own or face the prospect of being driven out. The members of this household, shrewd and extremely resourceful, had worked actively for the rival candidate who was a local Peasant and also the candidate selected by the Congress Party. But he was living at that time in Bangalore and could not offer protection in day-to-day situations to his supporters.

I have narrated elsewhere the visit in the summer of 1948 by a Shepherd who had settled down as a landowner in Kuderu near Chamarajanagar, after retiring from his career as an actor in a well-known dramatic company in Mysore. The Shepherd was a large and amiable man, and after his arrival, he talked to the Headman and a few others on a variety of matters. Everyone listened to him attentively, as he was talking to them about happenings in the world outside. After reminiscing briefly about his acting days and his present preoccupa-tions, he commented on the way in which Lingayats in his area—Kuderu was a Lingayat-dominated area—oppressed the others. He added that Brahmins had many faults and had done several unjust things when they were in power but they had certain inhibitions stemming from their respect for *dharma*. But unfortunately the Lingayats in his region were free from these inhibitions. I waited for someone to contradict the visitor but no one did. I wondered whether my presence came in the way of the group expressing its opinions about the way Brahmins used to treat the others. It was not unlikely that the visitor's day-to-day experiences in a village where Lingayat landowners exploited the others made him take a friendly view of the distant Brahmins. (His experience would probably have been different had he lived in a Brahmin-dominated area.)

It is only fair to add here that Lingayats felt oppressed in places and areas where they were in a minority. A Lingayat principal of a college who hailed from Mysore district once told me that his was the only Lingayat village in a region dominated by Peasants. And he added jocularly, 'We are in Pakistan'. Castes which were numerically very small experienced a sense of insecurity especially in villages where the leaders lacked a sense of fairness. A member of a minority caste invariably referred with pride to a village (or small town) where his caste was represented in strength. In such a place, a few of the caste-fellows there were well off and influential. An important temple was frequently located there and attracted pilgrims. The periodical festivals in the temple provided occasion for caste leaders to gather and discuss matters of common interest. In the case of Harijans, however, their minority status was greatly compounded by untouchability and economic dependence on the dominant castes.

CULTURAL CHANGE

When I was doing fieldwork, I concentrated my attention on reconstructing the traditional social structure which made me less sensitive to the factors making for change. This explains, at least partly, my failure to realize that the attitudes of the villagers with regard to disease, health and life-expectancy had changed because of the sharp decrease in mortality from the major epidemics of plague, smallpox and cholera. Plague and smallpox had almost completely disappeared while cholera was both much less frequent and destructive. The last occasion when cholera visited the village in epidemic form was in 1949. Prior to the World War II years, villages were visited by one or the other of these epidemics every few years. Preventive measures took time to reach the afflicted villages, and even when they were available, backwardness and superstition came in the way of their acceptance. The *amildar* was generally in charge of organizing the medical and relief measures. When an epidemic struck a group of villages in a severe form, he had to evacuate the inhabitants from their homes and settle them in temporary huts erected some distance away. They were allowed to move back only after the epidemic had died out.[3]

Traditionally, a person suffering from one of the epidemics refused to take modern medicine as it was thought to annoy Mari (called by many names). As could be expected of a deity who presided over these death-dealing diseases, she was quick to take offence, and a patient's only hope of recovery, slender though it was, was to throw himself entirely at her mercy. The twigs and leaves of the margosa (*Melia azadirachta*) were good for a person suffering from any of these epidemics, especially smallpox. Twigs were kept near his head, he was fanned with the leaves, and they were put into his bath-water when he had recovered from the disease. Only after a cleansing bath could he visit the shrine of the deity. Offerings of rice flour mixed with jaggery (*tambittu*), tender coconuts and betel leaves and nuts were carried on a tray to her. The *tambittu* was shaped like a pyramid with a flattened top, and sometimes, a depression was made in the flattened top to make possible its use as a lamp: the depression was filled with *ghi* and it provided fuel to burn a cotton wick light. The wick was allowed to burn itself out after which the pyramid was broken up and distributed as *prasada*.

Summer was the season for the epidemics and they invariably disappeared after the monsoon rains. The propitiation of the goddesses presiding over the epidemics was referred to as 'cooling' them (*tampu eriyuvudu*). The margosa was one of the trees which provided cool shade in summer and its leaves, twigs and oil were all believed to have medicinal properties. Margosa trees were frequently planted close to the temple of the village goddess, and the association between the goddess, tree and epidemics were close in the minds of people.

In 1948, the conquest of the killer epidemics, and of endemic malaria contrasted sharply with the failure to make maternity safer or less traumatic. No village woman went to a maternity hospital to have her baby delivered. A few rich villagers were able to secure the services of a midwife from either Kere or Hogur but most village women turned to their older relatives and friends for help during delivery. A woman felt most secure with her mother and this was why the first few confinements occurred invariably in her mother's house.

The Headman's wife died during childbirth a few months before my

---

[3] There is a graphic account of the *amildar's* using the shaman of a village goddess in order to persuade villagers struck by cholera to move into a temporary camp in N. Rama Rao, 1954, *Kelavu Nanapugalu*, Jeevana Prakatanalaya, Bangalore, pp. 354–8.

return to Rampura in 1952 and the Headman was naturally deeply affected by the event. She was his second wife and younger by several years, and the fact that her death was due to the midwife's incompetence made it all the more poignant.

One of my sad experiences in Rampura related to the death of an infant a few weeks after I had moved into the village. One day, all of a sudden, I heard a woman moaning continuously from the other side of the wall of my bedroom. Sometimes the moans were long and loud while at other times they were short and faint. There were even brief intervals when they were totally absent. This went on for two or three days. It slowly dawned on me that Mrs Karim, my neighbour, was having labour pains and her relatives and neighbours were busy visiting her. One night in particular, the moans were more or less continuous and were marked by frequent screams. I was unable to sleep a wink. I could not do any work the following day and I remember thinking unkind thoughts about Mrs Karim. Why couldn't women deliver babies with less fuss and noise? Why couldn't they be more reasonable? My work had made me thoroughly self-centred but even I noticed that I was the only one who was so surly and ill-tempered about having his sleep disturbed by Mrs Karim's pains and screams. Either the others slept much better than I did, or did not consider the matter suitable for comment. In any case, I am fairly certain that they would have thought it only natural for a woman to moan and scream during delivery. They would also have been more considerate to a mother having labour pains.

The baby came at last and a day or two after its birth, I found a distracted Karim wandering around with the half-shell of a coconut. I asked him what the matter was. He replied that the baby was hungry and that he was trying to get some cow's milk for it. Several hours later I heard Mrs Karim's loud and hysterical wailing. I also heard her friends trying to console her. An occasion such as this cut across the distinction between Hindu and Muslim for a few callers were Hindus. But it was entirely a feminine affair. No man, not even a relation, called on her.

The village doctor was not popular. In fact the complaint was occasionally heard that he only bothered about a few rich people and not about the others. As long as the doctor was assured of the Headman's protection, he could ignore the others. He played cards regularly with the Headman, Nadu Gowda and Kulle Gowda's father and that made it clear to everyone that he enjoyed the protection of the most influential men. His wife was coaching two boys in the Headman's household for the Lower Secondary examination. One afternoon he brought a few hot *chaklis* (fried savouries) for the Headman to taste. They were made by his wife, and it appeared that her cooking was even better than her teaching. The doctor practised the time-honoured tradition of propitiating the powerful and oppressing the poor.

One afternoon a man from a neighbouring village arrived in his cart at the Headman's house to obtain treatment from the doctor for some illness. The Headman gave a glowing certificate to the doctor's skills and then the doctor stipulated that he would agree to treat him only if a certain amount was paid in advance and an equal amount after the cure had been effected. The ingredients of the medicine were costly—he listed a few of the ingredients, and the time it would take to prepare it. A bargain was eventually struck.

The better off villagers went to an ayurvedic doctor in Hogur who had a good reputation, or to allopaths in Mysore. They were all enthusiastic about injections. A typical statement was, 'I went to the doctor in Mysore and he gave me an injection. Even as the fluid went in, I felt its power. An hour later, all my pain had gone'. In other words, the injection worked like magic. Urban doctors knew this weakness of villagers for injections and gave their patients what they asked for.

In 1948, there were two schools, one an 'incomplete' middle school for Kannada-speaking children, and an Urdu school for Muslim children. The former was housed in the official panchayat building while the latter was accommodated in a single-room structure with a thatched roof. The Kannada school was co-educational and attended by students from every group except Muslims. Girls generally attended school till they were eleven or twelve when they were withdrawn and stayed at home till they got married.

There were, however, a few village youths who had been to college who wanted to marry educated girls. But even they did not want girls who were 'too highly educated'. Adult girls who had been to school were suspected of having had affairs, and they were also likely to consider themselves too superior for rural life.

The Urdu school had less than thirty students and only one teacher. The right of Muslims to be taught in Urdu had been recognized in princely Mysore but where this meant founding schools using Urdu exclusively, the resources were too meagre to provide satisfactory teaching. This was particularly true of Urdu schools in villages.

As stated earlier, even in 1948 Rampura had only an 'incomplete' middle school, and local students who wanted to sit for the Lower Secondary examination had either to go to villages which had 'complete' middle schools or to a private tutor in Rampura. However, in 1948, education was becoming popular, and the bigger landowners made it a point to send their sons to high schools in neighbouring towns.

Prior to 1948, Rampura had produced four graduates all of whom lived outside. It was only those who did not have the minimum education required for a government job, who stayed back in the village. These were the young men who were dissatisfied with the existing state of affairs. They were politically alert, and disliked agriculture, indeed, all forms of manual work. They wanted to engage themselves in trade and commerce, and start small industries. They found village life cramping, and hated its petty discriminations and notions of high and low. They wanted change.

I have stated earlier that Nadu Gowda and the Headman went to school together—that must have been in the 1890s. In those days the only school in the village was the traditional *kooli matha*. The teacher was an Oshtama,[4] one of whose descendants, a boy of ten or twelve, was living in the village in 1948. All traditional schools were known for their liberal use of the cane, and even more barbarous forms of punishment which were meted out to unruly pupils. The teacher (*upadru*, a corruption of *upadhyayaru*) taught his pupils the three R's, and learning was synonymous with committing things to memory. The complex orthography of Kannada, rules of grammar, numerical tables, meanings of nouns, and poems and hymns, all had to be learnt by rote. Indeed, a good part of the time every day was spent with the teacher saying something and all the students chanting it after him. Advanced students had to learn to read, and understand the epics, and a few other classics.

The 'graduation' of students was marked by ritual. On the ninth day in the bright half of the month of *ashwini* (September–October) the graduating students were dressed in their best and went along the village streets singing and dancing. The songs sung on his occasion were referred to as 'Manoumiya Choupada' ('four-lined poems sung at Mahanavami') and some of them were irreverent if not hostile to the teacher. The man who had wielded the cane so liberally came in for rhymed abuse and scorn on the occasion of their emancipation. The songs and dances were regarded as entertainment and the houses before which the students stopped gave gifts to be handed over to the teachers.

The *upadru* was a poor man and each student had to pay an annual fee in cash and grain besides the customary gifts made on occasions such as initiation into writing. In spite of his poverty, the teacher was

---

[4] Oshtamas were also known as Satanis, and men from this caste were employed as priests in temples to Hanuman and Vishnu.

a highly respected member of the village community. The fact that he was usually a Brahmin added to the respect he commanded.

The incomplete middle school, like other schools of its kind in the area, celebrated the worship of two Hindu deities, viz. the Ganesha and Saraswati. The propitiation of Ganesha ensured the removal of obstacles in the path of everyone including students, while Saraswati was the goddess of learning. (In homes where the elders entertained educational ambitions for their children they were enjoined to worship Saraswati.) The annual *puja* of these two deities in school was popular with the students partly because of the tasty *prasada* which was distributed among them at the end.

During the Dasara festival in 1948, I was invited by the headmaster of the school to preside over the Saraswati *puja*. I suspected that my friend Kulle Gowda had persuaded the Headmaster to invite me, and I had no choice but to accept though I had no idea of my duties as 'president'. At some point in the proceedings I was asked to make a speech. I mouthed the usual platitudes about the need to respect elders and teachers, and to regard manual work as respectable if not elevating. I also urged the children to do something for the village when they became responsible citizens. But even as I was saying my piece I felt that I was an impostor who had used the occasion to please the few older men in the audience. Anyway, if my own boyhood provided any clues, the boys were probably impatiently waiting for me to end my speech so that they could share the *prasada*. To bring the events to a conclusion, the Headmaster asked the boys to sing the national anthem. I told myself that Independence had indeed made enough of an impact for the Headmaster of a remote village school to have trained his pupils to sing it. The boys stood up and sang 'God Save the King' with a strong rural Kannada accent. Either the Headmaster wanted me to appreciate his students' mastery of English, or he had not received an order from the Education Department informing him of the changes that had taken place in 1947.

Since the beginning of this century, significant changes had occurred in the villagers' material culture. I shall not, however, make an effort to describe all the changes but shall limit myself to changes in two items both of which concerned the body, and were visible, viz. dress and hairstyle.

The traditional dress of the villagers was a white dhoti with a coloured border which was wrapped around the waist like a *lungi* but unlike the latter its two ends were not sewn together. It covered the body from the waist to the shins. It was worn in such a way that the right side came on top of the left unlike in the Tamil country where the left side came on top of the right. An upper cloth of coarse cotton, or a woolen blanket worn round the shoulders, completed the outfit.

In the irrigated villages of southern Mysore, this dress gave place to a uniform of shirt and shorts. It is not known when exactly this dress came into vogue. However, by the 1920s shirt and shorts made from coarse dark grey or blue material had become so popular that it was a symbol of a cultivator. This dress was made by urban tailors, the poorer among whom worked in tiny cloth shops in the side streets. The shirt was collarless and the sleeves did not taper at the wrist or have buttons. The shorts were tapering at the knee-caps or, in a few cases, the shins.

Only the richer and more sophisticated villagers wore collarless shirts with 'proper' sleeves with buttons and button-holes. They were usually made from plain white cloth, or white cloth with coloured stripes, and a *dhoti* worn in the Brahminical style covered the region below the waist.

But the younger and more urbanized villagers had gone back to the *lungi* style though their *lungi* was different from that worn by their grand-parents. It came down to the ankles, and the cloth was fine to the point of being translucent. They also wore long, full-sleeved shirts with butterfly collars. A thin towel was invariably draped over the left shoulder. Most of them also wore thin, factory-made, effeminate sandals unlike their fathers who wore heavy hand-crafted ones made by Harijan leather-workers in Malavalli. Nadu Gowda, for instance got his sandals made by a particular cobbler in Malavalli, and he said no pair lasted him longer than six months. He was a huge man and the village roads were not kind on footwear. He was contemptuous of fancy sandals and their owners.

In the fifties, there emerged a small group of village youth all of whom were studying in high schools and colleges in Mysore. They dressed differently from everyone else in the village. They wore bush shirts, narrow trousers and Hawaiian sandals made of foam rubber. They tended to congregate in the house of one or the other of their small group to listen to film music over the radio or transistor. The bulk of the villagers regarded them as a privileged lot, boys who were supported by the hard work of their parents or uncles or older brothers. It was expected that they would have salaried jobs or stay in one of the cities when earning their livelihood.

In comparison with the men's dress, women's dress had undergone very little change—a phenomenon that was true of India as a whole, at least until 1970. The sari and blouse continued to be the standard dress of village women. But the saris were no longer bought in nearby fairs but in urban shops which displayed a variety of handloom and mill saris in different colours and patterns. Sophisticated silk saris from such well-known centres of weaving as Dharmavaram, Conjeevaram and Arni, and from factories in Bangalore and Mysore were sported by rich village women at weddings and festivals.

Before World War II, a close-necked and full-sleeved blouse from thick, grey cloth was popular with village women, or at least the poorer ones. This gradually gave way to half-sleeved and wide-necked blouses made from attractive, factory-made cotton material, and silks for weddings and festivals.

In 1948, the western-style crop was fast replacing the traditional tuft among the men and only the older and more conservative villagers retained a tuft. The Barber welcomed the crop as it meant less work than shaving the head of a man except for the crown adorned by a tuft. Conservative villagers had their faces shaved only when their heads were also shaved. The separation of the face-shave from tonsure was the result of westernization. Prior to that it was part of the total shave of the head and face, and those who had only their faces shaved were regarded as guilty of breaking pollution rules. However, matters became more simple when the crop became popular: the head was trimmed once in four or six weeks while the face was shaved once a week or fortnight, or before visiting a town. One of the village Barbers opened an urban-style shop on the Mysore–Hogur road where anyone could get a hair cut or shave any time during the day on payment of cash. While the traditional Barber did not perform his duties on inauspicious days the shop Barber ignored the prohibited days and timings. All this signified a weakening of traditional rules but even then very few villagers (perhaps, none excepting Pijja) used safety razors. The better off villagers felt that self-shaving was polluting (or at least their women-folk thought so) and bothersome while the poor ones did not have money enough to invest in the equipment and the frequent change of blades it called for.

THE STATE AND CHANGE

A long-range view of the changes which had occurred in Rampura revealed the crucial role played by the state. The economic development of the Rampura region was based on the two major irrigation canals,

Ramaswamy and CDS, which were planned and executed by the Hindu rulers well before the establishment of British rule.[5] After the defeat of Tippu Sultan at the hands of the British in 1799, and the restoration of the state, although truncated, to the earlier Hindu rajas, the administrative system became modernized slowly. The new administrative system enabled the state to undertake and execute development tasks for which the traditional system was not suited.

But just as it was obvious that on a long-term view the state's efforts at development were successful, a short-range view highlighted only the defects and inadequacies in its efforts. Some at least of the deficiencies seemed integral to any effort at improvement given the highly stratified nature of the society in which the people lived. The richer, influential and better-informed households were the first to take advantage of the new opportunities and their interests frequently clashed with those of the poor. Worse, frequently the enhanced power and resources of the wealthy made possible the more effective exploitation of the poor. The former were quick enough to sense when a new institution or improvement was likely to make the poor less compliant or more demanding, and opposition to such an institution was the result. The government's efforts to help Harijans to have tiled instead of thatched roofs for their huts were foiled by the manner in which the Headman dispensed the grants: he doled out tiny sums which the recipients spent on their pressing needs which included, in a few cases, toddy. It was common talk among the high castes that the Harijans had misused the money given to them for improving their huts. What else could one expect? The government's good intentions did not match its wisdom. Can anyone straighten out a dog's tail by tying a length of bamboo to it?

An egregious instance of the conflict between the rich and poor came to my notice in the incident of the transformation of a bull into bullock which I shall summarize here. Jogayya was an agnatic relative and client of the Headman. In fact, Jogayya's lineage had a client-like relation to that of the Headman's. One brother of Jogayya worked as a *jita* servant of the Headman's while another brother's wife had worked for a few years as maid to the Headman's mother. The Headman was in the habit of asking one or other member of Jogayya's lineage to do a job or run an errand at short notice. The latter could not say 'no'.

Early in 1947 the agriculture department of the Mysore Government

---

[5] See *Mysore Gazetteer*, edited by C. Hayavadana Rao, Vol. V, Bangalore, 1930, pp. 696–8.

embarked on a plan of improving the cattle in the State by giving to selected individuals in different villages quality bull-calves. The donees were required to feed and look after the calves, and after they were old enough, use them for stud purposes for at least five years. The recipient of the bull was again required to charge only one rupee for each service during the five-year period after which the bull became his. At least, that was the government's plan.

As could be expected, the Headman was given a fine bull-calf by the officials of the agriculture department. The Headman took it and then passed it on to Jogayya, asking him to look after it well. If he did look after it for five years, the Headman would see to it that the bull became his (Jogayya's). It was a good calf and would become a valuable bull in course of time.

In 1948, the bull was a fine-looking animal in 'active service'. I looked at the book in which Jogayya had listed the cows it had served. The cows had come from Rampura and several neighbouring villages. It looked as though the government's plan to improve cattle was going to be one of its more successful ones, assuming, of course, that Rampura's experience was typical.

Jogayya was one of those who used to drop in on me frequently and I found him a worried man. He was poor and the bull was expensive to keep. Besides green and dry fodder, the bull had to be given pulses and rice bran (*tavudu*) ground to a paste, and coconut and jaggery. He had looked after it as if it were his child. But he wondered whether it would not be taken away from him one day. There was no document to show that he was the donee and that it was he who was spending money and time in raising it. He had denied himself and his wife and children necessities in order to see that the bull got enough good food. Could I take a photograph of the bull with him and his son? It may come to his aid one day.

I admired the animal and I had long wanted to photograph it. But I had no intention of getting embroiled in a dispute between the Headman and his relative. I took a few pictures of the animal with Jogayya and his son, but I do not remember passing on a print to anyone. In any case, no one thought that I was scheming to make trouble for the Headman. The animal and its custodians posed before the 'Bullock House', within fifteen yards of the Headman's house. My own guess is that the Headman had not contemplated taking back the bull but Jogayya's was a suspicious nature.

When I returned to Rampura in 1952, one of the first questions I asked

Jogayya was about the condition of the bull. He seemed awkward and ill at ease and then smiled an embarrassed smile. After a couple of minutes' silence he told me that he had a big bullock and he needed another to make a team (*jodi*). It was not easy to find another which matched. Most reluctantly, he had to have the bull castrated. They now made an excellent pair and would fetch a thousand rupees. Thus ended the government's scheme to improve the quality of cattle, at least as far as the Rampura area was concerned.

Patience of an almost superhuman character, deep cunning and an ability to mask one's real feelings and intentions, were the only weapons which the desperately poor and exploited villagers had in their struggle against oppressors of all kinds, local landowners, tax collectors and invading armies. If they were unenthusiastic about an innovation which urban officials and local or foreign experts had thought up, it was because the latter were insensitive to the full implications of the innovation at the village level. While the ploughman thought of how well the new blade penetrated the soil, the worms underneath may be pardoned for taking a different view.

Another instance of the government's well-intentioned efforts going awry came to my notice in 1948. There was a young official whom I shall call Jangama and it was his job to promote rural welfare. His duties were unspecific and he addressed himself to many matters, in particular, hygiene and sanitation. I met him a few times, and I was at first told that he was an 'enthusiastic' official. It was only later that I understood the implications of this euphemism. He had urged the villagers to remove the unsightly manure heaps along the road and pointed out how they attracted mosquitoes and flies, and polluted the canal waters which were used for drinking. The villagers heard him out but went on as before. It was convenient to have the manure heaps near the owners' houses where they could be protected from thieves. Even more significantly, in the homes of most people it was the duty of the wife or daughter-in-law to carry domestic and cattleshed sweepings to the manure heap, and no woman liked the idea of a long early morning walk with a loaded basket on her head. It was especially difficult during the monsoon when it rained for days on end.

The Deputy Commissioner of Mysore had planned a visit to Rampura, and Jangama came a few days previously to ask the villagers to remove the unslightly manure heaps on the southern side of the Mysore–Hogur road. But the owners of the heaps took no notice. He became angry, and throwing caution to the winds, applied a lighted match stick to two or three heaps. They were all dry and caught fire easily and a favourable wind fanned the flames. The villagers had certainly not expected a young official to be stupid and highhanded enough to set fire to their precious manure heaps. Enraged, they went after him to beat him up. Jangama ran into the school house and bolted the door from inside. The villagers dared him to come out. In the meanwhile, word reached the Headman about the incident and he hurried to the school and asked the villagers to disperse. He made Jangama come out and then talked to him about the seriousness of what he had done on that day and the risks he had run.

Jangama had failed totally to appreciate the villagers' point of view regarding the manure heaps. He did not understand that a change in the style of life of villagers could only occur after agriculture had brought a measure of prosperity to everyone in the village, and the rules of hygiene and sanitation had become part of the school curriculum. To be fair to Jangama, he was doing only what was expected of him. The failure to appreciate the villagers' point of view stemmed from a much higher level in the government than his. Petty officials cannot be blamed for wrong policies.

The Quality of Social Relations

The principle of reciprocity was basic to rural social life. I have discussed earlier its expression in agricultural work. *Muyyi* was the term used for exchange of labour, and it was resorted to when the need for agricultural labour was at its peak.

Muyyi had also other meanings. For instance, it referred to the cash contributions made by relatives and friends at a non-Brahmin wedding. At any village wedding, sitting near the bride and groom were two men, one noting down the contributions made to the groom's household, and the other, the bride's. The richer households had these lists copied in big, bound notebooks. Each contribution had to be returned at a wedding in the donor's house. Elderly villagers recalled that in the old days anyone who failed to return the contribution was visited by the donor's debt-collector or *jita* servant. Such a visit meant that the defaulter had tried to get out of a solemn agreement. Since the sum involved was usually small, the defaulter was shamed. Village gossips were certain to pass the information to their relatives and friends.

The obligation to return *muyyi* cast a heavy social burden on the richer households. One or other member of such households had to be always on the move during the wedding season to return paltry contributions. The Headman's household were the worst sufferers in this matter. In 1948 and 1952, Lakshmana made frequent trips to villages near and far, after the rice harvest which ushered in the wedding season. Rame Gowda once confided to me that *muyyi* was outdated. His household had 'too many contacts' (*samparka jasti*) and it was not practicable to retain them. Indeed, some of the more educated and westernized individuals among the non-Brahmins made it a point to announce in their wedding invitations that *muyyi* and *tera* (bride-price) payments would not be received. They considered it embarrassing to receive and record the petty sums of cash made as *muyyi*, not to mention the trouble involved in repayment. *Tera* was denounced as the sale of a girl. The more sophisticated guests preferred to make gifts of silver tumblers, saris and dhotis and gadgets instead of cash. This was the general practice among urban Brahmins though close relatives some-times gave cash. (Payment by cheque was more prestigious than cash.)

The principle of reciprocity also expressed itself in unfriendly contexts. For instance, a man who had received an injury from another felt bound to avenge himself (*muyyige muyyi*). For instance, If A's straw rick was set fire to by B, A thought that he had to set fire to B's straw rick or inflict some other damage on him. Otherwise, his honour, if not manliness, was felt to be at stake.

Reciprocity also guided relations between close friends and relatives but this was obscured by the articulated sentiment that where there was affection there ought to be no calculation of return. In such cases reciprocity lurked underneath, surfacing only in crises.

The idea of reciprocity underlay cross-cousin marriage as also the marriage of a man with his elder sister's daughter. A girl went out of her natal home at marriage to join her husband, and she did not get a share in the ancestral house and land. She only got some jewellery and clothes. However, when her grown sons and daughters married their mother's brother's offspring, some kind of reciprocity occurred.

Underlying the broad idea of reciprocity in marriage was a more specific expression. While anyone in the preferred category of relatives enjoyed an advantage over an outsider, among the relatives themselves a man's father's sister's, or elder sister's daughter was preferred to his mother's brother's daughter. Such a marriage ensured the 'return' of the daughter of an outgoing female member to her maternal lineage. The loss of membership of her natal family which followed her marriage was compensated when her daughter came back. As the saying had it, 'the calf had to be brought back from the place where the cow had been given' (*hasa kotta kadeyinda kara tarabeku*).

Respect for the principle of reciprocity was not always easy, without emotional or other cost. For instance, in the summer of 1948 Millayya was under pressure from his younger brothers not to give his daughter (by his deceased wife) in marriage to Kulle Gowda's brother's son. Millayya's younger brothers pointed out that Kulle Gowda's brother was poor, while Millayya was one of the rich landowners of Rampura and his daughter could easily have married into a wealthy household. But then when Millayya had been given Kulle Gowda's sister in marriage *his* household was the poorer one, and it was therefore wrong for him to refuse to give his daughter when he was better off. Wealth and poverty were both transitory while moral rules were permanent. Many came to hear of the discussion among brothers, and Millayya was praised by one and all.

The preference shown for sons by the villagers was also based on reciprocity considerations. Traditionally, sons provided the best insurance against old age. They cultivated the family land and looked after their parents during old age. They also performed annual sacrifices to propitiate the dead ancestors which were essential for the latter's satisfaction and the lineage's continued well-being. The continuation of the lineage (*kula, annatammike, peelige, vamsha*) depended on the birth of male heirs in each generation. The disappearance of a lineage was viewed as a disaster. It resulted in the ancestral land's alienation.

The non-vegetarian castes in the village propitiated their dead ancestors on the ninth day (*marnoumi*) in the dark half of *bhadrapada* (September–October) with offerings of cooked meat.[1] The richer households slaughtered a sheep on this occasion while the poor had to be content with offerings of fowl. It was a big occasion. Each year during the *marnoumi* Nadu Gowda distributed twelve *khandagas* (khandaga = 180 seers) of paddy as charity to the village poor and mendicants. It gave him much satisfaction and he was proud of the fact that he had not stopped it even during the war years when rationing was at its worst. The annual act of charity, according to him, ensured that the living members kept good health and that the ancestral land continued to prosper. It was also an expression of gratitude to those who had worked unstintingly for their descendants: 'Where would we have been if they had not worked for us so hard?'

Reciprocity had also its subjective side. An individual felt compelled to do, or abstain from doing, something, because he had received a favour in the past, or because of the existence of a prior bond stemming

---

[1] A few of them, however, performed the propitiatory rites during the asterism, *makha*, which fell generally in August.

from the membership of a kin-group, village, caste, class, sect or religion. The word *dakshinya* expressed the sense of obligatoriness which moved persons to act in ways which were contrary to their immediate feelings and interests. The power of *dakshinya* was felt by one and all, excepting of course the minority of deviants. However, underlying *dakshinya* was the fear that if one did not do what was expected of one, others would not do what was in turn expected of them. But that was not the whole of *dakshinya*. It lay at the root of socialization, if not of all inter-personal morality.

Even when a man was not well enough to partake of the dinner at a relative's house he went because of *dakshinya*. And if he felt like cutting it, his host was certain to say, 'Just sit before the leaf, and make a pretence (*shastra*) of eating. That is enough.' The host on his side had to be certain that he had made every effort to secure the guest's presence. *Dakshinya* required him to put pressure on the guest. What applied to a dinner invitation applied also to more serious matters such as attending a wedding or festival, undertaking a journey, advancing a loan, giving or accepting a girl in marriage, and making a gift. *Dakshinya* made people do all kinds of things and this was acknowledged in the mordant humour of the saying, *dakshinyakke basaraguvudu* (becoming pregnant because of *dakshinya*).

A man who defaulted on his obligation was likely to be talked about. And continued indifference to obligations gave him a reputation for unreliability. In a small and closely meshed community, a reputation for unreliability was likely to have disastrous consequences. He would find no one willing to give him a loan, sponsor him for a contract or commercial transaction, employ him as a tenant and so on.

The multiplex character of rural social bonds was also a factor in restraining people from reneging on their obligations. Thus a labourer who wanted to stop working for a landowner had to take note of the likelihood that he might need a loan in the near future. Similarly, a landowner who wanted to sack a tenant had to restrain himself because he wanted the tenant's son as a *jita* servant. A reputation for ruthlessness did not enhance the landowner's popularity, and there were other landowners who were likely to take advantage of it. The ruthless landowner lost men to rival factions. In a multi-stranded relationship, the snapping of any single strand was prevented by the existence of the other strands. To this had to be added the constraints stemming from the value attached to enduring social bonds. There was always a tension between an uninhibited pursuit of one's interests and conformity to the restraining norms which were the expressions of other people's interests or desires.

As was made clear earlier, caste divided the villagers into different hierarchical groups, and the idiom of caste was extended to objects and even events in the external world to distinguish them into high and low. 'Are the five fingers equal?' was a rhetorical question that was asked whenever the government's intention to abolish untouchability was discussed. The inequality between the fingers on a hand symbolized inequality in God's creation, and the government's attempts to bring about equality were absurd and bound to fail. But paradoxically many of those who argued in this way found the Brahminical or Lingayat claim to superiority wrong and offensive.

While as between castes (or sub-castes) the idea of hierarchy was dominant, every man recognized some relatives and friends as his equals (*sarikaru*), and he was particularly sensitive to his image among them. Humiliation before them (*sarikara munde avamana*) was so grave a matter that at times it drove a man to desperate action.

The idea of equality also found expression, although indirectly, in occasional moralizing which was perhaps born out of envy. Thus a wealthy miser was criticized for his folly in behaving as though he was going to take everything with him on his head when he died (*ella tale mele hottukondu hoguttaneye?*). Lakshmi, the goddess of wealth, was notorious for her fickleness: a man who was favoured by her one day was likely to be deserted by her on another.

The villagers were aware that an individual's moral worth was not determined by caste: that is, that there were some very moral individuals among the 'low' castes and immoral ones among the high. There was a realization that character was different from caste but at the same time sentiments were uttered implying that the higher castes were (or ought to be) more moral. This was seen, for instance, in the lapses of a high caste man receiving more attention than those of a low caste man, though this was to some extent due to the former's greater visibility. Also, the existence of differential life-styles between the higher and lower castes was interpreted to mean that the former's was superior.

Sanyasis represented another expression of the equality idea. They were recruited from both high and low castes but they were all holy men entitled to universal respect. That, however, was only the ideal. In practice, the sanaysi's caste prior to his initiation was relevant in some ways, and in particular, in the composition of his followers many of whom came from his own, equivalent or lower castes. Where a sanyasi was the head of a monastery, the bureaucracy was particularly sensitive in matters of pollution and purity, and treated lay followers from lower castes differently from high caste followers. But a few sanyasis had truly cosmopolitan followings cutting across not only caste but religious divisions.[2]

There were also other expressions of inequality besides those arising from caste and landownership. Men were superior to women, and the older were superior to the younger. Some expressions of hierarchy, however, had not been institutionalized; the dark-skinned were regarded as inferior to the light-skinned, the uneducated to the educated, urban to the rural and so on.

The omnipresence of hierarchical ideas had led to the proliferation and refinement of the symbols of superordination and subordination. For instance, the different parts of the human body had superior-inferior connotations. From the point of view of mutual rank the head was the highest part of the body while the feet were the lowest. One of the deepest expressions of respect was the traditional act of salutation in which a younger man placed his head on the older man's feet: the most superior part of the former's body had come into contact with the lowest part of the latter's. Similarly, a devotee in a temple prostrated (*sashtanga namaskara*) before the icon. Prostrating at the feet of a deity or of a patron symbolized the devotee's or client's abasement before the deity or patron. Such abasement was regarded as essential for seeking help and protection. In addition, a devotee slapped his cheeks before the deity to express his repentance for sins of commission and omission. The left cheek was slapped with the right hand and *vice versa*.

A devotee in a temple took all *prasada* to both his eyes first before drinking, eating or otherwise disposing of it. Thus the camphor flame which was waved before the deity before being offered to the devotees, was touched, symbolically, with both hands which were then taken to the eyes. The *thirtha* (holy water) was received with both hands and then drunk, and afterwards, the hands were taken to the eyes and wiped on the hair. Similarly, a flower or *tulasi* leaf (*Ocimum sanctum*) given by the priest was taken to both the eyes before being tucked behind the right

---

[2] My comments apply only to 'traditional' monasteries and not to a modern organization such as the Ramakrishna Mission.

ear. Incidentally, receiving with both hands was obligatory. The use of only one hand was disrespectful while receiving with the left hand was forbidden. A child was taught never to put forward its left hand to receive anything.

The feet were not only the lowest part of the body but they came into contact with dirty and polluting things. Even in 1948, only a small number of men (and no women) wore sandals in Rampura, and a villager usually went into his house after washing his feet. His wife brought him a vesselful of water to the door, and the man washed his feet on the steps. A wife who failed to do this was not doing her duty.

The bodily positions which men assumed *vis-à-vis* each other had hierarchical connotations. As mentioned earlier, it was considered improper for a younger or inferior person to sit while his superior was standing while the opposite situation was proper. An inferior did not sit even when the superior was walking a few feet away. One afternoon Nadu Gowda was sitting on my veranda while the Headman was pacing the corridor below and Nadu Gowda told him jokingly, 'Why don't you go home?' The Headman understood what Nadu Gowda was trying to say and replied, 'I don't mind your stretching your legs.' Nadu Gowda retorted, 'You may not, but what will the people say?' Nadu Gowda was the Headman's senior by a few years but he still felt that he had to show respect to the head of the village.

When several men were sitting on a bench only the senior among them had the right to cross his legs. (The stretching of legs was allowed only when extreme age made prolonged folding of legs very painful.) If between two men, the superior was sitting with his legs crossed, the inferior usually sat on his haunches, and if the superior was sitting on a mat, the inferior sat on the bare floor. If the superior was sitting on the veranda, the inferior sat at a lower level, and sometimes even on the street itself.

In a group of men it was not difficult to spot the leader. The leader spoke and gestured differently from the others. When an important man such as the Headman was a member of a group, the others would not look him in the face but look down or away. And, frequently, when an inferior was with the Headman, his right hand went to the back of his head where it moved up and down in a scratching motion while the lips opened in a placatory simper before speaking. Once when I was walking with the Headman and Nadu Gowda on the road forming the crest of the tank bund, we encountered Pijja on a cycle, returning after a visit to Butagalli. As soon as he saw us, he jumped down from his cycle, removed his sandals, took them in one hand, and stood to a side of the road making room for us to pass. Even though Pijja had the reputation of being a rebel, he behaved like any other Harijan. Even non-Harijans who were in an inferior position had to remove their sandals and headgear before a superior.

Individuals who were economically and socially inferior seemed only too ready to agree with their superior, and flatter him when an opportunity presented itself. Agreeing with a superior and flattering him were approved if not prescribed ways of getting on, and every patron attracted one or more flatterers.[3] It is my impression that such flattery sounded more imposing in Sanskritized Kannada with frequent references to deities and incidents from Indian mythology than in plain, rustic speech.

The Headman asked me to go over to his house one morning to meet the elderly Brahmin accountant of Hogur and his son. Much of the land owned by the Headman lay inside the Hogur boundary. After I had been introduced to him, I invited him to have coffee and snacks in my house. I thought that I owed that courtesy to the Headman's guests. I was taken aback to find the accountant responding to my well-meant invitation with a snub: 'We don't lack anything as we are in the house of goddess Lakshmi herself. We have had fruit and milk and our stomachs are full.' From the way the old man put it my invitation appeared as an unfavourable comment on the Headman's inability to offer satisfactory hospitality to his guests. I sensed some hostility in the old man's reply—a feeling which was confirmed when I met him some time later in his house in Hogur—and more important, I felt upset that I may have given offence to the Headman by my thoughtless invitation.

Failure to show deference to the rich, powerful and old was to invite their wrath. Sarcasm was the first weapon used but sometimes a threat was also packed into it. For instance, 'How is it you are seen here? You must have lost your way', was simple sarcasm while, 'You must be wanting something, you are too busy to wander aimlessly' contained the threat that the man would not get what he wanted as he had not been

---

[3] The Maharajah of Mysore had professional flatterers (*hogalu bhattaru*) whose duty it was to proclaim his titles on state occasions. They went ahead of the elephant on which he sat during processions proclaiming his titles every few minutes. It is difficult to establish a direct link between institutionalized flattery at the princely level and the tendency of richer landowners to attract flatterers but it cannot be dismissed as accidental as it is one of the several instances of the correspondence between the two levels. Such correspondence points to the widespread desire to imitate royalty even in the days of poor communications.

available when he was wanted. Taunting (*hangisuvudu*) was cruder than sarcasm, simple or packed, and taunting meant that the taunted was being taken to task for not reciprocating. He had not given anything in return for the favours he had received. If even then he did not mend his ways he was certain to be punished. Such punishment took a variety of forms. If he was a tenant or sharecropper, his contract was not renewed, other landowners were told not to encourage him, pressure was brought upon his creditor to press for repayment of loans, and he even ran the risk of being accused of stealing someone's crop or letting loose his goats or bullocks on a neighbour's land.

But occasionally an inferior did stand up for his rights before a superior. I have seen poor and humble villagers shouting loudly before the Headman when they feared that their side of the case was being ignored. Indeed, I used to marvel at the patience with which the Headman listened to the ranting of disputants. I had expected him to be brusque and authoritarian but I found him allowing a man to make his point in his own way. Perhaps he wanted each disputant to have the satisfaction of stating his case before he gave his verdict. The implementation of the verdict of a village court depended largely on the support it obtained from the people and on its appearing reasonable to everyone.

The rich and powerful also had duties which included hospitality to visitors to the village. Visitors usually arrived without notice but they were invariably invited to a meal, and when they belonged to a superior caste the raw ingredients of a meal were supplied to them. No mendicant arriving at mealtime went hungry. The gifting of food (*anna dana*) was meritorious, and correspondingly, the failure to give it to the poor and hungry, a sin. Even those regarded as misers did not like to turn away a guest or mendicant arriving at mealtime. One of the worst criticisms of a rich man was to say that he turned away those who came hungry.

The advantages for travellers and visiting officials of the existence of such hospitality in villages which did not have inns and hotels are obvious. Even more important was the belief in the meritoriousness of sharing food in a system in which a few owned a great deal of arable land while the others lived on the margin of subsistence. During famines, which regularly visited the countryside, each big landowner took it upon himself to distribute some *ragi*-gruel to the starving. The feeding of hundreds of people at the weddings and funerals of the rich enabled the poor, who often had to go hungry, to have a free meal at which they could gorge themselves. Rice, which was a luxury for the poor, was served at such dinners, though with balls of *ragi*-dough. A good landowner walked along the rows (*pangti*) of squatting diners and made sure that each got enough to eat. (This had also its public relations side.) A full stomach had a special importance for those to whom it was not an everyday affair. The virtues of undereating make sense only to the overfed. The poor remembered the weddings of the rich principally by the kind of meals that had been cooked, and whether they were served as much as they wanted to eat or not.

The poor were exploited, and frequently mercilessly, by the rich. Or perhaps it would be more correct to say that the conditions of work accepted as normal in the village were harsh and exploitative. The only course open to a poor man who felt exploited and oppressed by a rich man was to curse the latter: 'May his house be ruined' (*avana mane halaga*), 'May his wife become a widow' (*avana hendati mundeyaga*), etc. There was a belief that when a poor man cursed a rich man out of the depths of his bitterness and hatred (literally, *hotte uri* or 'stomach fire') the curse would take effect. This was seen strikingly in the fear of a poor widow's curse, which, as described earlier, took the form of a long dirge. Thus two 'sanctions' were available to the poor against the rich: one was to curse, and the other, to run away.

FACE

The word *moka* (from the Sanskrit *mukha*) or face was heard frequently in conversation. It stood for a person's image before others and for his self-respect. It was one of his most important possessions. He had to behave in such a way that he was able to show his face to one and all and not have to hide it. When a man, or those intimately associated with him, did something wrong he felt he was unable to show his face to others, especially equals. When a man insulted another at a wedding, festival or other public occasion, his face was 'broken' before everyone (*ellara edurige moka muridubitta*). It was an insult which he could not get over easily. A man who was aware that he had committed a serious wrong was said to look as though 'his face had been beaten with sandals' (*moka ekkadadalli hodeda hagittu*). Similarly, a man who had managed to make some money for selling his sugarcane crop at a profit, or had just got married, was teased by his friends: '[Your] face has acquired a lustre' (*mokakke kale bandubidtu*). Similarly, an official who exercised power revealed it in his face (*mokadalli darpa ide*). Gentleness (*sadhu*), badness (*kettatana*), etc., were all discernible in a man's face. Another term that was heard frequently was *mana* which meant self-respect. A man with a keen sense of self-respect was referred to as a *manishta*.[4] He need not be rich. A comment that was heard occasionally was, 'We may be poor but we value our self-respect' (*navu badavaragira-bahudu adare manadinda baluttiddeve*). Similarly a rich man did not have always a strong sense of self-respect. A *manishta* was driven to suicide (or even homicide) because he felt he had lost his self-respect. *Avamana* was the loss of *mana*.

A *manishta* kept his word, and he also discharged his obligations scrupulously. He paid creditors on time, and he gave the gifts he was required to. He did not easily brook an insult. If he was not strong or aggressive enough to react instantly to an insult, he showed his resentment by silent non-cooperation.

Insulting a person's family, caste and village amounted to insulting him. In the case of 'The Potter and Priest', the Priest felt that his entire caste had been insulted by the Potter's declared intention to beat the priest till five pairs of sandals wore out. He pointed out there was only a small number of Lingayats in Rampura to take retaliatory action and they were dependent on the Peasants to safeguard the honour of their caste.

A friend of mine who was connected with rural development work in Mysore in the early fifties narrated an incident which poignantly brought out how strongly a group of poor Harijans felt regarding their *mana*. He and his colleagues had been invited to a puja in the Harijan ward of the village, and the hosts, after preparing sweetened milk (*khiru*) for the guests, discovered that they had too few tumblers and no one was willing to lend them a few more which they needed. At this the leader of the Harijans became so enraged that he emptied all the *khiru* into the gutter, saying, 'Where is our self-respect? We cannot even find enough tumblers for our guests.'

Individuals also had a sense of identification with their village and an insult to one's village had to be avenged like an insult to oneself, one's wife, one's family, etc. Disputes between villages did occur, and they were not always for material gains. The settling of inter-village disputes resembled international disputes in their tortuousness and sensitivity to issues of protocol. For instance, there was a dispute between some members of Kere and Bihalli at the annual festival of Madeshwara in Gudi in 1947, and the priests of the Madeshwara temple, and some leaders from Rampura and Hogur were all concerned

[4] *Manishta* had two near synonyms in *gauruvasta* and *maryadasta*.

to bring about peace before the Ugadi (Kannada new year festival generally falling during March–April) in 1948. A meeting was first fixed in Hogur but Kere leaders did not attend it as they felt insulted at being summoned to Hogur whose political and social standing was identical with Kere's. Both were *hobli* capitals and each had the same kind of traditional court, viz. *kattemane*, for the settlement of caste and other disputes.[5] The meeting had to be finally held on neutral and sacred ground, viz. the open space outside the temple.

In brief, *mana* was a basic value, and everyone was sensitive about his self-respect including those who were desperately poor. I have referred elsewhere to the traditional ceremony of the 'big betel leaves' (*dodda vilya*) at which sets of betel leaves and arecanut pieces were distributed at the weddings of Peasants and other non-Brahmin castes, and how they were notorious for giving rise to disputes regarding mutual precedence. The order in which each set of leaves and nuts (*vilya*) was distributed had to respect the seniority principle, and any departure from it proved explosive. Each guest received *vilya* as a holder of a particular role, viz. temple priest, Maharaja's representative (*amildar*, the official head of the *taluk*), caste headman, village headman, Brahmin, or representative of each village in the region. It was the last category that gave most trouble; the credentials of each claimant to represent his village had to be beyond dispute, and in addition, there was the thorny question of mutual precedence among villages. It was not unknown for two men to claim to represent the same village, and in such a case, the one who had the better claim was given the *vilya*. This naturally enraged the defeated man. The matter of precedence between villages was even more difficult, and a decision taken at one wedding could prove to be a source of continuous trouble for the caste. The distribution of 'big betel leaves' was frequently marred by shouting and angry exchanges. The expense of this ritual as well as its explosive character was responsible for the decision of Rampura elders to permit fathers of local brides to opt out of the ceremony on payment of Rs 8.25 to the village council.

Quite apart from the distribution of 'big betel' at weddings, the giving of betel leaves and nuts to guests was a prescribed courtesy (*maryade*) on certain formal and ritual occasions. The failure to do so was an insult. During the fifties there was a bitter and protracted dispute in Kere where

[5] For a discussion of traditional caste and village organization in the Rampura area, see my 'The Dominant Caste in Rampura', *American Anthropologist*, Vol. 61, No. 1, Feb. 1959, pp. 1–16. Also included in M. N. Srinivas, *Village, Caste, Gender and Method: Essays in Indian Social Anthropology* (OUP, 1996).

the dominant Peasants were divided into two factions, one supporting their caste Headman's right to receive, on ceremonial occasions, two *vilyas* and the other consisting of all those who thought he should receive only one *vilya* like everyone else. Most villagers were drawn, willy-nilly, into the dispute, and one could not talk to a Kere man for five minutes without the dispute turning up in some form or other. The Headman demanded two *vilyas*, one in his role as the Headman of the Peasants of the entire Kere *hobli*, and the other as the leader of the Peasants of Kere village. Kere, as I have said earlier, had a number of educated and politicized men, and they thought that the Headman's insistence on two *vilyas* was antediluvian and undemocratic. The Headman was wealthy, had a record of service to the village, and wielded much local influence while a few of the educated leaders of Kere were active in politics outside the village. The dispute dragged on for years and I do not know how, if at all, it was resolved.

There was an ugly scene at the wedding, in 1947, of the Headman's daughter in which Ningu, a guest from Kere, well known for his cantankerousness, walked out of the assembly (*sabha*) on the ground that he and all the other guests had been insulted. The 'insult' had occurred in the following way: As the wedding procession (*sabgast*) reached the Muslim area, a few Muslim leaders put jasmine garlands round the groom's and Headman's neck as an expression of their regard for them. No one objected then but after the procession had returned home, Ningu got up and walked out complaining that the assembly had been insulted. According to Ningu, only the bridal couple had the right to receive garlands at weddings, and not anyone else. The Headman, the chief host, should not have accepted the garland. By his acceptance, he had insulted the guests.

After walking out of the hall, Ningu walked to the gate of the Rama temple and sat down on a stone. The Headman, Nadu Gowda and a few Muslim leaders hurried after him to pacify him and bring him back. Ningu had raised an explosive issue, and the Headman's first task was to defuse it. He and his supporters assured Ningu that neither the Muslim leaders nor the Headman had intended any insult to the guests. The Muslim leaders had only thought of showing their respect to the head of the village, that was all. After much coaxing, Ningu allowed himself to be led back to the wedding hall and the hosts heaved a sigh of relief.

There was a general belief in the village that in matters of precedence the Shepherds were really the most finicky group. There was the saying: *kurubaranyaya kambli geddalu hididaru tiruvudilla* (Shepherds' disputes do not get settled even when the blankets on which they are sitting are being eaten up by termites). The arbitrators and disputants sat on *kamblis* spread on the ground and the arguments about precedence went on and on oblivious of the infestation of the *kamblis* by termites. In temples controlled by Shepherds, the order in which the leaders were to receive *prasada* was strictly laid down and any departure from it gave rise to a protracted dispute. To be fair, this kind of dispute could have arisen in the temple of any other caste in the area and the Shepherds were only more thoroughgoing and exacting. If, for instance, a Shepherd leader was absent at the temple on an important occasion, when his turn for *prasada* came, the priest mentioned his name and sprinkled the *thirtha* on a pillar before passing on to the next devotee. Failure to do so was to invite trouble.

A man's self-respect was damaged when he was called a 'bastard' (*hadarakke huttidavanu*) before others, and far more seriously when he was spat upon or beaten with sandals. In the latter case, both the aggressor and victim were punished by the village and caste elders, the aggressor because he had committed a serious wrong, and the victim because he had been polluted, and could only be readmitted after an elaborate purificatory rite. However, with the introduction of British law, this type of wrong became actionable under 'defamation' which was significantly translated as *mananashta* (loss of self-respect). Defamation was resorted to by villagers to strengthen sanctions for traditional offences. This happened to coincide with the weakening of traditional sanctions with increased spatial mobility, urbanization and westernization.

FRIENDSHIP AND ENMITY

Friendship (*sneha, dosti*) and enmity (*dwesha, vaira, hage, jiddu*) were both widely recognized relationships between individuals, families and lineages. Friends had frequent and pleasant interaction: they chatted together, went out on walks or journeys, ate in each other's houses, and occasionally, gave each other vegetables and fruits. With an enemy, on the other hand, there was a relationship of avoidance. When two men were not on speaking terms with each other they had a relationship of avoidance but this was still some distance removed from enmity. Enemies tried actively to harm each other in every possible way varying from malicious gossip, setting fire to straw-ricks, diverting water from, or flooding fields and filing suits in law courts to plotting murder.

Sometimes, inherited enmity gave place to friendship, and an outstanding example of this was provided by the friendship of the Headman and Nadu Gowda. It was significant that it was the village school which had brought the two together. The fathers of the Headman and Nadu Gowda were illiterate, and were thus denied the opportunity which the sons had of coming together every day for several hours at school. The boredom of learning the complicated alphabet, the multiplication tables, etc., for several hours every day in a crowded and dingy room, and the fear of the tyrant with the cane were bonds which bound all the oppressed.

As explained earlier, considerations of reciprocity did prevail among friends though the rhetoric of friendship stressed only affection. But reciprocity did not have to be on a one-to-one basis, nor did it mean that a material good had to be reciprocated with another good. Friendship occasionally spanned economic divisions so that while one side gave goods the other gave time, labour and 'loyalty' (*niyat*). But too great a disparity in status changed friendship into a patron-client relation.

Friendship was more visible among, if not more characteristic of, men. Grown men did not experience any embarrassment in showing their affection for each other. Two friends who had met after an interval of a few weeks held each other's hands, or one put his hand over the other's shoulder, except among the middle-aged and old. On a few occasions my friends arrived suddenly on my veranda and announced that they felt like seeing me. They were a bit embarrassed to find me working but I assured them it was nothing urgent. I invited them to have some coffee before we all went out for a walk. My friends were pleased that I had pushed aside my work for them. The only one to grouse was Kulle Gowda, 'You go, by all means go, have a good time. I shall sit here and work.' He was not the one to allow his light to be hid by any bushel.

Needless to say, friendship occurred within the same sex. A friendly relation between a man and woman who were not kindred to each other, or more specifically, between whom sex intercourse did not constitute incest, was usually interpreted as a liaison. The concept of a platonic relationship did not make sense to the villagers. They were too biologically oriented for that.

Friendships did occur across the lines of caste though here, as in the case of cross-class friendships, there were structural limits. For instance, friendships between Brahmins, Lingayats or Peasants on the one hand and Harijans on the other, were rare. Close relationship between members of one of the first three castes and Harijans invariably assumed the form of patron-client relationships. But I do know of friendships between Brahmins and Peasants, Lingayats and Peasants, and Brahmins and Lingayats. During the thirties I attended a wedding in Kere in which Mallayya, the Peasant friend of Seenappa, the Brahmin landowner-host, successfully 'persuaded' him to invite his (landowner's) cousin across the road. Seenappa was notorious for his obstinacy but Mallayya literally pushed him every step of the thirty yards or so between the two houses. Once or twice the host shouted at him, 'Mallayya, what are you trying to do? Don't force me to do what I don't like to'. But Mallayya handled Seenappa, his senior by at least a few years, and a Brahmin, firmly, like a father handling a wilful son. Seenappa finally reached the door of the cousin's house where he shamefacedly invited his relative to attend the wedding and bless the bridal couple. The incident provoked some mirth among the bystanders including Seenappa's relatives who commented, 'He listens only to Mallayya. None of us would have been able to persuade him to invite his cousin.'

Siddu, the Lingayat lawyer, and Swamy, Nadu Gowda's son, were close friends, but their friendship had to reckon with the pollution barrier. While Siddu was emancipated, his kinship group was orthodox, and as priests of the Madeshwara temple they were required to observe scrupulously the pollution rules. Swamy, his younger brother Kempu, and Japi used to visit Siddu in his big joint family house where he lived with his brothers and cousins. There was an immense wooden cot in the inner veranda of the house, and the visitors used to sit on it, leaning against the rolled up mattresses, while waiting for their friend to get ready to come out. But if Thammayya, the head of the lineage, saw the Peasant friends leaning against the mattress-roll, he insisted on its being washed. (Washing a mattress was neither easy nor tidy.) Only after a wash did it become pure enough to be used again by the members of the priestly household.

Siddu's wife was also a stickler for ritual purity. In the old days, she used to insist on her husband's having a bath after he returned from a walk with his Peasant friends. The latter came to know about it and protested vigorously to Siddu. Siddu, BA, LL.B., was able to persuade his wife that he had to respect his friend's feelings. But he dropped visiting the Madeshwara temple in view of his departure from the regimen prescribed for the priests. He only broke his self-imposed rule during the annual festival when every member of the lineage had to perform some chore in the *sanctum sanctorum*. Even this he dropped after he started practising as a lawyer. His secular status was too high to permit him to be a priest.

However, pollution rules were beginning to be relaxed in 1948. The urbanized Peasant youth of the village resented Brahmin and Lingayat pollution-consciousness, and also their exclusiveness in food, drink, etc. By 1952 even the more conservative Peasants were offering tea or coffee instead of boiled milk to upper caste visitors. Cooked snacks were offered to old friends like me, and Peasant hosts tended to be generous in their hospitality. Still later, educated Brahmin and Lingayat friends were expected to dine with Peasants on occasions such as weddings. Any guest who refused to dine on such occasions offended the hosts. No allowance was made for a queasy stomach. The least he could do was to sit before the heaped up leaf and eat a little.

A few Brahmins had, however, developed a taste for meat and chicken curries, and when they visited their Peasant friends they insisted on getting non-vegetarian food which, incidentally, they never cooked at home. But their departure from tradition was not always admired by their non-vegetarian friends. While it was understandable that conservative villagers should criticize meat-eating Brahmins, it was surprising to find even the urbanized youth criticizing them for having forsaken all Brahminical principles.

Friendship was indeed a value for the villagers, more for men than for women. Two good friends were said to be 'like brothers' (literally, 'like elder brother–younger brother', *annatammandirahage*). I heard this expression several times and I could not help recalling the statement of an elderly English colleague who had told me that he and his brother were very close and had written to each other every week. He had added, 'We are very good friends'. That is, friendship connoted intimacy in England while in Rampura (as in rural India everywhere), brotherhood conveyed intimacy. Adult brothers were frequently at loggerheads with each other and this was well known but apparently it was not enough to make a dent in the myth of fraternal solidarity. (The popular belief that the girls who came in by marriage into a family were responsible for its breaking up, was also derived from that myth.)

Friendship was a valued thing and the longer its duration, the greater was its value. By this test, the Headman and Nadu Gowda were indeed great friends. Nadu Gowda used to wax eloquent on this subject but on this as on other subjects the Headman was taciturn. But he had genuine affection for Nadu Gowda, and the two spent at least a few hours together every day. And as stated earlier, the Headman rarely went out of the village without being accompanied by his old friend.

GOSSIP

Gossip (*harate*) was an important activity in the village, and certain features of rural life such as nucleated settlement, the existence of multiplex ties, limited spatial mobility, availability of leisure, and the absence of regular recreation, all provided an ideal soil for it.

The fear of being gossiped about did act as a sanction against non-conformity. The words, 'the people will talk [about it]' (*jana matanadi-kolluttare*), were familiar ones. But there was a small minority in every village which seemed indifferent to local criticism. Nadu Gowda told me the story of the loose woman who was made to undergo an elaborate and expensive ritual of purification before being readmitted to caste. After she had bathed and worn new clothes, her tongue was singed with three kinds of needles, gold, silver, and iron, and she was given sanctified *vibhuti* by the guru who performed the purificatory ritual, to apply on her forehead. The woman, who was known for her tart speech, asked the guru whether it was not more appropriate to apply the *vibhuti* on the organ which had sinned instead of the innocent forehead. At the time I heard the story I was impressed by the villagers' ability to make fun even of things which they regarded as sacred. Its significance as showing the power of village society over confirmed violators of accepted norms came home to me only later.

The fear of gossip also did not restrain the Basava priest from doing what he wanted to. It was only when the Basava priest's mistresses tried to join the womenfolk of the Madeshwara lineage in cooking the dinner at the annual propitiation (*para*) in honour of the deity Basava that the Headman had to intervene.

A man who was outcasted for flouting the rules of his caste and of the local community generally tried to get back into the fold after a while. He did this when he tried to find spouses for his grown sons and daughters. No one in the caste wanted to marry the offspring of out-casted parents unless they themselves wanted to be thrown out. The only way out was for the outcasted person to apologize to caste leaders for protracted defiance and beg them to take him back. This was done after he had paid a fine to the caste and undergone the ritual of purification and given a big dinner. Many a rebel, after years of defiance, crawled back into his caste when he wanted to marry his son or daughter. In other words, sub-caste endogamy enforced conformity.

Among those who were loudest in their condemnation of gossip were the rich and powerful: 'What work do they (the gossips) have? They sit on the veranda and criticize others.' The revenue inspector stationed in Hogur told me that officials had always to be sensitive to what the gossips on verandas were likely to say. A State legislator once complained to Nadu Gowda that he dared not buy a new cycle for fear that gossips would say that it was a bribe from someone. (That he subsequently became wealthy is, however, another story.)

But while people in power claimed to be afraid of what the veranda critics said their actions often belied their words. The corruption of officials was a topic much discussed by all classes of villagers. The widely-held view was that with the arrival of popular government corruption had risen steeply and this was corroborated by officials who blamed politicians who interfered with the administrator's work to further their own ends. Ironically, homespun *khadi* had become, within a few years of Independence, a symbol of corrupt power instead of patriotism and self-sacrifice which it undoubtedly was during the freedom struggle when hundreds of Congressmen gave up their careers and courted imprisonment. During the early fifties, on one of my journeys by rail from Bangalore to Mysore, I was in a small third-class compartment, and at a wayside station, an elderly gentleman dressed in the uniform of a white homespun *kudta* (shirt), dhoti and Gandhi cap, entered our compartment. His clothes indicated that he was a Congress politician, and as soon as he got in, a volley of criticisms were hurled at the Congress. Corruption, the arrogance of power, indifference to people's welfare and many òther sins were laid at its doors. The poor man, a rural landowner turned politician, and perhaps that too only at the district level, was a model of patience and good humour, and he did his best to answer his angry critics. He admitted some misdeeds, explained the difficulties of politicians and bemoaned the villainy of middlemen (*pudaris*). Soon, he had succeeded in establishing a rapport with fellow-passengers, and the atmosphere in the tiny compartment was suddenly transformed into one of friendliness. All the passengers in the compartment were landowners, and I remember one of them, a young Brahmin from a village in Chamarajanagar, lifting his shirt and uncoiling from his waist several *ragi* plants, which had been wound round his dhoti like a belt. He strung out the plants, and measured them against his outstretched arms. They are indeed very tall plants, the tallest we all had seen. He explained that he had journeyed to a village near Bangalore to secure the seeds of this plant for his farm; the *ragi* plant was not only very tall but yielded more grain than other varieties. Everyone, including the Congressman, expressed their admiration for the *ragi*. The Brahmin farmer was delighted.

But I am digressing. The real point I wish to make is that I was taken aback at the swiftness with which the uniform of *khadi* had changed its meaning from self-sacrifice and patriotism to corrupt power. Everyone spoke of Congress *pudaris* and their misdeeds. They were everywhere, in government offices, educational institutions, law courts and hospitals. Along with the yellow press, which had proliferated in the cities, the *pudaris* were among the less savoury concomitants of popular government.

There was, however, a well-known norm, honoured more in the breach than in the observance, that gossiping was bad if not immoral. The saying *madidavara papa adidavara bayalli* (the sinners' sins lodge in the mouths of those who discuss them) was sometimes cited to discourage gossip. There was also the argument of prudence for abstaining from gossip. Everyone had something to hide from the others, and it was wise therefore to keep one's mouth shut. Even worse was the plight of those who pointed to the mote in someone else's eye while ignoring the beam in their own. As the Kannada proverb had it, 'there are holes in everyone's pancakes but in our house, the pan itself has holes' (*ellara mane dose tootadare namma mane kavaliyalle tootu*).

The men who kept to themselves and did not discuss others were praised by everyone including the gossips themselves. Some amount of verbal cannibalism was, however, an integral part of village life and those who kept out of it were respected.

There was a strong feeling that the unpleasant things occurring within a household should not be allowed to leak out. Every large household had its own complicated politics and its share of deviant behaviour, and neighbours and relatives tried to ferret out everything that went on in it. Every head of a household had to put up with hurts and insults from one or more members and learn not to complain about it. They were what was called in local parlance, 'blows delivered inside the veil' (*musukina olagina guddu*). They were poignant, as the blows came from those closest to one, and therefore, could not be discussed even with intimate friends. But when the pressure was too great a man's restraint gave way and he confided in a friend.

While some people were inveterate gossips and a few abstained altogether from gossiping, the others fell in between. The victims of gossip certainly condemned it strongly but that did not prevent the gossips from enjoying gossiping.

ENVY

Envy was a familiar phenomenon. A villager who owned valuable things such as a few acres of wet land, a pair of good bullocks, a milch-buffalo, a gold wristlet or a fountain pen, expected others to envy him and feared such envy. For instance, a villager whose new shirt got an accidental tear soon after it was admired by a friend was likely to remark, half in jest, 'What a foul eye you have! The moment you admired it, it tore'.

The eye (*kannu*) was an important locus of envy. A cow whose milk yield was high had burlap or cloth draped over its middle to conceal the udders from envious eyes. An attractive and intelligent child who evoked appreciative comments from relatives at a wedding or other occasion and became fractious soon after, was said to be suffering from *drishti* (or *kannu biddide*, i.e., someone's eye had fallen) or evil eye. The child's mother or other relative took in each hand a few chillis and salt crystals, took care to close the hands, and then waved them thrice before the child, after which the salt and chilis were thrown into the kitchen stove (*ole*). The chillis gave out an acrid smoke while the salt burnt. If the child became quiet soon after it meant that he (or she) had been really affected by someone's evil eye.

It was a rule of prudence, if not good manners, to refrain from praising another man's crop, orchard, house, cattle or child. For if any mishap followed the praise, the man who praised was certain to be credited with a bad or evil eye. A reputation for possessing an evil eye was no social asset. Everyone hid their valuable or attractive objects from him. Stories about the destructive powers of his eyes would do the rounds in the village, each narrator garnishing and improving the version he had heard.

The stomach (*hotte*) was another seat of envy. The envious experienced 'stomach fire' (*hotte uri*, or *hotte kichchu*) when anything good happened to someone they knew. Villagers frequently spoke of envious people resorting to malicious gossip or unfriendly action. A man whose straw-rick had been burnt down might exclaim, in bitter sarcasm, 'Their stomachs will now cool down' (*avara hotte tannagayitu eega*). The implication was that his straw-rick had attracted the envy of someone and its destruction must have given him satisfaction. Again, when a good bullock broke its leg during the agricultural season, the injured attributed it to someone's envy. He might then recall the latter's comment that the bullocks were fine animals, and that the price that had been paid for them was low. The owner of the bullocks would then reason that his good luck at the cattle fair had attracted the envy of the man in question.

The phenomenon of envy loomed large in the minds of villagers. The 'haves' kept referring to the covetous eyes and burning stomachs of others which resulted in anonymous petitions (*moogarji*) to officials, malicious gossip, lawsuits, and in extreme cases, sorcery (*mata*). I must add, however, that sorcery was only very rarely mentioned, and there was no one in Rampura who had the reputation of being a practitioner of the black art.

One of the Traders in the village, Sappa, was busy constructing a 'modern' house-cum-shop after pulling down his old mud house. The building was of brick and mortar, and the front portion of the ground floor was to provide for two shops, one for groceries and the other for cloth. The rest of the house including the rooms on the first floor, above the shops, provided ample accommodation for Sappa and his family.

Sappa had built his house-cum-shop on the model of Traders' houses in towns. It was the first house in the village to have an upper floor, the first to have brick-and-mortar walls instead of mud ones, and finally, the first to be roofed with factory-made 'Mangalore tiles' instead of tiles made by local Potters. Sappa was not a rich landowner but a poor trader. But according to Sannu and a few others who talked to me, a poor man ought to know his place and stay there. He ought not to aspire to doing things which were beyond him. Tongues started wagging about Sappa's foolishness. Many knew that he was building the house on borrowed money, Rs 3,000 from Millayya and some more from creditors in Mysore. A villager sympathetic to Sappa told me that he had saved some money and that it was not true to say that it was being built entirely on borrowed capital. Anyway, Sannu commented wryly that one of Sappa's creditors would eventually live in the house which he was taking great pains to build. Karagayya, Millayya's younger brother, said that Sappa was building like a townsman, paying for labour, and not like a villager who diverted his tenants and servants to do much of the labour. (He had not taken into account that Sappa was not a landowner with power over his servants and clients but only a Trader.) The village doctor, an inveterate meddler, criticized Sappa for the crest and motto which adorned the wall above the new shops. The crest consisted of two Indian flags, their handles crossing each other, and above them was the motto 'Shri Rama Sahayam', invoking the help of the deity Rama. The doctor told Sappa that it was wrong to mix up the national flag and Rama's name. The doctor was an 'educated' man, an urbanite and Brahmin, and poor Sappa got worried that he had done something wrong. The doctor then went round telling all and sundry what he thought about the Trader's crest. I found the doctor's behaviour childish and annoying, and in my annoyance, it did not occur to me to try and find out why he thought Sappa had done anything wrong. Was it because secular and religious symbols were being mixed up? The doctor may also have shared the widespread envy of Sappa, and also, he knew that the leaders of the village did not like Sappa's building a brick-and-mortar house. Voicing the sentiments of the rich and powerful gave the doctor satisfaction. That it also made him unpopular with ordinary folk did not seem to bother him.

It was envy which made villagers confidently predict that Japi's enterprise would be a failure. Again, envy lay at the root of the allegation made about every landowner that he had bought the land of poor Brahmins. It was true that by and large Brahmins had sold their land, and it had been bought by Peasants, but that was not the same thing as saying that everyone had prospered by buying Brahmin land at distress sales. Anyway, what was so wrong about buying it? How was it worse than charging 25 per cent interest to needy villagers or exploiting the labour of Harijans and very young boys?

A distinction may be made in expressions of envy on the basis of the social distance between the envier and envied. For instance, if one was rich and high caste and the other was poor and low, the latter commented on the meanness and exploitative nature of the former. If the rich man became ill or suffered a loss, then some poor man was bound to comment that 'God had showed [his anger with the rich man]' or 'What had been swallowed has now been vomitted'. When one of Rame Gowda's eyes became infected during the latter half of 1948, Kulle Gowda told me that it was due to the family's black-market activities. Since every landowner had indulged in black-marketing, according to his resources and daring, the selection of one person for punishment seemed invidious. It was only explicable on the ground that the wealth and influence of the Headman's family had attracted widespread envy.

Sometimes, a rich landowner was resentful of a tenant who was on the way up. The tenant had, by dint of hard work and saving over the years, bought a piece of land or built a house, and the landowner was then quick to detect signs of 'impertinence' or 'arrogance' in him. The owner perceived a threat to his future interests in the increasing prosperity of his tenant. The latter was likely to be accused of lacking in loyalty and gratitude, which was certain to drive the two further apart.

Envy from intimates, who were usually caste fellows and relatives, and frequently also peers, presented a more difficult problem. An intimate came home frequently, talked to different members of the household including old women, was invited to share pot luck, and on rare occasions, his advice was sought. At the same time, it was recognized that peers and intimates were given to gossip and envy apart from the possible clash of interests.

All this resulted in an ambivalent attitude towards intimates and equals. They were the people with whom a man relaxed, whose presence and cooperation were essential on occasions such as weddings and funerals but there was need for wariness in dealing with them. Bad news had to be kept from them as they were likely to convey it to everyone, and it was likely to be distorted and exaggerated in the course of circulation. Good news could not be conveyed to them till it was beyond doubt as otherwise they may prevent it from becoming a fact. The relationship between a man and his intimates was a complex one and contained an important streak of conflict.

SENSE OF HUMOUR

A sense of humour was an integral part of Indian village life even though anthropological studies show no evidence of it.

Mr Gorur Ramaswamy Iyengar is one of the leading humorists in Kannada, and his reputation is based entirely on the books he wrote on his beautiful, natal village of Gorur (in Hassan District) on the banks of the river Hemavati, a tributary of the Kaveri. While Mr Iyengar has an unfailing eye for the humorous incident and character, his writings are marked by nostalgia if not sentimentality, and this makes him miss the crudeness and cruelty which frequently flow through rustic humour. For instance, such physical shortcomings as stammering, lameness and muteness were occasionally the subject of 'humorous' comment. A half-wit was engaged in conversation solely for the entertainment his remarks provided to a small group of men who had time hanging on their hands. I have watched Kulle Gowda suddenly leave the work he was doing, to talk to the Rama priest's son-in-law, a man of subnormal intelligence, and whose freedom from any inhibitions in speaking about everyone including his relatives was a source of much amusement.

Kulle Gowda asked him several questions, including one or two about the Rama priest, and the replies sent the small knot of men around into loud guffaws. The Rama priest and Kulle Gowda were old foes, and the latter got some pleasure from the obscenities hurled by the son-in-law at his father-in-law. Kulle Gowda, also asked the son-in-law to carry a message to his former Peasant patron. The latter lived in a nearby hamlet, and Kulle Gowda and he had burnt the candle at both ends when they were much younger.

The damage suffered by an unpopular or unfair person gave widespread satisfaction, and the details of the incident were discussed and then passed on from person to person. Any trivial item of information was picked up and its humorous possibilities fully extracted. I wondered sometimes whether the disputes which occurred frequently were not a source of recreation for the villagers who saw in them welcome departures from the boredom of daily routine.

I remember the case of the widow whom her creditor Gulayya had tried to cheat. Kalamma the widow had borrowed Rs 50 (Rs 5 in cash and the rest in paddy) from Gulayya, and when a year later, her son-in-law took the money to the creditor he was flabbergasted to be asked to pay Rs 150. It had been changed from 50 to 150 and when the creditor was to produce the document it was discovered that the addition was in green ink while the rest of the 'document', a sheet torn from a boy's notebook, was in blue. On seeing the document Kulle Gowda pronounced that there was only one man in the village who used green ink and that that was P. M. Lingayya. The latter was a trouble-maker, much disliked, and his providing proof of his involvement in cheating was relished by many. (Lingayya tried to get out of the awkward situation by saying that while the ink was undoubtedly his, he did not know who had used his pen.)

Both Swamy and Kempu took Kalamma's side against the creditor. This followed Nadu Gowda's advice to Kalamma not to pay the money to Gulayya. Kempu told Kalamma's son-in-law in the presence of Lingayya that the son-in-law and Kempu should split the Rs 50 equally between them and let Gulayya go to a court of law to recover his debt. That he dared not go to a court of law after the attempt to cheat was known and relished by all. Gulayya's patron had roundly abused him for trying to cheat a poor widow, and this also got to be known. It was said that Gulayya's clumsy attempt at forgery was prompted by the desire to please his mistress, who was related to Kalamma and hated her. The news of the liaison, and Gulayya's stupidity in putting himself in a position where he could be sued for cheating, his suddenly taking fright and trying to hide all documents with him out of a fear of police investigation, all caused much merriment.

However, village humour was not always tainted by cruelty. The general admiration for Mrs Karim's debating abilities, for instance, was the tribute which ordinary folk paid to virtuosity of no mean order. Some of the admiration was due to the fact that a woman, and a Muslim at that, was able to assert herself before an assembly of men which included the Headman. It was a striking reversal of the role expected of the sexes, and it appealed to the villagers' sense of the absurd. The same reversal of roles occurred when the Harijan Pijja tied his Lingayat master in knots before the village elders. His cleverness at argument, quick repartee and penchant for apt simile or metaphor, were all admired. Talent and virtuosity were always praised, and more so when found in unlikely places.

That the villagers' sense of humour was a genuine one was revealed by their ability to laugh at themselves on occasion. This was brought home to me on several occasions. Once Virabhadra complained loudly to me about someone who had stolen vegetables from his vegetable patch (*menasi madi*). I told him that there should be deterrent punishment for vegetable-stealers. Virabhadra, who had a contrary streak in him, asserted that it could not be done. When a man was caught red-handed he was likely to say that he helped himself to a few vegetables as he was in urgent need and could not find the owner. Had he found the owner, he certainly would have asked his permission first. Virabhadra then explained to me that it was not just anyone who stole. A farmer took vegetables usually from someone well known to him. Taking vegetables from each other was therefore a sign of intimacy. As I heard Virabhadra explain, his original complaint appeared to me to be pitched in a high key if not altogether absurd. The same realization dawned on Virabhadra, and his dark round face split into a wide grin, his ear-rings offering a strange contrast to his impressive moustache. He had stalked into my veranda bursting with anger against the unknown thief only to depart like a boy who had had his hands suddenly stuffed with sweets.

Even the grave and silent Headman rarely missed an opportunity of teasing M. H. Chenna, the Shepherd leader who was probably the Headman's senior by a few years. He was not overwhelmed by the Headman and this made possible the exchange of badinage between them. Chenna's grown sons had separated from him and were living with their wives. As the Marnoumi approached, Chenna planned to buy a ram at the Saturday market in Kirgavalu to be sacrificed for the meal (*ede*) in honour of his dead father. Chenna asked his sons to share the price of the ram as each of them was getting a share of the sacrificed meat. But the sons refused: it was Chenna's duty to offer a mutton dish to his dead father and *not* theirs. Their turn to offer a sacrifice would come only after Chenna's death and not before. This was sound logic indeed though it did not seem to me appropriate to confront a living father with. The Headman and Nadu Gowda admired the sons' logic and laughed heartily. Chenna soon joined them, and if anything, his laughter was heartier than that of the other two. Chenna had a big hooked nose, pointed chin, and his mouth was in a recess between the two. He had several teeth missing and as he laughed, he looked like a Walt Disney cartoon.

On another occasion, Chenna narrated an incident in his household which shocked me, though he and his friends, the Headman and Nadu Gowda, regarded it as highly amusing. The fact that Chenna did not get along well with his wife was known to his close friends. This was responsible for his absence from Rampura for several weeks early in 1948 when he lived with his Vaishnavite guru in T. G. Koppalu, a hamlet seven miles away. Chenna found peace with his Guru and some of the peace might have come from marijuana-smoking to which the guru and his followers resorted occasionally.

On the occasion referred to above, the Headman teased Chenna about his wife complaining to her friends about his still being a 'boy' (*hudugu*). I did not catch the meaning but later I was told that while Chenna continued to be ardent his wife thought they were too old for sex. Their sons and daughters were adult and married.

Chenna's urban son-in-law was visiting the village at that time and Mrs Chenna was solicitous of his needs, a fact which only exacerbated her husband's annoyance. To please her sophisticated son-in-law, Mrs Chenna made an urban, middle-class breakfast for him comprising *uppittu*, a savoury dish with broken wheat, and coffee. She took the hot breakfast to her husband who asked her what it was. When she answered him, he told her to pour the breakfast down her vulva. Chenna narrated all this calmly and cheerfully. The Headman and Nadu Gowda burst into loud guffaws on listening to this piece of conjugal dialogue, and as usual, Chenna joined his friends in the laughter. The three old men, laughing for all they were worth, in the middle of the street presented indeed an odd spectacle. I was the only quiet one and I was not certain whether it was proper for me to show my appreciation of Chenna's sense of humour. The guffawing old men were oblivious of the attention they were attracting from passers-by. It was very unusual to see the Headman so cheerful.

Even the poorest and oppressed villagers were not without a sense of humour. I cannot easily forget the laughter and the barbed humour of the Headman's *jita* servants whom I saw every day for at least a few hours, and some of whom slept on the cowhouse veranda. While it was true that the laughter was more marked among the boys, even the older men, excepting for Mada, had their lighter moments. Savukana Ninga was an old Harijan and he had spent his entire life as a *jita* servant. Unremitting labour in all seasons and weathers coupled with continued hunger and malnutrition had so emaciated his body that it was a bag of skin and bones. He had a sharp, knife-like face with a hooked nose, and I can recall his leathery, unshaven, white-bristled face even now. Ninga narrated a few incidents from his life, and his humour stood out sharply against a background of poverty, misery and oppression.

One hot summer morning when I was walking along the CDS Canal, about thirty feet to the north of the bridge on the Mysore–Hogur road, I saw several workers, men and women, engaged in digging up silt to enable the smooth flow of water when water was let in, in June. This was an annual summer activity and it, like road repair, provided employment to some villagers during the leanest part of the year.

I stopped near the workers and started focussing my camera on them. One woman, who was carrying a basket of earth on her head, and perspiring freely in the sun, commented, 'Had we known that we were going to be photographed, we would have worn our good saris'. The comment provoked loud laughter. Villagers invariably wore their best clothes for the camera but they were not ideal for canal-digging!

A few men in the village were known for their freedom from normal inhibitions when talking to some women. Karim cracked loud jokes with the Harijan women who worked regularly for the Headman. Sannu, the priest, was another and he was, on occasion, extremely obscene. For instance, he and Chari, the accountant, ran into Oilwoman Loki, sitting by the road and selling fried *Vades*. Sannu sat down and started teasing her. He asked her about the functions of each part of the female genitalia. After a while Loki got annoyed and said, 'Oh Priest, does your bottom itch?' The question was a warning to Sannu to shut up.

Kulle Gowda had a dry wit but it showed itself only with his equals and inferiors. When he was teased, he came out with a profanity or obscenity, or an astringent observation that amused those around him.

He was also one of those men who talked freely to women though he did not go as far as Sannu.

A sense of humour probably enabled the poor and exploited to accept the conditions under which they were living, and it may also have been a substitute for more destructive expressions of inter-personal violence. But it is also possible that I am giving it far more importance than it really had. Another sociologist less desiccated and more compassionate might have given it a much less prominent place. And it is even possible that had I stayed among the Harijans instead of with the Peasants, I would have accorded a lower place to humour in village life. But as I write these lines I recall that Pijja and Savukane Ninga, both of whom were Harijans, had a keen sense of humour.

Religion

INTRODUCTION

Foreign travellers, missionaries and administrators who have written on Indian religion have concentrated, by and large, on the exotic and sensational elements in it such as the multiplicity of deities, their bloodthirstiness and cruelty, fantastic shapes and forms, and their immorality; on the outlandish beliefs and customs, excessive ritualism and wasteful expenditure at weddings and funerals; and finally, on the sense of hopelessness, despair and fatalism, induced by the endless round of birth and rebirth. Westernized Indians have been, as a rule, critics and reformers of folk religion, and with rare exceptions, have dismissed it as 'superstition'. One hundred and fifty years of sustained attack on their traditional culture and religion have put westernized Indians permanently on the defensive. This led to among other things, an emphasis on those aspects of culture and religion which presented a 'good' image of India to foreigners and a denigration if not repudiation of the other aspects. Even attempts at reform seem to have been reinforced by a desire to present a decent cultural shop-window to foreigners.

The efflorescence in Indological research in the nineteenth century also led indirectly to downgrading folk religion. The translation of Indian scriptures and philosophical literature into English and other

European languages, and the excitement which they caused in western academic circles, brought considerable satisfaction to educated Indians. An overemphasis on the scriptural-theological dimension of Hinduism and its sects was the natural result.

Yet another factor worked towards the ignoring of folk religion. Educated Indians, by and large, hailed from the higher castes, and they had a built-in prejudice against ritual involving the bloody slaughter of animals, consumption of native, low-status liquor, and of fire-walking, hook-swinging and other cruel customs. It is not surprising that their accounts of religion underplayed these features and highlighted those which were flattering to the national ego.

If any category of scholars could have redressed the balance in favour of folk religion it ought to have been Indian anthropologists and sociologists. But unfortunately their success in this has not been conspicuous. For one thing, the study of religion did not become fashionable in the two disciplines until recent years. And even now religion is important only in the relation it bears, largely negative though, to two concerns which are felt to be paramount to developing countries; economic development and modernization. Further, leading Indian anthropologists and sociologists profess to be rationalists. In brief, the prevalent academic climate has not been conducive to treating folk religion seriously.

I have stated earlier that I had a visceral aversion to watching the spilling of blood, and to ritual involving cruelty to man and beast. But I was aware of my prejudices and considered them deficiencies in one wanting to study a sub-culture different from his own in some respects. But I did have an interest in ritual and religion though I wish I had had the time to make more systematic observations than I was able to. Above all, I had a deep respect for the religion of the people, and I had no desire to change it. When I examined my own faith, I found that it contained many elements which were present in the people's, and I did not regard this as something that I should be ashamed of.

Much has been said by foreign observers on the crippling effects, for individual and social endeavour, of the fatalistic ideology of Indians, in particular of rural folk. I wonder whether 'fatalism' did indeed have such effects on nineteenth-century Indians, but if my own experience of Rampura in 1948 is any guide, it was likely that the foreign observers had misunderstood the part played by 'fatalism'. It came in handy usually as an explanation of a disaster that had already occurred and not as inhibiting present or future action. For instance, when a villager had lost a bullock at the height of the agricultural season, or his wife had died suddenly leaving behind young children, and then he or his friends explained his misfortune by reference to *karma* or *hane baraha. Karma* was only very occasionally used in its ordinary sense, viz. the kind of deeds a person performed in a particular incarnation (*janma*) determined the pattern of his life in the next. *Hane baraha*, the idea that what was written (by Brahma or fate) on the forehead would come to pass, was again used with reference to past events. I did not hear any villagers talking about Brahma, the Creator, recording each man's future on his forehead as soon as he was born, but a sudden misfortune or combination of misfortunes invariably prompted someone to refer to the 'writing on the forehead'.

Misfortunes were only too frequent in village India. The villager's pitiful resources, economic and intellectual, and his continuous struggles with the forces, natural and human, ranged against him, made him a frequent victim of disaster. The lack of any medical attention coupled with the total ignorance of the rules of sanitation made childbirth hazardous, and their frequent epidemics which carried off large numbers of people gave a chancy character to life. If to this were added undependable rains, insects and other pests, and vermin, extortionate landowners, usurious moneylenders and corrupt officials, we get an idea of the risks faced by farmers in growing a crop and the demands they had to meet. It was indeed a miracle that they managed to survive.

Living by immemorial custom offered a sense of security to the villagers but this was not without a price. Strict conformity was demanded from everyone, and the non-conformist who dared to violate custom ran the risk of being ostracized. Ostracism was particularly harsh in a small, face-to-face community where everyone knew everyone else. The community was also linked by agnatic, affinal, economic and other ties with neighbouring villages so that news travelled quickly along established networks.

Individuals were expected to spend as lavishly as they could on such occasions as weddings and funerals. The rich had naturally to spend far more than the poor. Failure to do so meant accusations of meanness or impiety. While tight-fistedness was the rule in everyday life, it had no place at weddings and funerals. The above norms were built into a villager from very early in life and internalized. Individuals were powerless to alter the value-system of the community. It could change, if at all, only as a result of the impact of powerful external forces as, for instance, when the leaders of the village introduced a few reforms in the thirties.

It is pointless to blame individual villagers for indulging in wasteful if not suicidal expenditure at weddings and funerals. It is understandable for foreign observers to be struck by the 'irrationality' of such behaviour but the same cannot be said of westernized Indians who are themselves given to wasteful expenditure at weddings and funerals.

The villagers were heirs to a rich and complex religious life. The richer households among the Peasants usually had a more Sanskritized style of life than their poorer caste-fellows and this meant that they spent more time and money on their religious duties.

It is difficult to characterize the complexity of the religious life of villagers beyond stating that there was a multitude of deities and festivals, and that life-cycle crises were marked by rituals, which were sometimes elaborate as at marriage and death. The deities included gods as well as goddesses, some of whom demanded blood-sacrifices. The calendrical festivals were common to the region while some of them had even an all-India spread. The festivals of village deities were, on the other hand, purely local in character, and they generally lasted several days, and were frequently characterized by blood-sacrifices and by the performance of *pavadas* or 'miracles' in which the priest or other participant became possessed by the deity and answered questions.

There were also pilgrimages to the shrines of 'house deities', and to the great centres of Sanskritic Hinduism in south India.

Finally, no account of village religion would be complete without a brief reference to the phenomenon of possessions by deities and spirits (*gali*).

As stated above, marriage and death were marked by elaborate and complex ritual. Marriage itself began with the search for a bride and ended only when the wife joined her husband for good. Each step in this process was regulated by custom and interwoven with ritual. Mourning ritual began with death and ended only on the thirteenth day when a feast was given to relatives. The dead man (or woman) joined the body of apotheosized ancestors who were propitiated annually during the 'ancestors' fortnight' (*pitru paksha*) prior to the Dasara festival while among the Brahmins and a few other castes, the annual propitiation was on the anniversary of the actual day of death. The ritual surrounding birth ended on the eleventh day when pollution ended for everyone except the mother. The puberty of a girl resulted in her becoming impure for fifteen days at the end of which she was dressed in her best sari and jewellery, and made to sit on a wooden plank while women relatives performed some ritual, sang songs and offered her sweets and other good things to eat. As it was usual among the higher castes to have girls married before they came of age, consummation took place a few weeks after puberty. An auspicious day was selected by the astrologer for the ceremony, and relatives and friends were invited to a pre-consummation feast. The groom left his wife's bedside early in the morning, and stole away quietly to his house, without seeing any member of his wife's household.

There were variations between castes in life-cycle ritual, Brahmins, Lingayats and other Sanskritized castes spending more time and money on ritual than the others. The life of Brahmins in particular was permeated with ritual. Every Brahmin household had a domestic altar where *puja* was performed before the morning meal was eaten. Every adult Brahmin had to perform certain ritual acts daily (*nitya karma*), and besides, even acts like shaving, bathing, eating, defecating and urinating were accompanied by ritual. During the last few decades, however, the process of secularization had gone far enough to reduce the time spent on ritual as also the hold of ideas regarding purity and pollution. In 1948, for instance, of the three Brahmins in Rampura only the Rama priest lived like a Brahmin. The other two were preoccupied with their jobs. However, I should be surprised if they did not worship at the domestic altar every day before the morning meal.

I have discussed the ideas of purity (*madi*) and pollution (*mailige*) in my account of inter-caste relations. But these two linked ideas are also important in analyzing life-cycle and daily ritual. But I shall not consider them here as I have discussed them at some length in my Coorg book,[1] and they apply more or less fully to the situation in Rampura.

The division of labour between the sexes expressed itself in ritual also. For instance, women cleaned the domestic altar and *puja* vessels, prepared the food or other articles to be offered to the deities, and lit the lamps while the men performed the actual worship. This was particularly true of worship which was complex and lengthy among the Sanskritized castes. The priests, both those who were in charge of temples and the specialists in life-cycle ritual, were always men.

Older men and women were usually more ritual-bound than the younger, and the presence of an old woman in a household meant its

---

[1] *Religion and Society among the Coorgs of South India*, Clarendon Press, Oxford, 1952, pp. 101–22.

adherence to a traditional mode of life. There were several old women in Rampura like the Headman's mother. The women adhered more closely to the rules of pollution and purity than the men, and the kitchen, which usually included the domestic altar, was the heart of the purity-pollution system. The women kept the men on the pollution track, and this was probably related to the fact that the social world of women was synonymous with the household and kinship group while the men inhabited a more heterogeneous world.

The subject of the complexity of village religion cannot be complete without a reference, however brief, to its 'underworld', viz. sorcery and witchcraft. Rampura in 1948 did not have a single sorcerer or witch though I did hear people citing the instances of individuals who had sought to acquire supernatural powers by spending nights in grave-yards, digging up corpses, sitting on them and performing gory rites. But these were only stories which they had heard from someone or the other and no one in the village practised them. However, the bulldozer driver who was levelling the Headman's land in the summer of 1952 was a practitioner of the black art. He even gave a black magic performance just as the wandering group of Garudigas had done in the summer of 1948. The bulldozer driver was a Tamil non-Brahmin. His powers so impressed the second son of the Basava priest, a maverick, that he enlisted himself as a pupil. Modern machinery had also brought black magic to Rampura. (Students of modernization only emphasize the machine.)

THE MANY KINDS OF DEITIES

The villagers propitiated a wide variety of deities from the high gods and goddesses of all-India Hinduism in their various manifestations, incarnations and identifications to local ones presiding over epidemics such as smallpox, cholera and plague, and others who had an intimate association with lineages and households. Indeed, the number and variety of deities seemed bewildering at first sight but was much less so if they were grouped into a few categories on the basis of well-recognized principles.

There was specialization among the deities and the degree of specialization varied from deity to deity. For instance, the deities presiding over epidemics were the most specialized of all and they were propitiated elaborately during epidemics or at their periodical festivals. It was their job to protect the village from the epidemics in return for propitiation. Before modern public health measures reached the villages, epidemics were frequent, killing substantial numbers. The generic name for the deity presiding over epidemics was Mari though she was also occasionally known by other names such as Kali. The Maris of different villages were distinguished by prefixing the village name to Mari. Thus the Mari of Kere village was known as *Kere Mari*. Sometimes she was merely referred to as *amma* or 'mother'.

As described elsewhere, the rains, their occurrence at proper times and in proper quantities, as well as their failure, were a most important preoccupation of the villagers. Basava was the deity primarily concerned with rains since he was responsible for the welfare of cattle. Madeshwara of Gudi also came into the picture probably because he was regarded as very powerful. He was prayed to to ensure the safe delivery of cows. This function was perhaps derived from the fact that the main Madeshwara temple in Kollegal *taluk* was a centre for cattle trade during the four calendrical festivals (Shivaratri, Ugadi, Dasara and Deepavali) when villagers from far and wide flocked to it.

Other deities were also prayed to during a drought. The fact of caste was also relevant in this context, and I expect that Brahmins worried by the drought would pray to Rama or some other Sanskritic deity. In a grave crisis they would have the arduous *parjanya japa* performed by a group of Brahmins proficient in the ritual.

The continuity of the household was also of supreme concern to the villagers. This required that the women coming in by marriage were fertile and that the children born to them survived into adulthood and kept reasonable health. Without the household surviving, the family farm would lie fallow, thus underlining the link between human and chthonic fertility. One of the worst curses in the armoury of a villager, was 'May the *ekka* (*arka, Calatropis gigantea*) grow on your house'. The plant grew wild and one of the signs of a decayed house was the sprouting of the *ekka* plants all over the abandoned site. A more direct and less symbolic form of the curse was, 'May your house come to an end'.

Another category of deities concerned with the well being of the household (and lineage) were the 'house deities' (*mane devaru*). I shall consider them later and rest content here with stating that if the 'house deities' proved unhelpful, the villagers approached any deity who they thought was likely to help. This kind of situation provided a door for the introduction of new deities, cults, and even of sanyasis, gurus, and charlatans who promised all sorts of benefits. I have referred repeatedly to the popularization, since the 1930s, of the cult of Tirupati Srinivasa.

Again, in the neighbouring village of Kere I saw what was perhaps the beginnings of the cult of Sathyanarayana. This deity was popular over a great part of India, and propitiating him regularly by reading an account of his doings was believed to benefit the devotee both materially and spiritually.

Each temple in the village had a special association with a particular caste or group of castes. The Basava and Madeshwara temples, for instance, had Lingayats for priests, and attracted devotees from non-Brahmin castes. The latter part of the statement is, however, subject to two qualifications: Harijans were excluded from the temples of caste Hindus and castes which were staunch followers of Vishnu had either nominal or no association with the Basava and Madeshwara temples which were Shaivite. There were at least three non-Brahmin castes which had a Vaishnavite orientation: one tiny household of Oshtama which traditionally supplied priests to Anjaneya (or Hanuman) temples; the Trader households which had as their lineage-deity Narasimha (half-man, half-lion), an incarnation (*avatara*)[2] of Vishnu, and finally, the Swineherds who had Srinivasa of Tirupati as their lineage-deity.

The division into Shaiva and Vaishnava sects was sharper in south India than in the north, and was found at different levels of the caste system. Among Brahmins, the Sri Vaishnavas (popularly called Iyengars) and Madhwas were both exclusive devotees of Vishnu while, among non-Brahmins, the Lingayats were exclusive devotees of Shiva. (Not long ago, orthodox Iyengars used to boast that they had never stepped into a Shiva temple.) Even when a whole caste or a section of it were not followers of a sect, individual households could develop an affiliation to a sect either directly or indirectly. Thus attachment to the Madeshwara temple resulted in increased contact with Lingayat priests, gurus and a Shaivite life-style, while association with a temple to Narasimha meant usually increased contact with Iyengar (or Madhwa) priests and a Vaishnavite life-style. Individuals from every non-Brahmin caste were free to join either the Vaishnavite mendicant order of Dasayya or Shaivite order of Jogayya. I shall discuss this later.

At the main village temple to Mari the priest (*gudda*) was a Peasant. (As mentioned elsewhere, the Harijans had a separate temple for Mari at which one of their castemen was priest.) This temple, like certain

[2] The deity Vishnu, who has the role of protector in the Hindu pantheon, incarnated himself repeatedly to crush evil forces which assumed the form of demons. Incarnations are not, however, confined to the mythic past: the pious believe that they occur whenever evil increases.

others in the village, was really active only on a few days in the year when a votive or other propitiation was taking place or a regular festival was being held. For instance, the Mari temple at Rampura did not have an elaborate annual festival as at the Mari temple in Kere but was only propitiated when an epidemic of smallpox, chickenpox or cholera was about. In addition, any household in which a child was affected with chickenpox took the child to the temple after recovery, and worshipped the deity.

The duties of the priest in any one of these temples were not particularly onerous except very occasionally. Ordinarily the priest was expected to keep the earthen lamp in the *sanctum sanctorum* lit every evening or on a particular day in the week, considered sacred to the deity. Sometimes, on the weekly sacred day, the priest was expected to have a bath, change into washed clothes and worship the deity before having his morning meal. I do not know how scrupulously such rules were observed in each case but I am certain that not every priest obeyed the rules expected of him. For instance, I do not remember the earthen lamp in the Mari temple being lit except on a few rare occasions, and it was in some ways an important temple. In this respect, the Madeshwara, Basava and Rama temples were different. The priests had to perform *puja* every morning and evening, though they, if they wanted to, abbreviated the service, and skimped on the offerings to be made. It may be recalled here that each grower gave the priest of each of the temples a headload of rice-in-the-straw and this was to ensure that the daily offerings were kept going everywhere. An honest priest offered a rice-dish every day to his deity, and he distributed at least some of it to the devotees present. Villagers felt that not only was the deity being deprived of something which was his due but the villagers of their share. Only at festivals and other special occasions was cooked food offered on a big scale but then additional collections were made for them. Here again, ordinary villagers complained of the meanness of priests who distributed minuscule portions to poorer devotees while taking care to send sizeable parcels to the leaders. The rule of reciprocity was being broken everywhere: between man and god, and between the priests and the villagers. I have a feeling that I heard complaints only about the Rama priest partly because villagers resented the attention which he paid to his land, and which, they believed, was at the expense of his other duties. On the other hand, the idea of Lingayat priests cultivating land did not appear grotesque.

The God's House lineage had a shrine to their tutelary deities in their ward, and an old member of the lineage was priest at the shrine. The deities had a reputation for fierceness and the priest was particular about bathing every day and lighting the lamps in the shrine.

The Rama temple had been endowed with two or three acres of rice land (far less than either the Madeshwara or Basava temple) and the priest had built for himself a hut on the vacant ground opposite the temple. The Rama Navami, marking the birth of the deity, was the most important of the annual festivals celebrated in the temple. It was next in importance only to the annual *jatra* of Madeshwara at Deepavali which attracted thousands of devotees from dozens of villages, and which brought in a considerable amount of money to the villagers in various ways. The priests were of course the biggest beneficiaries from the fair.

While in the old village the Rama temple had a close association with the Brahmins living in the *agrahara*, in 1948 it was the Peasant leaders who were in charge of it. They had raised the money to rebuild it: it was the most handsome building in the village, and it must have taken a few years to build it. The Headman and Nadu Gowda personally supervised the collection of contributions, in cash and kind, for the Ugadi and Rama Navami festivals. The priest was aware of his dependence on the two leaders, in particular the Headman. If the priest was tolerated in the village it was because of the Headman and Nadu Gowda.

It is likely that when the village had several households of Brahmins, some of whom were rich and influential, they controlled the Rama temple. But after their exodus to the cities, the temple came completely under the authority of the Peasant leaders, and its linkage with Brahmins was snapped.

The Madeshwara temple belonged really to Gudi people but as Gudi was a 'dry' and poor village, the priests had sought the patronage of the powerful leaders of Rampura. Sannu narrated to me how his grandfather moved from the tiny, ancestral hamlet of Chaudhary Koppal, located to the north of Gudi, to Rampura when the Headman's father was a young man. The latter agreed to their staying in Rampura and allotted them a site. Sannu told me that his grandfather heard the growl of a tiger at night during the first few nights of his arrival. Madeshwara rode a tiger, and the growls were interpreted as an auspicious symbol. The main temple of Madeshwara (of which the Gudi temple was an imitation) was situated in dense jungle, and the association of tiger and cobra with the awe-inspiring deity was only appropriate. But paradoxically the deity who rode a tiger, and whose hair was adorned by a coiling cobra, was also a protector of cattle. I did not inquire whether this came from the identification of Madeshwara with Shiva whose 'vehicle' is a bull (Nandi), or because of the cattle fairs held at the deity's festival, or because of both.

The linkage between Bire *devaru* (or Birappa, as he was popularly called) and the Shepherds was an intimate one, and the favourite animal for sacrificing to him was sheep. (Another way of stating the relationship was sheep: Shepherd: Birappa.) Periodical festivals lasting several days at which elaborate ritual was performed, were held in honour of Birappa, and the Birappas of a region formed a hierarchy. Once in several years, a festival was held in which all of them were involved, and the ritual, which was even more elaborate than the festivals of individual deities, reflected the hierarchy. A sharp sense of protocol between the deities characterized the festival which was in some ways like a drama, the processions of two deities meeting and then going to meet a third and so on.

There were temples to Birappa in neighbouring villages though not in Rampura. One of my neighbours, a very old man, was a priest (*gudda*) at one such temple. He was referred to as *Devaraguddayya* (literally, 'god's priest'), and he cooked his own food because he was a vegetarian while his daughter and her husband, with whom he stayed, were not. I used to see the old man, returning home in the evening after a day's work on the farm, with a headload of *jowar* stalks on his head. He was a man of few words, and he was respected for his vegetarianism and teetotalism. His only luxury was chewing betel leaves and nuts, which must have been an effort, for some of his front teeth had dropped out. Even though twenty-six years have passed, I can still recall his face, with its steel-grey, walrus moustache, lined with age and unremitting work and shining with sweat as he walked up, single-mindedly, to his house.

I have referred earlier to the discrimination to which the Smiths were traditionally subjected in this region. The caste deity of the Smiths was Kali, usually referred to as Kalamma, and only in towns or large villages in which they were represented in large numbers were there temples to her. (There was a Kali temple in Mysore, for instance.) Traditionally, Smith marriages were performed either at pilgrim-centres or in Kali temples.

Rampura, like most other villages in the region, did not have a Kali temple. But a few at least of the traditional disabilities had vanished as, for instance, was evidenced in the Headman's households treating Smith and Brahmin married women on an equal footing during the Rama Navami festival.

Other castes in the village which did not have temples of their own were the Traders, Swineherds and Basket-makers. The last-mentioned were really temporary immigrants who were expected to return to their home-town after spending a few years in Rampura. They seemed to be Vaishnavites in the sense that they were devotees of Srinivasa at Tirupati. The Swineherds had spent a much longer period in Rampura than the Basket-makers, and also many households from other castes, but, for reasons mentioned earlier, they seemed marginal to village social life. They had come from Telugu-speaking areas adjacent to Bangalore, and if their names were any indication to their faith, they were Vaishnavites. The Traders were integral to the village economy and society and they were all Vaishnavites, the men colourfully indicating their allegiance by decorating their foreheads, every morning, with *namam*. Their names suggested that their 'house-deity' was Narasimha.

As stated earlier, the association of a caste or group of castes with a deity did not prevent them from seeking the aid of some other deity when it was necessary or expedient to do so. Thus during a smallpox epidemic everyone, including Brahmins, sent their offerings to Mari. I was told of Brahmins even making animal sacrifices to Mari through their non-Brahmin friends, though I personally did not come across any instance of it. I was also told of Muslims who sent votive offerings of milk and buttermilk to Madeshwara in thanks for the safe calving of their cows. Similarly Hindus, even urban, educated Hindus, visited the graves of Muslim *pirs* in the hope of having their wishes granted.

Castes whose temples were located outside the village did also develop an allegiance, over a period of time, to local deities and temples. It is here that the tendency of Hinduism to add any number of new deities to the list already worshipped, proved so convenient. Gradually, over the decades, the links with old deities became weakened as it happened with old friends with whom interaction had ceased. But when a member of the family died suddenly or fell seriously ill, or there was a series of inexplicable disasters, then an old man or woman in the kinship group asked the rhetorical question. 'What else could be expected when new water flushed out the old water, and old gods were no longer worshipped?' The afflicted family then visited the neglected deities, begged their pardon for long neglect. Old ties were renewed.

But when a caste had strong sectarian loyalties, or the basis of its formation was sectarian as with Lingayats, Sri Vaishnavas and Madhwas, there was a built-in resistance to worshipping deities from another sect. Similarly, Brahmins had resistance to worshipping deities to which animals were sacrificed, and high non-Brahmins to deities who not only demanded meat but liquor. And, of course, caste Hindus did not worship a deity associated with Harijans exclusively.

THE CHARACTER OF THE DEITIES

Deities differed from each other not only in their functions but in their personalities and character. This was particularly seen in the contrast between the mild, vegetarian deity Rama and the fierce Mari who was traditionally propitiated with the sacrifice of bull buffaloes. (Indeed, in those parts of South India where the male buffalo was not used as a draught animal, its only use was to be decapitated before Mari.) The villagers were so scared of Mari during an epidemic that they prayed to her to leave them and go away.

The propitiation of Mari during the hot summer months was called *tampu ereyuvudu* (cooling her). Her shrine was decorated with *margosa* (*Melia azadirachta*) twigs, and the margosa was well known for cool shade during summer. Married women (or virgins) carried trays each containing a green coconut (*elnir*), *kalasha* (a brass vessel containing some water whose mouth was stoppered with a coconut and a few betel leaves placed between the nut and vessel's rim) and *tambittu* (a dish of rice-flour sweetened with jaggery) and a set of betel leaves and arecanuts. Frequently, a hollow was scooped out in the flattened top of the rice-flour pyramid and filled with *ghi* in which a cotton wick was inserted and lit. This kind of lamp was generally made in fulfillment of a vow (*harake*), and the members of the household each ate a piece of the votive flour after the wick had burnt down.

Mari roused in her devotees craven fear and not love, and this fear rose to terror when an epidemic was actually on. Tradition-minded villagers afflicted with smallpox or cholera refused to take any allopathic medicine for fear that it would anger the deity further. Margosa twigs were kept near the patient, he was fanned with them, and after he had recovered, the leaves were put into the cauldron in which water was heated for his bath. It was only after this purificatory bath that he visited Mari's temple to express thanks for his recovery. Mari was indeed an odd kind of 'mother' (*amma, avva, tayi*), one who killed her offspring right and left when she was angry with them. Mari was a different kind of mother from the human mother.

The villagers were afraid of not only Mari and other deities who demanded blood-sacrifices, but even of some vegetarian deities. For instance, Madeshwara evoked respect bordering on fear from his devotees. He was a celibate and misogynist. According to local tradition, the original site of the temple in Gudi was much higher than it is now, and the tower of the Chamundeshwari temple cresting the hill in Mysore was visible from there. Madeshwara was so incensed at the sight of that offensive tower that he pressed the land down into a hollow from which it was invisible.[3]

Before World War II, pilgrimages to the main Madeshwara temple, in Kollegal Taluk in Mysore district, were undertaken on foot. Villagers trekked across miles of dense jungle in long convoys during the pilgrimage season. They had to carry their food with them, and drinking water was difficult to find. They had to be in a state of purity, and sex relations were tabooed during the pilgrimage. Husband and wife were required to address each other as 'brother' and 'sister', and women who expected to be in their 'periods' before the journey had been completed did not undertake the pilgrimage.

I must digress here briefly. At various places in the book I have stressed the great hold Madeshwara had over the minds of villagers in Mysore and Mandya districts. The simple yet total faith which they had in the deity, and the risks they took in undertaking the pilgrimage to his main shrine—and many of them went every year— were most impressive. And the Madeshwara cult was the source of an ethic and world-view which was contrary to the villagers' natural acceptance of the biological dimension of life. (There were similar cults elsewhere in south India, Shasta's in Kerala being an outstanding example.) This means that villagers were subjected to two contrary value pulls, one propelling them towards the total acceptance of the bodily appetites, and another, away from them. Hence the deep reverence in village culture—indeed in Indian culture as a whole—to the sanyasi, or holy man who had conquered his bodily appetites. Bodily processes symbolized and limited the human condition while conquering them was a mark of divinity.

The kind of relation that obtained between Madeshwara and the villagers was illustrated in an incident which occurred in the summer of 1952 when a new *teru* (elaborate wooden chariot in which the deity was taken out in procession at festivals and other special occasions) was being built. Much energy was spent in searching for the right kind of

---

[3] The Sanskritic identification of the jungle deity of Madeshwara is neither complete nor clear. If it were complete, the goddess Chamundi (a manifestation of Parvati) would be his wife.

wood, and of course, at the cheapest possible price, and Sannu's older cousin, Thammayya, whose turn it was to be priest for the year, went round likely villages in his search of timber. He ended up by buying a big tree in Ganjam, and I shall pass over the problems of felling it and cutting its branches to suitable lengths and hauling them to the temple site. A carpenter with the necessary skill was brought in from another village for making the *teru*. But he had to have assistants, and Virachari, a local Smith, was asked to help him. He was an old man, and he had been running a temperature. At least, that was what he told Sannu's cousin when he was asked to assist the master-carpenter. But he nonetheless presented himself at the temple on the following morning. And he had a tale to tell. He found himself waking up before dawn, shivering and perspiring, for he had felt the sharp swish of a thin cane (*chadi*) across his back. He took some time to realize that it was only a dream but that did not help in preventing him from shivering with fright. He concluded that Madappa (that was how the deity was ordinarily referred to by the villagers) had been angry at his reluctance to turn up for work on the *teru*. He told all this to me later in the evening and I could sense the fear on his face even as he recalled the swish of the cane on his bare back.

The deity Srinivasa of Tirupati, to whom the richer villagers were fast developing an allegiance, had also a reputation for sternness. A promise made to him had to be kept and he did not treat broken promises lightly. He also granted favours to those who believed in him.

In contrast to Mari and Madeshwara, Basava was a mild deity. I do not have in mind here the fact that he was incapable of controlling his lecherous priest as such a charge could also be levelled at some other deities with a reputation for extreme sternness. (Indeed, in the wider society as a whole the corruption, cynicism and greed of priests was a part of the folklore.) I have in mind the villagers' belief that Basava had migrated to a temple in a village across the river because of anger over the priest's conduct. Basava had done a similar thing a few years previously. Going away from a place because one was angry was more typical of women than men, and that the symbol of unbridled masculinity, the bull, should behave like that only sharpened the paradox.

The sanction at the disposal of Basava was withholding rain but even here his was not a case of exclusive jurisdiction as, for instance, Mari's was over epidemics. Madeshwara, and even Rama, could be appealed to for rain.

However, Basava was not entirely without a stern element in him. I was told that during a cholera epidemic, several people heard, late in the night, the ringing of a cow bell and the sound of the ground being pawed by a bull to the accompaniment of angry snorts. A few men got up from their beds and went out to investigate the matter. Nowhere did they sight a bull. In the morning, they compared notes and concluded that Basava was angry and had to be propitiated.

I do not think a deity who was totally devoid of sternness could have won the allegiance of villagers. He was most likely to be ignored.

I must here refer to the concept of 'satya' (literally, truth) as applied to deities. A deity who answered the devotee's prayer had *satya*. I generally heard it mentioned in positive contexts and not in negative ones. That is, such-and-such a deity had *satya* while another had 'much satya' (*bahala satya*) but I did not hear of any deity as lacking in *satya*. Either this was due to the fear that such a charge might provoke the deity in question to retaliate, or because of an unstated assumption that all deities had *satya*. I can even imagine a situation in which a few devotees debated as to which of the various deities known to them had the greatest *satya*, but not one in which they debated the question of which deity (or deities) lacked *satya*.

Implicit in the idea of *satya* was the ability of deities to answer the prayers of devotees, to grant them the things they wanted such as good health, children, good harvests and money. In return for the sense of security and other benefits which they received from their deities, devotees propitiated them.

This way of stating things might appear crassly mercenary but it should be remembered that the ordinary villager was engaged continuously in a life-and-death struggle with his environment, natural and social, and his religion and gods had to be relevant to his struggle. He had no time for high-faluting theology. His reverence for the sanyasi who had renounced the world was undoubtedly genuine, but he did not consider it cynical to expect returns from hospitality and reverence to sanyasis. In popular thinking at any rate, sanyasis were credited with having powers which ordinary mortals did not.

HOUSE DEITIES AND SECTARIAN ORDERS

The institution of house deities (*mane devaru*) had an importance even outside religion. When several households had the same house deity (or deities), it was frequently indicative of the existence of an agnatic linkage between them. This was useful in tracing links between the poorest sections of the village population which tended to have shallow genealogies. House deities were also useful in finding out the village from which a household or group of households had migrated to Rampura. For the bond between a household and its deities was a persistent one though the kind and intensity of contact varied from one household to another. It also varied according to the nearness of the original village, length and residence in the new village, the economic position of the household, and the kind of treatment which the household had received from the deity. In the case of the largest agnatic kin-group in the village, viz. God's House lineage, it was far more convenient to have a shrine built locally than for the thirty odd households to make the difficult journey every year. Another leading household which was otherwise scrupulous in the observance of its religious obligations, did not maintain any relation with its house deity except to name one of the sons after him, the reason being the death, many years ago, of a male child when the members were on a pilgrimage to the deity's temple. It was regarded as a particularly hostile act on the deity's part.

The intensity of the contact with the house deity varied from annual visits to once in every few years. But there were also some who had not visited their house deity for several years. Periodical visits were not, however, the only way of keeping contact with the house deity. For instance, an offering could be sent through a kinsman or friend. And even those who did not visit the house deity followed the custom of naming one of their children after him. At the hands of a man who had an intimate knowledge of the region, the names which regularly recurred in a genealogy provided clues to the identity of the house deity, and occasionally, to the lineage's sectarian orientation. There was also a negative rule regarding names: two living members of the household were not allowed to have the same name. Usually this meant the male child being named after the father's father (if the latter was dead), and the female child after her father's mother. In many genealogies, the members of alternate generations had the same names. But among the richer and more urbanized households names had begun changing. Such traditional names as Mada, Sidda, Beera, Kempa, Javara and Kala were giving way to Srinivasa, Ramaswamy, Narayana, Krishna, Srikanta and Shankara. (Interestingly enough, in the urban areas, the educated upper castes were busy changing from these names to secular names such as Ashok, Sanjay, Ravi and Mohan.)

With the non-Brahmin castes the house deity was frequently a village god or goddess demanding blood sacrifice. With some households, however, the house deity was a high god of Sanskritic Hinduism. Thus one Peasant household had as its deity Chenna Keshava of Belur and another, Narayana of Melkote. Where a Sanskritic god was the house deity, his consort was also worshipped, and her name was given to female children.

Under certain circumstances, a household sought protection from a new deity. The latter was referred to as '*mare bidda devaru*' or 'deity from whom shelter was sought'. Sometimes, the new deity completely eclipsed the old. Occasionally, new and prestigious cults were added to the old ones: I have referred to the increasingly popular cult of Srinivasa of Tirupati, and as the villagers' contacts with the wider world increased and diversified, there were likely to be further additions.

In fact, in the case of the richer and more influential families the cults observed were a layered whole providing an account of their religious evolution from the propitiation of strictly local village deities to all-India gods and gurus and sanyasis.

The household (and the lineage) was also the channel through which other religious traditions besides that of the house deity were perpetuated. I have earlier shown, for instance, how the special association between a particular caste and a temple was perpetuated through the household. This was not only true of the households which supplied one male member as priest (*gudda*) to the temple but of the others.

The household and not caste was the principal institution for perpetuating sectarianism. In fact, even the local section of a *jati* was not always homogeneous from a sectarian point of view. But where the entire caste was homogeneous, individual households did not have any elbow room except very occasionally when the head of a household came under the influence of a guru or monastery or temple belonging to a different sect. This had happened, for instance, with Shepherd Chenna whose caste was Shaivite in orientation but had come under the influence of a Vaishnava guru and monastery. The Oilman brothers had come under the powerful spell of a great Shaivite pilgrim centre. And so on.

Sectarian differentiation had occurred in Hinduism right from its earliest days, and during the medieval period, south India was the centre of some significant departures of doctrine. To begin with, the great Hindu theologian Shankara propounded the theory of *advaita* or monism (the idea that the individual soul was identical in nature with god, and that its eventual destiny was to merge in the latter). Ramanuja, coming two centuries after Shankara, had criticized *advaita*, proposed in its place *vishistadvaita* or qualified monism, according to which the individual soul did not totally merge in god but retained a sense of its identity even when united. Ramanuja was followed two centuries later by Madhwa, who advocated *dvaita* or dualism in which the individual soul and god were regarded as distinct entities. *Bhakti*, or devotion towards god, was far more important in the doctrinal systems of Ramanuja and Madhwa than in that of Shankara; incidentally, Shankara was a devotee of Shiva while Ramanuja and Madhwa were both devotees of Vishnu.

Another significant development in the field of sectarianism came from Basava, the founder of Virashaivism (militant Shaivism), popularly referred to as Lingayatism. Basava was roughly contemporaneous with Ramanuja, but he was not preoccupied with theological niceties and system-building. He was a forthright advocate of *bhakti* towards god (represented by the symbol of Shiva, the *linga*, which every Lingayat, male and female, had to wear round his neck), of the equality of all human beings irrespective of caste, and of the importance of manual labour for all. A corollary of the importance of *bhakti* was the downgrading of ritualism and of the authority of the scriptures, including the Vedas. Lingayatism was far more important than the three other sects founded by Shankara, Ramanuja and Madhwa, if judged solely by its influence on the masses, including those from the lower castes.

The perpetuation of sectarian ideology and practice was assured by the transformation of sects into castes, or a congeries of linked orders. Sectarian affiliation was a crucial principle of caste differentiation among Brahmins in south India while the Lingayats subsumed a number of caste distinctions which, however, are nowadays getting blurred under the impact of democratic politics. The monasteries of the four sectarian castes are presided over by sanyasis (referred to as 'Swamijis') who are highly respected by the people. Each sect has more than one monastery, the Lingayats having a large number of monasteries, especially in the northern and western parts of the State. While all the sects have an interest in popularizing their ideology, the Lingayats have been more active as well as more successful in their evangelizing efforts than the others. Entire castes, or sections of castes, have been absorbed into Lingayatism.

All this is preliminary to a brief description of the Dasayya and Jojayya which are two popular priest-cum-mendicant orders among the non-Brahmin castes of rural Mysore. The Dasayyas are a Vaishnavite order while the Jogayyas are Shaivite.

The order of Dasayyas was open to all men of the non-Brahmin castes, including Harijans. A hereditary guru from the Sri Vaishnava

(Iyengar) caste performed the ritual which included branding the shoulders of the initiate with the twin symbols of Vishnu's conch (*shankha*) and discus (*chakra*), and teaching him a secret *mantra*. A Dasayya had a uniform, an elaborate one, consisting of a white gown, a coloured cummerbund, a turban, dhoti worn in the Brahminical way, a copper begging bowl slung from the shoulder (*bhuvanasi*), a conch shell for blowing, gong and striker, and a necklace of *tulasi* (*Ocimum sanctum*) beads. He decorated his forehead with the *namam*, and begged on days sacred to Vishnu in the Hindu calendar, such as Saturdays, especially Saturdays in the lunar month of Shravan (August-September). On such days he had to eat food prepared from the grain collected by begging. Among the non-Brahmin castes, a Dasayya was invited on such life-cycle occasions as naming ceremony, wedding, and death when he worshipped the symbols of his sect after which he was given a meal.

While the institution of Dasayya was ideally voluntary, there was a marked tendency for it, as for most things in the village, to become hereditary. At least one son joined the order to carry on the family tradition.

The guru visited his disciples once every few years if not annually. Such a visit was called *shishyarjane* as its main purpose was to collect cash and grain from disciples. It was also the occasion for initiating new candidates and to settle disputes among followers. When a village had several Dasayyas one of them was nominated the head and the guru generally functioned through him.

The guru had also inherited his position: he was a descendant in the agnatic line from one of the men whom Ramanuja, the founder of the sect, had entrusted with the authority to recruit followers. The authority and power of the gurus was therefore derived from their birth in branches descended from the original office-bearer and not from the head of any monastery. Each guru operated in a particular area, and on his death, his sons divided it among themselves. The right to work as guru in an area was treated like any other alienable property, being liable to be sold, mortgaged, rented or inherited. This was the case with other village offices also, religious as well as secular.

The order of Jogayya was the Shaivite parallel of Dasayya. His uniform was an austere one consisting of a shirt, dhoti worn in *lungi* style, and turban, all ochre-coloured. The Jogayya's begging 'bowl' was a cloth-sling (*jolige*) suspended from the shoulder, the food and grain given by the people being deposited in the sling's bottom. Three horizontal stripes decorated the Jogayya's forehead. Many a Jogayya had a repertoire of songs and stories about Shiva which he sang while keeping time with his cymbals. Some ballads were indeed long as, for instance, the one about Madeshwara, which could last several nights. A Jogayya frequently repaid hospitality by singing a religious song or ballad on the veranda of his host, and a few villagers sat round him listening, and incidentally, adding to their store of merit.

The initiation of an individual into the Order of Jogayya was carried out in a monastery, and the initiate (or his sponsor) had to pay the expenses of the rite as also a fee. The monastery had a hierarchy of officials the lowest (*chooradararu*) of whom visited villages to collect the annual fee payable by Jogayyas.

Even as recently as the 1930s, respectable Peasants did not like to marry into households which had a tradition of providing recruits for their Order and I was unable to find out why such households were considered inferior. Perhaps the reputation which Dasayyas and Jogayyas had for consuming liquor as part of their duties was responsible for the low esteem in which they were held. I was assured, however, that the consumption of liquor occurred only among those castes which already did so as a matter of custom. It was much more likely that the low status of Dasayyas and Jogayyas was due to their being required to perform priestly and mendicant duties. It is relevant to recall here that priestly households among Brahmins had a low status, and among priests, those who officiated at death were regarded as singularly low. Dasayyas and Jogayyas both had ritual duties at death, and at periodical ancestor propitiations. Again, Dasayyas and Jogayyas were regarded as low only among the landowning and trading castes, and not among the poorest sections of village society. To the latter, on the contrary, membership of the Orders provided a link with high caste organizations and resulted in the Sanskritization of customs and lifestyle, paving the way to social mobility.

ASTROLOGY

Astrology is woven into the fabric of Hindu religion as it is lived from day to day. I have already described the institution of reading the forecast for the coming year at the Ugadi festival, but I should add that the experts who prepared the almanac did not all follow a single system of calculation. There were different schools, and the cognoscenti argued among themselves as to which almanac was the most reliable. In princely Mysore, the Maharajah had his own astrologer, and the palace almanac commanded more prestige than the others. I wonder whether the authority of the Maharajah rubbed off onto the almanac.

The almanac was a necessity for an orthodox Hindu but in Rampura only the Brahmins, the priestly Lingayats and a few others had almanacs in their homes. When a poor and illiterate villager wanted to start an important job he found out from the Rama priest a suitable date and time for it.

But the Rama priest's knowledge of astrology was minimal, and those who wanted more expert advice had to seek it outside the village. Since only the Brahmins and a few others had their horoscopes cast at birth, the astrologer answered his clients' questions on the basis of the time of asking the question. (In the cities were to be found specialists whose income was derived mainly from practising this type of astrology. These astrologers were rated according to the reliability of their predictions.)

The life of the villagers was regulated by three calendars, the Julian, lunar[4] and solar. As already mentioned, one of the most important dates in the villagers' calendar was 10 June when the gates of the reservoirs were opened releasing waters into the irrigation canals. The village school, the government offices in the *taluk* and district capitals, and the shops and firms in the cities all regulated their activity principally with reference to the Julian calendar.

The agricultural, social and religious life of the villagers was largely based on the Hindu lunar calendar. I have already commented on the importance of asterisms in predicting the seasonal rains. A few of the older and more Sanskritized peasants knew the names of those which had unfailing association with rain. Most villagers and even some urban folk commented that such-and-such an asterism was certain to 'give' rain.

In the lunar year, the four months beginning with *ashada* (roughly from mid-June to mid-October) were inauspicious for performing weddings, house-warming and other ritual. They were the rainy months when Vishnu slept on his serpent-couch at the bottom of the ocean. He woke up four months later, on the eleventh day of the bright half of *kartika* which marked the coming of winter. The month of Pushya (January–February) was another inauspicious month for those who followed the lunar calendar.

The solar calendar was nowhere as important as the lunar for the religious life of most villagers. Only the Sankranti was based on it. However, Brahmins had to resort frequently to the solar calendar to per-

---

[4] Muslim religious life was guided by the Islamic calendar which was lunar but which differed from the Hindu lunar calendar in that there was no provision in it for a quinquennial intercalary month. But many village Muslims had knowledge of Hindu festivals, the dates on which they occurred, etc.

form some kinds of ritual. Offerings of sesame and water were made to ancestors on the first day of each solar month (*sankramana*).

Rampura did not have a resident astrologer. In many villages of the region, this role was performed by the hereditary chaplain (*purohita*). Rampura's chaplain was resident in Hogur, and was not easily accessible to local folk, that too the poorer ones. His place was taken by the Rama priest whose competence did not extend beyond consulting the almanac.

An old Lingayat priest, Shantiviraradhya, from another village, enjoyed a local reputation for his knowledge of ritual and astrology, and the headman and a few other peasants and Lingayats consulted him. The village elite had also access to experts in other villages and in the towns.

Regulating social and religious life resorting to three calendars appears extremely complicated but it was not really so. The seasons, and the opening and shutting of the reservoir gates set the pattern for agricultural activities while the almanacs printed in the cities gave them the dates of their feasts, fasts and festivals. However, for most villagers, the priest and astrologer made consulting an almanac unnecessary. But the Brahmins found it necessary to consult the almanac frequently.

BASIC RELIGIOUS IDEAS

Certain ideas are basic to the understanding of the day-to-day religious life of the people in Rampura and neighbouring villages. It is interesting that each of these ideas is a part of a linked pair. Thus purity (*madi*) is linked with its contrary, impurity (*mailige*), wrong conduct (*tappu*) with right (*sari*), justice (*nyaya*) with injustice (*anyaya*), and sin (*papa*) with good or meritorious conduct (*punya*). Another pair of linked ideas is *dharma* (moral conduct) and *karma* (actions have consequences in subsequent incarnations), and it differs from the other pairs in this that one is not opposed to the other.[5] But this statement needs to be qualified: *dharma* in common parlance means, among other things, good deeds, while *karma* is used for acts which are wrong and even evil. According to the Kannada proverb *dharmakke kola, katti karmakke mosale bittaru*

---

[5] The opposite of *dharma* is *adharma*, i.e. the violation of the rules of law, morality and religion. *Adharma* is the antonym of *dharma* but it is a literary term and used only very rarely in ordinary conversation.

(dig a pond and gain *dharma*, and leave a crocodile in it and earn *karma*).

I shall not discuss here the concepts of pollution and purity. They were fundamental to the organization of the social and religious life of the villagers but I must hasten to add that it was not possible to draw a clear line between the social and religious. In a sense, all social life was religious as it came under the sway of pollution and purity ideas.

Tappu and *sari* were again important, and each term had a range of meanings: *tappu* referred to technically incorrect action, violation of the rules of conduct (e.g., talking back to elders, or having sex relations outside marriage), or breaking a rule of ritual or religion (e.g., not offering blood-sacrifices to a dead ancestor). It also referred to a fine levied on a person for the wrong done. A caste or village elder was occasionally heard telling someone, somewhat aggressively, that when a particular rule was broken a fine had to be levied on the guilty person (*tappu vasuli madabeku*).

Sari meant 'correct' (way of doing a thing), proper (manners), appropriate (e.g., paying tit for tat), and also right in a moral sense. *Sari* also meant 'even' as opposed to 'odd' (*besa*) when referring to numbers. In that sense it also referred to sameness of level. When a person wanted to stress that a paddy-plot or the floor of a room was a perfect level he said *sarisamawagide*. *Sama* meant 'level' and *sari* was used as a prefix to emphasize the perfection of the level.

All properly brought up children were expected to have the power to discriminate between right and wrong. Implicit in such discrimination was the knowledge that choosing the wrong course of action had unpleasant consequences. For instance, a man who made passes at a married woman and got thrashed by the husband, became the target of gossip and scorn: 'The thing he did was like eating mud' (*mannu tin-nuva kelasamadida*) and he deserved what he got. Another comment on such an occasion was 'whoever ate salt had to drink water' (*upputindare neeru kudiyabeku*) implying that the man ought to have stayed away from eating salt in the first place.

Villagers knew that the ability to discriminate between right and wrong was distinct from the actual choice of the right. Many a man chose the wrong course because of greed, lust or love of power. In fact, those who invariably chose the right were very few. They were referred to with respect bordering on reverence, and at other times with irreverence as 'Dharmaraya', after the eldest brother of the Pandavas, who never swerved from the right, and never told a lie. Such conduct was admirable in one way but was impractical in that it was detrimental to one's interests.

A man who chose the wrong but got away with it, was a clever man while the one who got caught had to pay the penalty. In other words, in actual fact, not everyone who ate salt had to drink water. But this was as much due to luck as to cleverness. When his luck ran out, however, he was caught and punished. Hence the proverb that 'a thief's wife was bound to become a widow one day' (*kallana hendati endiddaru munde*).

Villagers were keenly aware that a rich man was able to escape punishment for his wrong deeds while a poor man did not. Money and power bought many a man's co-operation, compliance or silence. In any discussion of right and wrong villagers cited instances of rich men doing what they wanted to, without having to pay the price for it because they were able to frighten victims and witnesses, or bribed the police or other officials. The poverty of the poor was made worse by oppression by the rich. It looked as though moral maxims were meant only for the poor and the weak. But then something happened out of the blue and the rich man suffered a disaster or great disgrace, and villagers suddenly perceived the vulnerability of even the mighty before the justice if not the wrath of the gods. These events helped to reaffirm the faith of the villagers in divine justice and in the reality of moral rules.

Two other terms which were heard frequently in the villagers' talk were *nyaya* and *anyaya*. *Nyaya* meant 'according to law or rule, right, just, fair, moral' while *anyaya* was the opposite of *nyaya*. A point made by one of the parties to an argument may be fair or according to rule (*adu nyayavada matu*, i.e., 'it is a just point') or outrageous (*adu yava ooru nyaya?*, i.e., 'the rule of which village is it?'). It was not only the points and arguments advanced by disputants which were either *nyaya* or *anyaya* but the decisions of arbitrators. The corruptibility of arbitrators was a perennial theme of village life, and one of its functions, apart from any element of truth which it may have had, seemed to be to enable the defeated disputant to accept an unfavourable decision. Kinship links, and economic, sex and power considerations frequently distorted the procedures and decisions of village courts as some arbitrators themselves admitted occasionally.

Nyaya and *anyaya* were used freely in disputes, and disputes were frequent enough for sensitivity to the subtler points of customary law and procedure to be widespread among villagers. The disputes also provided occasions for the display of forensic skill and for beating old rivals. They were the intellectual equivalents of wrestling bouts with this difference that decisions in the latter were fairer as a rule.

Nyaya was also used as a synonym for a dispute that came up before arbitrators. Thus *dodda nyaya biddubittitu* meant that a big dispute involving difficult issues had arisen. As mentioned earlier, the Shepherds were notorious for their love of disputes, and sensitivity to questions of mutual precedence.

Dharma had both an ethical and religious referent. Its different meanings, 'correct', 'right', 'moral' and 'merit', all formed a continuum, and the same term connoted different things on different occasions. Similarly, even a term like *tappu* was capable of being used in a religious context: a man begged forgiveness from his god for a lapse (*tappu*) and paid a fine (*tappu kanike*) or performed some other action to atone for it.

The moral did not exist as a category independent from the religious, and one who violated a moral rule was also doing damage to his soul, and angering the gods. Thus deceiving another person was not only morally wrong but sinful. A trader who cheated his customers was inviting disaster upon himself or one of his family members. When the news of his cheating a customer got around, someone was bound to remark, 'will god keep quiet?' or 'does god keep his eyes shut?' Cheating defenceless persons like widows or minors, and embezzling village funds (*urottina hana*) or temple funds, was more heinous than ordinary cheating.

Looking at the situation from the religious side, certain sinful acts (and omissions) were also immoral. A son who did not perform his dead father's obsequies, or a priest who neglected his temple duties, was behaving unethically. This was compounded when the son had inherited property from the father, or the temple had been endowed with land. The rule of reciprocity had also been broken in such a case.

A man who had performed acts of *dharma* (*dharmada kelasa*) was respected by all. Having a well or pond dug near a temple, building a hospice (*chatra*), erecting bamboo and palmleaf booths (*aravattige*) for serving refreshments to pilgrims, and planting avenue trees for the benefit of wayfarers were all acts of *dharma* or *punya* (religious merit). The repair of a temple, and ensuring the performance of daily ritual by endowing it with land, were popular acts of *dharma*.

Dharma was also used in a relative sense varying according to status and role. Thus a king's *dharma* differed from his subjects', and each caste had its own *dharma*. A priest's *dharma* was different from a layman's, and a father's different from his son's. At the same time, there was also a common *dharma* which transcended differences of status and role.

Villagers, especially the older ones, saw the glaring discrepancy between the norms which they were taught in their childhood and the profound changes which had occurred in recent years. For instance, it was no longer true that all Harijans were landless labourers or village servants. Some were teachers in schools which were attended by high caste pupils, and there were also Harijan officials, lawyers, doctors, legislators and ministers. Many Brahmins had given up painting caste marks on their foreheads, shed their sacred thread, and even ate meat and drank liquor. Girls from Brahmin and other high castes no longer married before puberty but instead studied in colleges, and took up jobs outside the home. Some villagers thought that things were indeed topsy-turvy (*tale kelaku*, i.e. standing on head). The current (and absurd) idea that all men were equal was satirized in the local pun *onde mataram*. In 1948, I did not find a single adult villager, even among those under thirty, who thought that Harijans ought to be allowed to enter high caste temples or draw water from caste Hindu wells.

However, there was respect for such virtues as truth-speaking, honesty, kindness and sympathy for the poor, whomsoever they resided in. A Brahmin who was hard-hearted was criticized, 'What kind of Brahmin is he? He ought to have been a butcher'. Similarly, an honest and kind man belonging to a 'low' caste was respected and praised. But there was a belief that the higher castes possessed, or ought to possess, good qualities in greater measure than the lower.

But as mentioned earlier, common sense dictated that goodness or virtue ought not to be carried to excess. It was all right for a sanyasi or other holy man to speak the truth always, but not for ordinary men. That was suicidal. One certainly could not afford to tell an official or even a neighbour how much he had grown or sold. Losses and expenses had to be exaggerated, and yields and income reduced. In fact, even rich villagers dressed shabbily to give the impression of being poor. All this was part of the strategy of survival.

My discussion of *dharma* as I think it was understood by villagers might appear confusing but this was partly at least due to there being no hard and fast lines between its different meanings, 'correct', 'right', 'lawful', 'ethical' and 'meritorious'. Not infrequently it was used in different senses within the space of a minute or two. To make matters more complicated, though ethical and religious behaviour had a large overlap, it was possible to speak of a man's virtues without reference to their religious dimension and *vice versa*. For instance, a kind and honest man who was not ritually minded was contrasted with one who was very religious but exploited, economically and otherwise, those in his power.

Karma, which was paired with *dharma*, was a religious idea with far-reaching ethical implications. A man's present position was determined by the kind of life he had led in a previous birth (*janma*), and this was stressed especially when there was a hiatus between his qualities and his position. Thus a rich man who was mean and miserly was said to owe his wealth to the good deeds he had done in his previous incarnation. Similarly, a good man whose only son died prematurely had probably committed a grave sin in his previous incarnation. Such arguing from cultural hindsight was not infrequent. But it was interesting that the fear of misfortunes in a subsequent incarnation did not seem to have any effect on people's conduct in contrast to the fear of punishment, and the hope of rewards, here and now. God had in his hands the power to punish as well as reward, and if he wanted to command the loyalty of his devotees, he had to make a judicial mix of both like a good headmaster, or even a politician. He had also to make his presence felt by occasionally granting prayers. A god who was above the villager's concerns did not make sense. He may possess wonderful qualities but villagers wanted to know how he was going to be useful to them. Max Weber would have been disappointed in Rampurians: they were *not* soteriologists. Salvation was only the goal of saints and sanyasis. They wanted gods with whom they could bargain, and from whom they could obtain benefits. Even from saints and sanyasis they wanted benefits. They did not think it cynical to ask for benefits.

The idea of *karma* did not come in the way of undertaking activity or of initiative. As I have said earlier, *karma* was mostly used to explain misfortunes and calamities which had already occurred. Fear of punishment in another incarnation did not present itself as an immediate threat. It did not prevent the land-grabber from his continuing efforts to grab the land of the poor, the womanizer from coveting other men's wives, and the miser from levying usurious rates of interest. Any change in their style of life was more likely due to some sudden disaster or the influence of a guru or other holy man.

On any fair reckoning, villagers had to be regarded as activists. Considering their proneness to disasters of all kinds, their poverty and ignorance, and the fact that the planting of each crop was really an act of faith, it was indeed astonishing that they were activists. Withdrawal from all activity made more sense in their situation.

Karma did offer solace to the villagers in that it helped them to survive the all-too-frequent disasters. A drought may burn up seedlings, or torrential rain destroy the harvest, an enemy burn up the straw-rick, or smallpox or plague take away the only son, but the villager continued his activity. *Karma* provided an explanation for the misfortunes which had occurred. But the importance of *karma* in preventing immoral action is open to question. However, other people's immorality provided an opportunity for gossips to lick their chops and sermonize. Gossip, which was abundant, provided an opportunity for the discussion and clarification of norms.

Papa (sin) and *punya* (religiously meritorious) were primarily religious terms but they also had ethical overtones. *Papa* referred to any sinful act but it was also an expression of pity or sympathy towards another person who was suffering or was deprived of a benefit or faculty. It is only with the former sense of *papa* that I am concerned here.

A sinful act might be related to a particular role of a man or woman, or it may be role-free. Thus a host who served more of a choice dish to one guest than to the others had committed the sin of *pangtibheda* or discriminating among the guests seated in a row. A paternal uncle who cheated his minor nephews of the property that was their due had abused a position of trust, and this was a graver sin than cheating a stranger.

There was a certain amount of castewise difference with regard to the perception of sin. Thus a Brahmin regarded all slaughter of animals as sinful since it involved the destruction of life while a meat-eating non-Brahmin regarded it as his religious duty to offer a blood-sacrifice to his dead ancestors or deities. Again, it was a sin for a Harijan to enter a high caste temple while it was a good thing for a high caste man to do so. (I am here referring only to traditional ideas.)

But there were also acts which were *papa* or *punya* for everyone, irrespective of caste, kinship, locality, class and sex. The sanctity of human life was a value which everyone had to respect. Visiting pilgrim centres, feeding the poor, endowing land to temples, and digging wells and planting trees earned *punya* for all. Men who performed these acts were respected just as cheats, usurers and adulterers were disapproved of.

I must reiterate that what I have written so far about the basic religious ideas of the villagers is drawn from my experience of the 'touchable' Hindu castes. But I think that it is true of the Harijans also, though they are likely to regard with scepticism, if not reject, at least some parts of upper caste ideology and world-view. In this context, it may be pointed out that Sanskritized individuals in each caste articulated the ideas discussed above more clearly than the others. (Of course, the clearest articulators of the ideas were not always well known for putting them into practice.) Of the few Harijans whom I came to know reasonably well, Pijja was the most Sanskritized, and he expressed the ideas of popular Hinduism better than many a high caste man. Kullayya, the Harijan headman who was given to few words, was respected for his piety. It is not unlikely that these men were the vanguard of a more thoroughly Sanskritized culture for their caste as a whole. But the question then arises, what were the religious ideas of the less or least Sanskritized Harijans? Only an intensive study of the religious beliefs of the Harijans and other lowly castes would answer the question. Unfortunately, I did not feel the need to do it when I was in Rampura. In fact, with the limited time at my disposal, I could not concentrate on any single caste before gathering a modicum of information on each.

MAN AND GOD

Man and god, or to be more precise, men and gods, were in intimate relation with each other, and this relationship was characterized by inequality. Gods were powerful and could grant favours or cause disasters while men were weak and in dire need of protection from the myriad, hostile forces around them. The situation was much worse before modern medicine, communications, education and scientific methods of agriculture began to reach the villagers. The life of the Indian villager was indeed nasty, brutish and short, and if one may add, disaster-prone at every point.

Every landowner paid at harvest a headload of paddy-with-straw to each of the priests of the Basava, Madeshwara and Rama temples. These three temples were the richest and most prominent in Rampura. The deity Basava both represented and, in a sense, was in charge of the world of cattle and their welfare. In practical terms, it meant that they should be healthy and have enough fodder throughout the year. Since the most important sources of fodder were paddy and *ragi*-straw, *jowar* stalks and some green fodder during the rainy season, adequate rains at appropriate times were essential to keep the cattle well fed.

The deity Madeshwara was also a protector of cattle. Was not his 'vehicle' (*vahana*) the Nandi bull? He was the lord and master of Nandi.

Rama was a generalist among deities, people praying to him for pretty nearly everything they wanted. He was a good deity, and he did not evoke in his devotees the fear which Madeshwara or Mari did. He was also somewhat distant from the farmers' concerns. He was the god, *par excellence*, of the Brahmins, and of a few better-off Peasants and others.

As stated earlier, there was a division of labour among the gods, and villagers generally addressed their prayers to appropriate deities. Thus a prayer for the welfare of cattle was rarely addressed to Rama and never to Mari but to Basava or Madeshwara. Taking the Rampura region as a whole, men with skin diseases went on pilgrimages to the shrines of cobra-deities such as Mattitalayya, and the Subramanya shrine near Kalastawadi on the Mysore–Seringapatam road.

The deified spirits of male ancestors were propitiated annually, and the welfare of the living members of the lineage, and the farm, house and cattle were their concern. But these matters were also the concern of the house deities. Overlapping jurisdiction did, however, occur frequently, and in such cases, villagers took the safer path of praying to all the deities concerned.

From the foregoing, it is clear that villagers viewed their relations with deities in much the same way as they viewed their relations with each other. There was this difference, however, that the deities were vastly more powerful, and also more difficult to understand and predict than human beings. When one deity failed a devotee he approached another in much the same way as when one patron failed him, a client approached another.

Changes were occurring, however, in the religious world of the villager. New cults, deities, and gurus were swimming into the villagers' ken as a consequence of increased contact with urban forces and the mass media. For instance, I am fairly certain that over fifty years ago, only a few Rampurians, most of them Brahmins, had heard of the famous pilgrim centres at Tirupati, Madura, Rameshwaram and Banaras, and even among them probably not more than one or two had visited them. In those days, a pilgrimage to Banaras was regarded as a hazardous enterprise though much less so than in the nineteenth century when a pilgrim's successful return from it was a fortuitous accident.

It was only during the post-Independence years that Rampurians, like others in neighbouring villages, started visiting the major pilgrim centres in the state and outside. Improved health services had wiped out smallpox, cholera and plague, the epidemics over which the deity Mari in her various forms presided. The effects of these changes on the cults of village deities is important for study, and it is probable that the increased popularity of Sanskritic gods, ritual, and forms of worship was due to the forces mentioned above.

Reciprocity was a fundamental principle underlying the relations between man and god in the same manner that it was between human beings. To put it crudely, devotees expected to benefit from propitiating deities, and the benefits sought were health, wealth, children, good crops, victory over rivals, and a sense of security. They were also 'negative' in the sense of freedom from sickness and ill-health and from possession by evil spirits (*gali*, lit., 'wind', or *devva*, the opposite of *deva* or deity). Some deities were able to only grant one type of favour as, for instance, Mari or Basava whereas some others were more versatile like Rama and Madeshwara.

While the theologian conceived of god as immanent (*sarvantaryami* lit., inside everything), having knowledge of past, present and future (*trikalajnani*, lit., knowing three 'times'), ineffable (*anirvachaniya*) etc., the villager dealt with him as he dealt with his powerful patron or his Trader, Smith, Barber, Washerman or Potter. He wanted benefits and favours from the deities he propitiated. Sometimes he made a deal with a deity as when he made a vow promising to go on pilgrimage to his shrine if he was (for instance) cured of an illness, or his wife bore him a son. To remind himself of his vow, he took a piece of cloth, washed it, dipped it in a solution of turmeric, and after the cloth had dried put a coin in it and tied it to a pole in the kitchen roof. Sometimes after he had been granted the favour he had asked for, he made the pilgrimage.

A family shifted its allegiance from a traditional to a new deity when the former failed to grant a favour, or inflicted an injury while the latter proved to be helpful. Reciprocity underlay such a shift: the traditional deity had failed to observe the rules of the reciprocity game while the new one had. Reciprocity, or more appropriately, its content, varied from deity to deity, and this was contingent upon the personality and attributes of each deity.

When a devotee suffered a serious misfortune and his prayers to his deity were of no avail, he felt cheated. On occasion, however, he was so enraged by his deity's conduct that he abused him. When, for instance, the old priest of the Madeshwara temple, father of Thammayya, was arrested and taken to jail during the Ganjam revolt in the 1890s, his wife went to the temple, stood before the icon, and berated the deity, 'I will heap stones on you, I will heap thorny cacti on you'. Stones and cacti

are the opposite of sweet-smelling flowers with which icons are decorated and worshipped. This incident was recalled nearly sixty years
later.

In some cases, there were standard terms of abuse which angered
devotees could use. Thus Shiva was addressed as *makkalu tindukonda-
vane*, i.e. 'You killer of children', referring to Shiva's destruction of
Kama, the God of love. Rama was addressed as *hendati kaledukonda-
vane*, i.e. 'You who lost your wife', referring to Ravana's abduction of
Sita.

It look me time to understand that opposition to a deity was a regular
form of relationship like adoration or worship just as friendship and
enmity were recognized forms of relationship among human beings. In
this connection, it is significant that Hindu theology recognizes both
adoration and opposition as legitimate forms of relationship with god.
While most devotees chose the path of love and adoration, a few, very
few, chose the path of opposition. A celebrated instance of opposition
is provided in Hiranyakashipu, the puranic demon-chief, who was slain
by Vishnu in his *avatar* as Narasimha (man-lion). Hiranyakashipu's
hatred of Vishnu prompted him to prevent his young son Prahalada from
worshipping him. According to folklore, Hiranyakashipu had the choice
of attaining union with Vishnu through practising the path of love or
opposition and he opted for the latter as it was the shorter. The path of
love would have meant more incarnations (*janmas*) than the path of
opposition. Approaching god through opposition is called *virodha
bhakti* or adoration through opposition, and it is regarded as a closer
relationship than that of love. In adoration through opposition, the
devotee is unable to shake god out of his mind while in the other his
mind could wander.

Rampurians lived in a theistic universe in the sense that everyone in
the village believed that god did exist, or more precisely, deities, male
and female, and spirits, did exist. I do not think that elderly Rampurians
had come across an atheist in the course of their lives. Faith in a
particular deity might have been shaken but that only prompted an
individual to seek protection from another deity but not reject all deities.
A rationalist and atheist simply did not make sense to Rampurians. The
only two occasions when I found that I had annoyed my good friend Nadu
Gowda were (1) when I expressed my preference to be a bachelor even
though I was past thirty, and (2) when I refused to answer his questions
about my religious beliefs, and instead, parried them with counter
questions such as, why should people believe in god? It was one of those

few occasions when I behaved with deliberation as I thought that it would be interesting to get Nadu Gowda's reactions to atheistic views. I persisted in my stupid cleverness, little realizing that I was annoying him in matters which were of profound concern. It was then brought home to me forcibly that where religion was concerned I could not count on Nadu Gowda's indulgence.

Nadu Gowda was in some respects an exceptional man but in certain others, as for instance his deep religiosity, he was typical of the villagers. Even Kulle Gowda, a non-conformist in many areas of behaviour, was religious but, characteristically, he wore his religion far more lightly than others. In fact, even those who were known for practising usury, lechery or deceiving others as a matter of habit, were not irreligious. But it was wrong to conclude from this that there was no relationship between morality and religion. Lechery and dishonesty, for instance, were both wrong and sinful. Those who broke the moral rules were aware of what they were doing, and in some cases at least, their religiosity might have been prompted by awareness of their wrong doing.

God existed, and evidence for this was available in the miracles that occurred in certain temples on certain occasions. For instance, many a villager narrated to me how, at the annual festival of the lineage goddesses of the God's House lineage, a party of devotees from the salt-maker (Uppaliga) caste from a nearby village broke open a number of coconuts on their shaven heads. This was an old custom, and it was referred to as 'pavada' or miracle. How was it that these men were able to do it while ordinary men were not?

Another miracle was walking on nails (*mullamige*), or rather, walking with sandals through the soles of which were driven nails so that the sharp ends came into contact with the walker's soles. One of the priests of the Mikkere Virabhadra temple donned the *mullamige* during the Ugadi (New Year) festival when the deity's icon was taken to the Kaveri river for a bath. He walked about before the deity on the sandals, carrying an open sword in hand, and he answered questions put to him by devotees. (The questions related to health, birth of children, monetary problems, etc.) Several villagers told me about how painful it was to wear the *mullamige* and one young boy even challenged me to try them on. I did not accept the challenge: the nails were not only sharp but rusty.

The behaviour of some bulls (*basavas*) dedicated to the Shiva temple was also cited as evidence of the power of the deities concerned, and indirectly, of the existence of the latter. For instance, the bull dedicated to Mikkere Virabhadra (or of the deity Nirappa of Hunjanakere) tried to gore a devotee participating in the festival, and it later transpired that the person in question was in a condition of impurity and ought to have abstained from attending the festival.

I must here pause to add that while the villagers cited supernatural events and happenings as evidence of the handiwork of god, they were not a credulous lot. They were shrewd, commonsensical and hard-headed, and this trait of theirs was seen repeatedly and in a wide variety of contexts. I shall illustrate what I mean by reference to a frequent form of divination, viz. the institution of flower-asking (*hu kheluvadu*). There is more than one form of flower-asking but I shall confine myself to that which is common in Rampura.

When an individual, or a group of villagers wanted to take a decision and were unable to do so on the basis of the facts available or commonsense, or they wished to know what was likely to happen in the future on a matter of great importance to them, he or they went to a temple, and after worshipping the deity, prayed to him requesting that he 'give them a flower' (*hu koduvudu*). The priest was informed in advance, and he washed the deity and stuck water-wet flowers all over the icon before the arrival of the devotees. *Puja* was then performed, the last act in it being *arati*, the waving of lighted camphor (or cotton wick dipped in oil) before the deity. The priest then offered the light to each devotee who took both his palms to it after which he touched his eyes and then saluted the deity with folded palms. Then the leader of the party of the devotees formally requested the deity to give a flower. If a flower on the right half of the deity fell in response, it was interpreted as a favourable answer while a flower on the left side falling indicated a 'no'. However, if no flower dropped, it indicated that the deity did not wish to answer.

Since I was on very friendly terms with the villagers and I felt certain that they would not mistake me, I tried to point out that the fall of a flower which was stuck into a crevice cavity in the icon was governed by chance and that no significance ought to be attached to it. But I was told that the fall of any flower did not count but only of those which were wet and stuck firmly in. They explained to me that the *garbha gudi* (*sanctum sanctorum*) where the deity's image was housed was always without a window. The lighted lamp in that room along with incense sticks and camphor produced warmth and this resulted in the fall of flowers. But only the fall of wet and firmly stuck flowers was relevant.

Sometimes, however, after the deity had refused to give a flower at the first session, the devotees tried a second time, usually on the following morning. This was termed 'asking for a stale (or overnight) flower' (*tangalu hu keluvudu*). In such a case, only a flower which had been used on the previous day mattered and not any other.

Villagers assured me that they had, on rare occasions, witnessed flowers being 'thrown' (*eseyuvudu*) by the deity instead of merely falling. Sometimes a sceptical devotee even asked that a particular flower decorating the deity's icon be 'given' in indication of an affirmative answer. A great deal depended on the truth or power (*satya*) of the deity, the conduct of the priest, and perhaps also the faith of the supplicant.

To Rampurians, deities were as real as their friends, neighbours and relatives. However, relatives existed as human beings while gods existed sculpted in stone, wood or metal. (Some village deities inhabited even plain unhewn stones.) Each deity had his own personality, his special likes and dislikes, just like each villager who was not infrequently identified by his quirk or oddity.

The complexities of the flower ritual, and the reality and immediacy of deities to Rampurians, were brought home to me when in the summer of 1948 I accompanied a party of elderly villagers to the Basava temple to ask the deity whether the drought would be broken. It was a scorching afternoon, and we all trooped into the stone-paved compound of the Basava shrine. Each one of us had covered his head with a towel to protect ourselves from the heat and glare of the pitiless summer sun. Nothing I had witnessed in Brahminical temples, or even in Coorg, had prepared me for the 'interview' which followed between the villagers and the deity. Once or twice, the absurdity of the situation seemed overwhelming but I managed to keep a straight face, and more important, the earnestness of the villagers gathered in the narrow anteroom outside the *sanctum sanctorum* made a profound impression on me. I shall quote the 'interview', with slight alterations only, from my field-diary as a summary would fail to convey its quality:

Monday, 3 May 1948: Today some elders went to Basava to find out (ask the deity) whether it was going to rain (or not). Kulle Gowda's father, Nadu Howda, Kobli's father and a few others comprised the party. Sannu joined later. On the way, I asked why Basava's temple had been chosen and not any other. I was told that was because it was the oldest. The Madeshwara temple belonged really to Gudi. The Rama temple was not either as old as Basava's or the department of rains did not come under Rama.

The Basava temple is in the old village site, and the temple has not been shifted like Rama's. Inside the temple is a stone pedestal on which sat Basava (figure of a recumbent bull). . . . On either side of Basava was a much smaller image of him. . . .

The old priest's younger son substituted for his father on this occasion. The image had been washed etc., decorated with daubs of sandalwood paste, and flowers and *bilva* (*Aegle marmelos*) leaves, still wet with water, had been placed all over the face and neck. (Care had been taken to see that none were likely to slide down easily.)

It is believed that there is an intimate relation between Basava's *para* (feast) and rain. When (the first) monsoon rains occurred, the feast was given, and it is said that formerly rain followed the feast washing off the leaves used in the dinner.

After we went in, *puja* was performed, lighted frankincense (*dhupa*), and camphor were waved before the deity and then offered to the devotees. Flowers and *bilva* leaves were also given. (Sannu, his son, and I sat in the inner shrine while the others sat in the covered veranda outside.)

Kulle Gowda's father, Made Gowda, was asked to make the request to the deity for a flower. I had imagined that everyone would stand up and bow silently beseeching almighty god for a sign which they could understand. But the proceedings were as different as possible from my expectations. Made Gowda stood up and said, 'You are famous as Rampura Basava. Do you wish to retain your reputation or not? Please give us a flower. We have not performed your *para* because of lack of water. Give us rain today and tomorrow we will perform your *para*'.

'In Edagai, Kapi and other villages your are famous as Rampura Basava. It has rained all around us, in Hogur, Hundi, etc. Why has it not rained here? Tell us if you are angry. Why should you be angry with us? We have seen to it that you do not lack anything.' (Nadu Gowda here mentioned that there was something wrong with the priest which he would not mention then but later.)

Another elder almost barked, *appaneyagali, yatakke kadastiya* (Give us your order, why do you torture us? Give it early.)

Nadu Gowda was irritated, 'Give us a flower on the left side if you so wish. Why do you sit still? Are you a lump of stone or a deity?'

Someone chimed in, 'He is only a lump of stone; otherwise, he would have answered'.

Nadu Gowda added, 'We will say that there is no god in the temple and that you have left the village'.

Someone else took a different line: 'We are not entirely dependent upon you. On 10 June, canal water will be released by the government. And anyhow it will rain a little later (after the south-west monsoon had set in). Even if it does not rain, we won't starve. Rampura people eat rice (grown with water from the irrigation canals) and not *jowar* (sorghum grown on wholly rain-fed land). So give us a flower'.

I sat in the inner shrine looking at the flowers. They seemed glued to the deity. There did not seem to be an earthly chance of any flower or leaf coming down. I wondered at the faith of these people. They were all in earnest (but) the atmosphere was not that of a group of men in awe of a great god but that of a number of reasonable men trying to coax a man lacking in good graces into right behaviour. It resembled a veranda scene where a dispute was being settled, and an unreasonable party was being told what was right.

I asked the villagers whether if it rained that evening (after the deity's silence), they would conclude that Basava had given it. They said 'no'. . . .

Again, I told them that the flowers and leaves had been pressed into cavities (in the icon). They ought to have been loosely placed. They dismissed my idea. What was the point of placing them loosely? Only when firmly-placed flowers came down had the deity given them.

Nadu Gowda narrated to me an incident in his life when two of his grandsons contracted cholera and the doctor told him that they were as good as dead. Then his second son had a dream in which he saw a *bhairagi* (holy man in ochre robes following a Shaivite Order) who told him 'it is all right, go'. The son also heard bells ringing. Nadu Gowda went on the following morning to the Basava temple and asked for a particular flower. It fell at once and the grandchildren survived. . . .

I then asked the elders what was the next step. They told me that they would visit the temple on the next morning to ask for a stale (*tangalu*) flower. The priest would stand outside the door, wave lighted camphor before the deity and then everyone would wait for a flower to fall. If no flower came down then it meant that the deity had left the village.

Abusing and taunting one's favourite deity was again understandable because it was common among people bound together by close ties and interests such as relatives, friends, masters and servants, and patrons and clients. A man who did not give a thing when he was asked might part with it when he was taunted, and taunting implied the pre-existence of close ties. The villagers' relations with deities paralleled in some ways their relations with patrons.

The fact that Basava was a deity to whom they had gone to plead for rain did not inhibit the villagers from speaking to him forcefully and uninhibitedly. The incident recalled to me the manner in which even the humblest villagers stood up for their rights when they felt that their rights were being trampled upon by somebody.

After the infructuous interview with Basava, a few younger Rampurians went to Madeshwara and asked him for a flower. The flower was given soon, and a heavy shower fell during the night. The grateful villagers quickly raised funds for a silk umbrella for Madeshwara, which had been promised him in return for rain, and took him out in a gala procession.

As far as the villagers were concerned the most important thing was that deities did exist, that they could be prayed to for obtaining certain desirable objects, bringing about desirable events, or avoiding or preventing the materializing of undesirable objects or events. Deities provided the necessary sense of security, and the source of hope for undertaking the multifarious activities essential for day-to-day living. But deities had to be worshipped, offered sacrifices, and made much of. Devotees had to be in a condition of ritual purity to approach and worship them. Failure to propitiate, make offerings, and observe the rules of purity and pollution was likely to result in punishment. However, the elaborate system of ritual, myth, belief and action which had been developed over the centuries to cocoon the villagers from all-too-frequent disasters, had set up its own anxieties, stresses, strains and guilt feelings.

Farewell

As November progressed, I began to worry about the diminishing time available to me for work. I was expected to be in Oxford by the middle of January which meant that I had to reach there at least a week before. It was my first teaching job, and I was worried, to say the least, about my lack of preparation. But while in Rampura I could not think of anything else but the yawning gaps in my data. There was so much to be done. I went round during the day collecting information in a hectic way but when I went to bed I started thinking about the work still to be done and the unprepared lectures.

I had started my work in the village feeling strange, and wondering how it would go, but as the weeks went by, I felt that I had no reason to feel despondent. Information did not come in steadily but in sudden gusts, and after a while, I got used to the pattern. Village life, which at first seemed chaotic, gradually became more coherent. Perhaps more important was the fact that I enjoyed my work and my encounters with villagers from different castes and classes. True, there was always the feeling at the back of my mind that the time at my disposal was woefully short for studying so complex an entity as Rampura. My anxiety increased rather than diminished with such success as I had in the collection of data. I would list the number of things to be done in the coming week or fortnight and fret if I did not fulfil the targets I had set for myself. At times my anxiety reached a point when it prevented sleep and I usually solved the problem by running away to Mysore for two or three days. This had the effect of renewing my curiosity and zest.

In spite of frequent outbursts of anxiety, I enjoyed my fieldwork. I was curious about everything concerning the villagers, and by and large, I liked them. I had mixed feelings about a few with whom I came into frequent contact but I tried, as far as possible, to see their point of view. I had a few close friends, and I liked talking to them, and being with them. I also knew that they liked me.

I felt real affection for my village friends, and during my entire stay in Rampura, I cannot recall feeling the need for intellectual company. (I realize that this is also a comment on me.) My friends could discuss the events and institutions in the village with subtlety and humour which made me respect their intelligence. They understood that I wanted to learn about village life and institutions, and they took the trouble to answer my questions, however naive or ignorant they appeared. With only a few villagers such as Nadu Gowda, Sannu, Pijja, Washerman Kempayya and Hakim Sab did I have formal sessions at which I collected information on a variety of matters. With most others, my meetings were informal.

I suffered from two kinds of deficiencies in collecting information: I did not want to embarrass, let alone upset, my informants by asking them questions on financial, marital or domestic matters. Only if the informant himself touched on any of them, did I try to probe further. I usually obtained information on sensitive areas by keeping my eyes and ears open when people were talking, and by occasionally intervening with a question or two to give a focus to the talk. Even then, I took care not to appear nosey. I was aware that I was being circuitous but being endowed with a temperament which made me dread asking embarrassing questions, I had no choice. I am ignoring for the moment the likelihood of the villagers being put off by direct questions.

There was a considerable amount of gossip in the village about extra-marital sex relations and some of the reported liaisons were across the lines of caste. I felt that I should know about them and the only way to get the information was to ask my friends. But even with them I had to be circumspect as they could mistake me for being a garbage-collector which would have affected my standing with them. It was only when I was out walking with my friends that I asked them the questions which I wanted to, and after I had taken care to steer, as inconspicuously as I could, the conversation in the direction of my interests. I thought that I ought not to believe everything that I had heard or was told and that I should sift the chaff from the grain. Also, how could one get 'evidence' to substantiate a rumour? But my talks with my friends failed to yield the 'evidence' which I was seeking. My friends had of course heard the rumours which I had, and they believed them to be true. But the only thing I could conclude from all this was that rumours about extra-marital relations were widespread and widely believed in. This was only what was to be expected in village society where every bit of gossip moved along well-established networks and the networks of different individuals intersected at many points.

But the entire process of deliberately bringing out my questions about the seamy side of village life during walks with my friends made me uneasy. I felt that I was taking unfair advantage of them. Yet, on the other hand, I felt that I ought not to rest content with rumours, but seek certain information. I was bothered all the time about the propriety of what I was doing.

Perhaps one of the reasons why the villagers liked me was due to the contrast between their expectations about me, and my own behaviour: they had assumed that as an educated, urban and well-off (by their standards) Brahmin, I would behave like the officials who, during their brief visits to the village, met and talked with only a few leaders. In contrast, I went to everybody's house, talked with them, and took pictures. This they liked, and perhaps they did not appreciate enough the fact that I had to be informal with everyone in the interests of my work.

One of the results of knowing everyone in the village was a diffusion of my energies. I found it difficult to walk uninterruptedly from the Bullock House to wherever I had work. I had to stop and make conversation with my friends and acquaintances as otherwise there was the likelihood of their misunderstanding me. This was annoying but there was nothing to do but to put up with it. Sometimes, however, such chats yielded 'leads' about important matters which I had to follow up later. But whether they yielded information or not, they kept me in touch with a wider range of people than I had close relations with, and helped create a reservoir of goodwill for me.

The village represented a distinct olfactory world. Some smells were pleasant such as harvested paddy and jowar stalks, hedges, straw-ricks, and the smell of earth after the first rains. The smell of the Bullock House was, however, an acquired taste. I was used from childhood to cowdung smell—there was a colony of milkmen behind our house in Mysore—but living in the Bullock House, where eleven bullocks were tethered from early evening till the following morning, produced an overpowering stench of cowdung and cow urine, which was a phenomenon of a different order. There was no escape from this smell in the village for in most houses the animals were tethered in a part of the main living room. Anyone who had grown up in a village probably found the urban, middle-class home a sharp olfactory contrast. I did find the Bullock House smells overpowering to begin with but after a while I not only became used to them but even liked them.

Manure heaps also exuded a strong smell but strange as it may seem I did not find it unpleasant. I disliked them, however, because they attracted flies, mosquitoes and other insects. I remember a big manure heap at about a hundred yards to the north of Gudi, along the path to Kere. I had to pass by it when I walked to Kere, and I recognized it not by looking at it but by the smell issuing from it. It was a landmark for me, and not an unpleasant one.

But what I never got used to was the revolting practice of children defecating on the village streets. I hated walking on the village streets in the morning as I was certain to come across one or two children calmly defecating by the roadside. I welcomed the swineherds' pigs as they left the village cleaner unlike the dirty domestic fowls which only pecked at the piles of ordure and deposits of human phlegm on the road. This made me understand why the Sanskritized, non-vegetarian castes refused to eat fowl, and regarded mutton and fish as food of a higher order.

As my fieldwork progressed, I began to view the village and its environs more like a native than an outsider. Not only did I get used to smells, dirt, dust, heat, winds, noise, the insects and vermin, and the lack of privacy, I learnt to distinguish good land from bad and the various properties of the plants and trees commonly found in the area. I knew the life-histories of several individuals, the details of major disputes, and the main local events. In fact, I was occasionally able to correct my friends and acquaintances on matters pertaining to the village. There was an element of the show-off in me, and I was aware that my interventions would provoke someone to say, 'You know much more about our village than us.' This was a compliment no doubt but it was not free from a trace of concern. A few of my more knowledgeable friends told me that they had never imagined that I was going into every aspect of village life, and in the detail I did, and added, half-jokingly, 'Our secrets are now with you.' 'We don't know what you are going to do with all the information you have collected', and 'You can get many into trouble' were the other expressions which I heard occasionally. It was true that I knew of instances where individuals had benefited themselves at the expense of the government, but the last thing that I would have thought of doing was to harm those who had trusted me and given me of their friendship.

But not all the compliments of the villagers could convince me that I had done anything more than only scratch the surface as far as gathering information was concerned. In fact, paradoxical as it may appear, the compliments served only to remind me of my failures and of gaps in my data. But it was impossible to convey this to the villagers. But my conscience would not be lulled to sleep by the compliments even though sometimes I knew that I had in a way invited the compliments from them.

As my stay drew to a close I had also to worry about my social obligations. Word had got round that I would be leaving shortly, and I was stopped while on my rounds by everyone I knew to be asked when I was going, how long I would be away, when I would return, etc. If I happened to drop a remark about English weather or food, I was certain to the detained longer. The villagers clamoured for more information, and after my exposition wondered how human beings could live in England. They might have been discussing Eskimos in the deepest Arctic.

My friends were sad at the prospect of my departure. They discussed every little detail of it, and told me repeatedly how they would miss me. They feared that I would forget them in the preoccupations of my work and social life. Would I write to them? It was enough if I wrote once a month about my safety and welfare. After all, I was going to a country thousands of miles away.

A few even asked me the price of an air-letter, and were shocked when I told them. The villagers were a frugal lot, and only wrote on post-cards cramming as much information as they could into each. For instance, Nadu Gowda, who was extremely fond of his youngest son studying in a Mysore college in 1952, had instructed him to write once a month and only on postcards. But, quite inconsistently, he himself wrote me a few air-letters during the thirty months I spent in Oxford and I valued them as evidence of his great affection for me.

Nadu Gowda's son Kempu wondered why I had to go to a country so far away to get a job. Could I not get one nearer home? As far as he was concerned, it would be good if I became an officer in Mysore State, preferably as Deputy Commissioner of Mysore district. I would then be useful to him and others in the village.

Two friends who seemed particularly affected by my departure were Kulle Gowda and Nadu Gowda. The former's unhappiness was to some extent understandable. His self-interest was bound up with my continued stay in Rampura. I was a source of occupation and income to him. The occupation also gave him a sense of importance which was necessary for one who had come down in the world, and who was, in addition, vain. He was one of those who wanted me to write to him regularly. He kept nagging me, 'Once you get there you will forget us', but at the same time took care to see that I would have to write to him. He told me that he would keep copies of the documents which were drafted by him for those who sought his services as scribe, and record disputes. He intended doing a survey of Gudi, to which I have referred earlier, and this would also keep him in touch with me. As a parting gift I gave him a wrist watch. It was a foolish gift for I ought to have known that Kulle Gowda would part with it when he was next in need of money. A few villagers criticized the gift as they thought that I should have given something more valuable.

Nadu Gowda was the one most upset by my impending departure, and unlike Kulle Gowda, his self-interest was not bound up with my stay. If anything, I had made demands on his time and energies though in the process I had helped him spend his leisure, and perhaps also added to his entertainment. I could not help being surprised at the fact that we had become such good friends. Our friendship had grown steadily during the year, and was free from the occasional doubts and conflicts which had marked my relationship with the others. I had become very fond of the warm-hearted, grandiloquent and occasionally imperious and hierarchical old man. For several days before my departure, he spent hours on my veranda looking woebegone and telling me how bad he felt. He had even toyed with the idea of giving me an acre of wet land to induce me to settle down in Rampura. But he realized that I was 'as expensive as an elephant', and that an acre of land was pitifully inadequate.

I was touched by Nadu Gowda's generous thought, and I could appreciate what parting with an acre of wet land meant even to one who had over forty acres. But what I did not then realize was that it was the highest ever evaluation of my friendship, keeping in mind the fact that I had offered nothing in exchange. I wonder if the fact of my being a Brahmin had influenced him. He was the kind of man to whom a gift to a Brahmin would have appeared meritorious. He knew that my style of life was far removed from that of a pious Brahmin but I was a scholar, a profession which he probably associated with Brahmins. He once told me in his characteristic style, 'The kind of property you are acquiring lasts thousands of years unlike the property which we acquire.' He was, of course, referring to knowledge.

On the day before my departure, Nadu Gowda was sitting on my veranda leaning his heavy bulk against one of the dark-green modern pillars, carved by the village Smith. He was looking even more depressed than usual while I was busy packing. The headman walked across from his house, smiled a wise smile and said, 'I knew he was a "paper cap" (*kagadada topi*), and would leave us all one day. That was why I took care not to become too friendly whereas you observed no such caution. You see how his departure is affecting you.' It was an eloquent comment on the headman's nature, and also an explanation of why he had maintained a distance with me.

My last few days in Rampura were miserable. I was by temperament a stay-at-home but I had been forced to shift my residence periodically as a result of the profession I had chosen. The process of uprooting myself from a settled routine and established relationships with a known group of people was deeply disturbing, and in the present instance Rampura represented only the first stage in the snapping of my bonds. Leaving Mysore was going to be worse and then there was Bombay where I had several friends. The prospect of leaving the warmth and sun of Mysore for the cold and wet of an Oxford winter was not exactly exciting. (My previous winter in Oxford, the 1946–7 one, was the worst for several decades, and it was compounded by a power cut from 8 a.m. to 12 noon, and from 2 to 4 p.m.) As I thought of all this, I was full of self-pity. I envied the villagers who spent all their lives in one place, whose relationships were stable, and whose routines never varied. The village appeared a snug and cosy place, and lucky indeed were those who inhabited it even though they were ignorant of their good fortune.

My younger friends insisted that I should have 'tiffin' with them on the eve of my departure. The group included Swamy, Kempu, Siddu, Millayya's brother Karagayya, Congress Puttaswamy, and probably one or two others. They were the modernizers, and they got the tiffin prepared at Hotel Mollayya's teashop, the leading local teashop. Mollayya was a Peasant, and it was he who had prepared the snacks for the party given by the young dissidents to the visiting minister earlier during the year. My friends had done me proud: the thick *chapatis* literally dripped with pure *ghi*, and so did the sweet made with broken wheat. The best variety of bananas had been bought, and there were betel leaves and arecanuts after an over-sweetened tea.

I tried hard but I could not eat more than one *chapati* and a few spoonfuls of the rich sweet. My friends assured me that everything was made with pure *ghi*, and that I should eat a little more. Were the dishes not to my taste?

I could not tell them that I did not have an appetite, and that rich food did not agree with me. The talk around me was hardly more to my taste: it was about my going away, my forgetting my poor friends in the village, and finally, did I know how long it would be before I returned home? All the questions that I was pushing away from my mind were being thrust before me.

It was sweet of my young friends to have given me a party, and I was deeply appreciative of their affection and kindness. As I returned after dark to the Bullock House and to my packing, the thought crossed my mind that I had not been given a party by the headman. Was he annoyed with me? I was certain that he would have heard of the party given by my younger friends and I did not know what he would conclude from it.

But soon I was too busy with the last stages of my packing, the brunt of which was being borne by Nacha, assisted by a few neighbours. Kulle Gowda walked in and out barking instructions to Nacha, much to the latter's annoyance. My furniture, bedding, vessels, etc., were being sent to Mysore in Karim's cart, driven by his son Alimia. An old tenant of my acquaintance from Kere, Kari Ninga, was travelling in the cart to make sure that the things would safely reach my house. It was going to be an all-night journey.

I was due to catch my bus at about 10 a.m. on the following day and I had to wait by the roadside with the luggage I was carrying with me. There was usually a scramble to get into a bus, and sometimes the bus arrived in Rampura overloaded, which meant that local travellers had to wait for another bus. As breakdowns were frequent, the timings of buses were not predictable.

I was suddenly summoned to the Headman's 'office room' an hour or so before my departure. I went in to find that several men had already gathered there including the Headman, his sons, Nadu Gowda and Karim. The room had been swept clean, and the chairs, benches and table had been dusted and rearranged. At the back, near the wall, was a table, and behind it were arranged three chairs, while the benches were arranged in front. The owner of the Brahmin teashop was making coffee and snacks in a corner, and I found the smell of coffee competing for supremacy with the more pervasive one of paddy in gunny sacks, and dust. I was invited to take the chair between the Headman's and Nadu Gowda's, and as soon as I had sat down, the serious business of eating began. It was done with concentration. The teashop-owner was praised for preparing tasty snacks. My hosts did not neglect me either and pressed me to eat more. The teashop-owner was urged to look after me. But before we had finished with eating, music suddenly burst on our ears, music made by *nadaswaram* pipes and *dolu*. The musicians had come from Kere. The party must have been planned at least a day in advance. I felt mean at the uncharitable thoughts I had entertained about the Headman on the previous evening. But I was not left to my reflections for long as Lakshmana suddenly stood up and made a speech praising me. It was a speech in the accepted style of farewell speeches: my virtues, real and not-so-real, were listed, the affection and esteem which the villagers had for me was stressed, as also the fact of my being missed, etc., etc. The end of the speech was marked by loud applause. A thick garland was produced from somewhere and Lakshmana put it round my neck and we did *namaskar* to each other. Karim followed Lakshmana, put a garland round my neck and poured a couple of handfuls of crystal sugar and almonds on my head. I stood up after the garlanding and confetti and thanked the villagers for their kindness and hospitality and for treating me as one of them.

As Lakshmana was speaking I suddenly turned to the Headman and said, 'I feel terrible when I hear praise like that.' The Headman replied, 'That is how the worthy feel.'

The bus arrived, and strangely enough, on time. But the Headman's emissaries had told the driver that I was travelling and that a seat had to be reserved for me. The driver started using the horn to remind us that it was time. I panicked at the sound of the horn. I wanted to leave the room at once and run for the bus. But the Headman asked me to take it easy. The bus would wait. I replied that the driver might become impatient and leave. Someone in the audience dared the driver to do that. They would see how he would visit Rampura again.

We continued to make small talk while the driver hooted the horn more persistently and I became more and more restless. After what appeared a long time we all got up and made for the door. Lakshmana instructed me to put on the garlands which I had deposited on the table. I obeyed him, and the procession formed outside on the street, with the musicians in front, followed by me, flanked by the Headman and Nadu

Gowda on either side, while the others brought up the rear. The musicians played for all they were worth, and the villagers got on to their verandas to watch the procession. I felt very self-conscious as I saw the grinning faces on the veranda. It was a little more than a hundred yards to the bus but the journey seemed slow and protracted. There was a big crowd around the bus, and many villagers greeted me with the traditional good-bye: *Hogibittu barutira?* ('Will you go and come back?'). A front seat on the driver's row had been reserved for me, a tribute to the Headman's power over the bus owner. I was standing near the front left wheel saying good-byes when the driver told everyone concerned that he had really to be going. I got ready to climb into the bus when Lakshmana came and hugged me, north Indian style, with his right shoulder touching my left, and *vice versa*. He had his green Nehru waistcoat on, and like his dress, the bear hug which he gave me was also characteristic of the politicians.

I got into the bus at last and kept my hands folded in greeting as everyone around wished me farewell. The bus started after a great deal of stuttering and coughing. As the bus gathered speed I turned towards the Harijan ward where several men, women and children were watching our progress, and I greeted them. Suddenly I recognized, in the crowd, the emaciated and deeply creased face of Doni, my friend: 'Are you going away?' she cried out, and I started to reply. But the words choked in my throat. My self-restraint which had held so long threatened to give way and I turned my face away from her. At once, the small man sitting between me and the driver, whom I had not noticed so far, asked me, 'You must be an officer and very popular. It was a big send off.' I told him somewhat coldly that I was not an officer, and turned away from him, and looked on either side of the road. I wanted to be by myself for a while. It was going to be my last journey down that road for some time, and I wanted to drink in every detail of the vanishing countryside. The terraced rice-fields spread around me in all directions and clumps of trees were dotted about the rice-fields breaking what would have been otherwise a sheer stretch of paddy. The fields were in varying colours from green touched with yellow to gold and brown. The slightest breeze caused a ripple in the fields, and the plants swayed and bowed before returning to their vertical position. Occasionally, a gust of strong wind disturbed several plots momentarily ruffling the pattern of colours.

It was a sunny and breezy day, typical of the season and I wondered when I would be returning to the village. I feared that it would be many years and the thought depressed me. I tried to take my mind off my departure and take in the scenery. Feeder canals, clear and shallow, flowed rapidly through the fields, their banks lined with the *hongé* trees bright with shrill green leaves. The land dipped and rose, and went round sudden rises, while the bus rattled along, jolting us at every turn and twist, and dip and rise. Through it all I had brief and tantalizing glimpses of the shimmering Kaveri flowing in the distance.

Index